THE LIVING WORLD OF KNOWLEDGE

The Living World series comprises:

The Living World
OF
KNOWLEDGE

London   COLLINS   *Glasgow*

This Impression 1970

ISBN 0 00 100101 9

CONTENTS

CONTENTS

CONTENTS

THE SCIENCE OF GEOLOGY

We do not need to keep our eyes very wide open to realise that earth is more than the dark brown stuff in our gardens, and is not at all the simple " element " which the Ancient Greeks believed it to be. For instance, our own house may stand on clay but a friend's on gravel or sand. If we dig down through the layer of *topsoils* we may come to soft, white chalk or hard, grey granite or one of the many different rocks.

MINERAL DEPOSITS

Now these differences are more than just curiosities. It is unlikely that our back gardens conceal coal or natural gas, ironstone or gold, but an expert with his instruments can tell from the lie of the land where it would be worth while prospecting for valuable minerals. The nature of the upper layers of earth affects the way the landscape looks. You don't have to be much of a gardener to know that roses grow better on some soils than others, or much of a naturalist to associate pine trees and bracken with sandy heaths, and smooth, grassy downs with chalk.

Furthermore, when we look at the buildings in the different regions of Britain, we find that each place has its own special architecture depending on the kind of stone available. In Cornwall, for instance, the older houses are of rough granite, but along the Welsh border of a warm, red sandstone. In a belt stretching along the Cotswolds the houses are built of a beautiful easily-carved limestone; in another belt they are mainly of flint. Where there is no local stone at all, the houses were built of baked-clay bricks. Even these differ in size, shape and colour from county to county.

Yet, in a sense, all earth was once the same; for our Earth began as a globe of white-hot, molten material, weighing about 6,000 million, million, million tons, that split off from the sun, perhaps 5,000 million years ago. (We cannot really imagine spans of time as vast as this but if, for comparison, one year was squeezed into a second then 5,000 million years would be represented over a century and a half.) Gradually the surface of the Earth cooled and hardened into a crust about 20 miles thick. Below this, in a zone which scientists are now hoping to explore by drilling very deep *moholes*, there is believed to be another 4,000 miles of *magma*, or molten rock, held under tremendous temperatures and pressures, much as it was when it was first formed.

The outer crust, on the other hand, has changed enormously and in very complicated ways. The unravelling of the problems of the rocks—which is the function of geology (meaning " earth-study ") has been one of the great achievements of modern man.

SHRINKING OF THE EARTH

To see how geologists imagine that the Earth took shape, let us begin with that hot, molten globe spinning in space. Hundreds of millions of years passed, and slowly the surface cooled and solidified. The skin then began to thicken, growing inwards, until a section through the Earth would have looked rather like a slice through a soft-centred chocolate. Now when things cool they shrink and the greatest shrinkage occurs at that moment when a liquid becomes a solid. So, if the crust of the earth had solidified into a perfect globe, there would have been a gap inside between it and the still-molten centre.

But the pressures that built up before the gap could be created were vast and caused the crust to crumple up like the skin of a rotten apple. The " wrinkles " on the earth's surface formed hills and valleys although these were quite different from the ones we know to-day.

Much of the rock produced when the earth cooled remains unchanged to-day. Granite is a familiar example of this kind of rock which is called *igneous* (from a Latin word meaning " fiery "). These igneous rocks are mainly made up of the common elements, silicon and aluminium, combined with oxygen but they do not all look the same because different rates of cooling produce different varieties of the compounds. But they are all alike in that these early rocks are harder and denser than rocks produced by later events.

WEATHERING

About 2,000 million years ago, when the temperature of the earth's surface fell below boiling point (100°C.), a most important series of events took place. The huge clouds of steam that had surrounded the earth began to condense into water to form lakes and seas. Now there began " weather " much as we know it to-day.

The heat of the sun sucked up water vapour from the oceans; the winds carried the vapour from place to place; the vapour condensed to water in the clouds over the cooler mountains; the water rained into rivers that ran to the sea, eating away at the land as they went; the sea and its storms lashed the rocks at its edges and pounded the stones that fell into it. As the Earth cooled further, the water froze in the cold regions, cracking open rocks; icebergs ground away

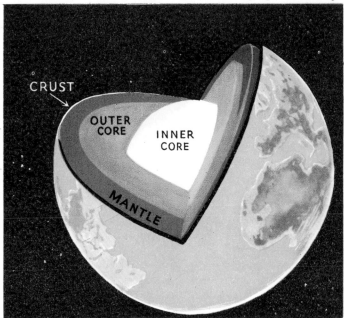

A cross-section of the earth, with its various layers exposed. The crust on which all life exists is only 25 miles thick.

The crust consists of several different geological layers, or strata, normally arranged in order of their age.

at the earth and all these agencies contributed to the breaking up of the rocks into smaller particles.

The weather those thousands of millions of years ago did, in fact, what it is still doing to-day; it acted like sandpaper (and sometimes like a sledge-hammer), breaking the rocks up and grinding them down to pebbles and then to fine powders. And at the same time compounds such as salt, which dissolves in water, were carried down to the sea and generally lost to the land for ever.

FOSSIL REMAINS

Then, about 1,000 million years ago, another great force made its appearance—life. The first living thing arose in the sea in a simple form and was probably soft-bodied; when it died it left no record of its existence. Fossil remains from about 500 million years ago, show us that life in the ocean had developed into the form we know to-day as Invertebrates, which include the shellfish. Like shellfish to-day, perhaps they could extract calcium from the sea water and absorb it into their skeletons and bones. When they died their chalky shells fell to the sea-bed and formed layers, eventually to be pressed into rocks such as the limestone family which is chemically quite different from the rest. Later still, great forests grew up on land, died and laid down layers rich in the life-element of carbon—layers which form the " fields " of coal, oil and natural gas which we rely on to-day.

The depositing of these *sedimentary* rocks was only the beginning of their story. They generally started in a powdery form and the weight of the oceans or of other rocks settling on them later, and the heat from the centre of the earth, made them rather harder and more compact so that sand turned to sandstone and clay to shale. If we were to extract a slice from deep into the earth's crust, we should see a sandwich of several " decks ", with different geological layers, or *strata*, neatly arranged in the order of their age, the youngest on top.

Geologists recognise about a dozen main periods for the formation of these sedimentary rocks, which were laid down over a lower and older igneous stratum. They range from the sandstones and limestones of the pre-Cambrian age of more than 500 million years ago to the Quaternary gravels which were formed only a few million years ago when man had already appeared on the earth. In a typical part of the earth's surface (for instance, under London), the sedimentary rocks are in all perhaps a mile thick. But it is very rare to find even a fairly complete series of strata—and often they do not appear to be in the right order.

DETERMINING AGE

Before we see why this should be we should explain how it is that scientists can be reasonably certain about the ages of things which have existed for more than a hundred times longer than there have been men on earth. There are several ways of dating the main events we have described: by discoveries of astronomy, by the rate at which rivers are still taking salt into the sea, by the rate of weathering on stone, and so on. The *radioactive* method, described in another article in this book (*see* Archæology), has, in recent years, given much-needed data. All these results agree well with each other. But some of the most interesting evidence of all comes from the study of fossils.

STUDY OF FOSSILS

Fossils are the remains of living organisms which have been preserved inside rocks, and anyone who has studied them would agree that they are not dull and dusty things. It is true that we usually see them only in museums, for, although some rocks consist *entirely* of fossils, the conditions which allow their being preserved for perhaps a 1,000 million years are not very common. However, if we are lucky we may discover on the face of an old quarry the print of a sea-snail or a fern which died 400 million years ago. Sometimes scientists can recognise the creature from a clue like a footprint or an egg.

What has happened in all these cases is that the dead plant or animal, or some trace of it, was buried in a soft substance like clay. The remains lay undisturbed, the clay preserving the shape while they were gently being changed by heat and pressure into hard rock. This left the *outline* of the creature which had fallen into it, even though the creature itself had long since rotted away leaving a hollow mould of its shape —though in many cases the hollow was filled in by a later rock, and in recent strata the actual bones of animals may be discovered.

Now, at the same time as geology was becoming a science, naturalists were discovering how various forms of life had developed from each other. Many of the creatures found as fossils are now extinct, of course—but they resemble living creatures. Even without the specialised knowledge of a biologist we can guess that a worm evolved before a fish, a fish before a lizard, and a lizard before an elephant—with a similar " family tree " for the plant kingdom.

So, from these fossil remains, we have extra evidence about the *order* of the rocks. Only physical methods can give us the *actual* dates. Thus geology and the science of fossils (which is called *palaeontology*, or " the study of old life "), help to check each other's calendars.

MOUNTAIN RANGES AND FAULTS

After the sedimentary rocks had been laid down and perhaps hardened, they were seldom left unaltered. For all the forces which we have already looked at were still at work 2,000 million years ago—as they are at work to-day. The centre of the earth went on cooling and contracting, for instance, so that the crust was subjected to new stresses which had to be relieved in one way or another. All the mountains and valleys we know to-day were formed well after the surface of the earth had cooled and apparently set. In fact, the higher and more jagged mountains such as the Himalayas and the Alps are generally younger than such comparatively gentle ones as our own Pennines. The seas we now know, too, are very different from those into which water first fell, and according to one theory the continents themselves have drifted half-way round the world.

The stresses which these movements set up were relieved in two main ways, of which the simpler was for a whole pile of strata to crack—usually in a slightly diagonal direction— and then for one side to slip in relation to the other. Sometimes there were two cracks, in which case a whole slice of the earth's surface might drop hundreds of feet below the rocks on either side. Catastrophes of both kinds are called faults, and we do not need to look very long at a map of Great Britain to guess that the Great Glen, which carries the Caledonian Canal in almost a straight line across Scotland, is an outstanding example of a fault.

The other important way in which strata have been distorted is by *folding*. If we think of the various layers of rock as being pushed by great sideways pressures, we realise that eventually the layers will start to form a " hump " that will go on rising up until the hump topples over on its side. If you were now to dig down through the fallen hump, where before you would find only one set of layers of rock, now you would find three—two made by the sides of the hump and one the original set of strata. Obviously, the top set and the original set will have their layers arranged in the same order downwards while the middle set would have its order exactly reversed.

But we know that rocks are hard things that crack more often than they fold and so another thing can happen. When the hump starts to rise, the set of strata cracks through the hump. If the sideways pressure continues, one edge of the crack will then slip over the other and one set of strata will come to lie on top of the other, both sets being in the same order.

EROSION AT WORK

Supposing the rocks folded in this way were to have remained unchanged to this day, it would be fairly easy to see how they had been folded. But other great forces, those causing *erosion*, have been at work all the time. Winds have been eating away at the land (only by a fraction of an inch a year, it is true, but by thousands of feet as the centuries went

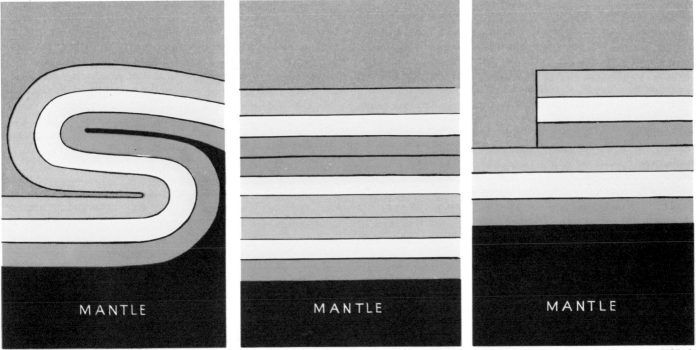

Layer distortion. Left: *Folding—top and bottom layers are in the same order while the middle layer is reversed.* Centre: *folded layers in position.* Right: *Slipping—due to sideways pressure one layer has slipped over another.*

11

The Giant's Causeway, composed of thousands of basalt pillars, is thought to have been formed from cooling and cracking lava.

by); rivers have changed their courses and laid down new sediments; and tides have eaten away at cliffs. All these forces were attacking sometimes the older and sometimes the younger rocks. At one period large areas of the world (including Britain), froze up completely and glaciers scoured deep ruts. At other times, volcanoes were very active, throwing out an igneous rock which solidified quickly and so was different from granite (this rock is called basalt, and there is a good example of it at the Giant's Causeway in Northern Ireland). Often there were earthquakes and landslides, which would make even the worst of those which we read of in the papers, seem small affairs.

Sometimes, in fact, these upheavals brought a recent, near-the-surface sedimentary rock back to a depth where it met great heat (because it was near to the molten magma) and pressure (because of the weight of rocks above and perhaps a sideways thrust from earth-movements too). Then it became changed—physically rather than chemically, and to all intents and purposes became a new material. Rocks which have passed twice through the fire in this way are called *metamorphic* and an example is marble, which is far harder, denser and hence more valuable as a building material than the chalk from which it came.

While we are considering especially useful rocks, we ought to note that compounds of comparatively rare heavy metals like copper were to solidify out of the magma later than the silicon and so on which are fairly evenly spread over the earth. (Even most jewels or gem-stones are made up of common elements, and are only rare because the conditions in which they crystallised slowly, under great pressure, were rare). So these metal ores were forced up late in time into local cracks in the earth's surface—fortunately for the men who can to-day dig them out in a fairly pure state. Even the more common iron is usually found concentrated, though there is probably a huge amount of it left in the liquid magma.

In summary we can say two things about geology—that it is a complicated study and that it is a useful one. In addition to the ways mentioned above, geology helps the civil engineer to dig tunnels or raise skyscrapers, the archaeologist (or student of early human civilisations), and many others. Anyone who thinks he has only to dig a hole at the bottom of his garden to find all the earth's strata in the right order is certainly in for a disappointment. Since more people live in old river valleys than on stony heights he is more likely to meet a few inches of topsoil (which is not of great interest to a geologist) and then several strata, each hundreds of feet thick, of clays and sands not very different from each other. But it is not difficult even for a beginner to see geology " in action " if he does not look downwards so much as *around* him, particularly when he travels more than a mile or two from his home.

For Great Britain has more changes of geological structure (and hence of landscape) in a small area than any other part of the world. It has, in fact, given names such as Devonian to characteristic rocks or ages. Look at a railway cutting where on top of the chalk there is a layer of *conglomerate* or *boulder* clay with rounded pebbles in it. Is this how a very recent upthrust of the sea-bed appears? Then travel across London from the Chiltern Hills to the North Downs. Do you have a suspicion that these are so alike that both are *outcrops* (or places where a stratum reaches the surface) of a saucer of chalk which dips right under the Thames and so has become filled up with clays and sands? And above all look closely whenever you see the face of a quarry or cliff where the layers have become exposed—and ask yourself questions.

Then check your guesses with a simple book on geology and (just as important) a map showing Britain coloured so as to demonstrate its rock formations. Bit by bit your sense of wonder will grow, not only at the strange things which have happened to the earth in its thousands of millions of years of history, not only at the ways these affect our life and work to-day, but also at the cleverness of the men who in the last few generations have worked out most of the mysteries of the story of the earth.

12

Civilisation and Culture
ANCIENT EGYPT

Egypt has long been the paradise of archaeologists. It has rewarded them, step by step, with the revelation of one of the grandest of the world's ancient civilisations, and its dry air and sands have rejoiced their hearts by preserving from decay an abundance of eloquent remains.

It is an old saying that " Egypt is the Nile ". The ancient civilisations of the Near and Middle East have all arisen in river valleys, where a sufficiency of water and fertile land has encouraged early man to settle. The development of the Nile valley thus parallels those of the valleys of the Tigris and the Euphrates in Mesopotamia. The Nile makes Egypt what it is by its annual rise and fall. Regularly every summer its waters, swollen by the rains of Central Africa and the melting snows of the Abyssinian plateau, flood their banks. Afterwards, just as regularly, they drain away and deposit a wide belt of rich black earth on either side of the valley. There, from the earliest times, the inhabitants have raised their corn and other produce. Though modern Egypt is more than four times the size of Great Britain, practically the whole of its population is congested along the banks of the life-giving river. The rest of the country is mostly a parched and sun-scorched waste of sand and stone, volcanic mountains, and limestone, sandstone and granite cliffs from which the Egyptian builders quarried their stone.

Father Nile nourished two types of people. In Lower Egypt (the fan-shaped region of the delta), trading and cultural contacts with the Mediterranean countries and beyond developed in the inhabitants the enterprising spirit that was to make Egypt a pioneer in many works of progress. In the Upper Egypt of the south, isolation from the world encouraged a more passive and strongly conservative temperament. Of the actual origins of the primitive Egyptians, all that can be safely said is that they were a blend of native with other African and Western Asiatic strains.

THE EARLIEST EGYPTIANS

We can dimly trace the beginnings of their story in the flint implements they have left behind them from perhaps 10,000 years ago in the Old Stone Age. From the time of the New Stone Age onwards the tale becomes fuller and richer as the primitive peoples gradually developed into a civilised nation. Having ceased to be wanderers, they built themselves houses of reeds, and mud and settled down in village communities to fish and hunt and farm for their living. They learned to weave linen for clothing and to make crude pottery and baskets and boats. They started to regulate the Nile floods and reclaim the sodden land by dykes and irrigation canals. They began to use copper instead of stone for their tools and weapons. The artificers acquired skill in making stone vessels and carved and sculptured figures in stone and ivory. Painting began in the decoration of finer pottery with vigorous representations of plants, animals and men. Buildings of sun-dried brick were erected. The craftsmen made bracelets and rings and other ornaments, as well as fine furniture—and the people played at ninepins and marbles.

Meanwhile their wise men studied astronomy and worked out a solar calendar of 365 days. The year was divided into twelve months of thirty days, with five days added to " complete " the tally, though of course, it left out just over a day in every four years. In their religion, besides honouring a crowd of local deities, mostly represented in the form of animals, the people worshipped a sky-god. And, from the articles discovered in their burial places, for use in the next world, we know that they believed in life after death.

Another great forward stride was taken in these prehistoric times. They began to evolve a picture-language in which each sign (originally based on a drawing of the object mentioned) represented a syllable or a word. In the course of time this system of writing underwent several developments. The original pictorial signs, called *hieroglyphs* (sacred carvings), continued to be used for sacred and other special purposes; but, being very elaborate, they were found too slow for use in ordinary writing. Accordingly, sets of simpler forms, known as *hieratic* (priests' writing), were evolved from them, chiefly for priestly and other literary work. Later still, an even simpler kind of script, the *demotic* (people's writing), was employed for everyday purposes. Actually, long before this, the Egyptians had discovered the principle of the alphabet, in which a small number of letters—in their case twenty-four—serves instead of the hundreds or thousands of signs needed in a picture-language. Strangely enough, however, they made only a limited use of this bright idea. Other early civilisations, such as the Sumerian and the Hittite, used picture-languages; but the Egyptians were the first—at all events in the Western world—to produce the materials for true writing: reeds for pens; ink; and strips of the papyrus reed for paper.

The diadem and ear-ring were once Tutankhamen's; the necklace belonged to the daughter of Senusit II (900 B.C.).

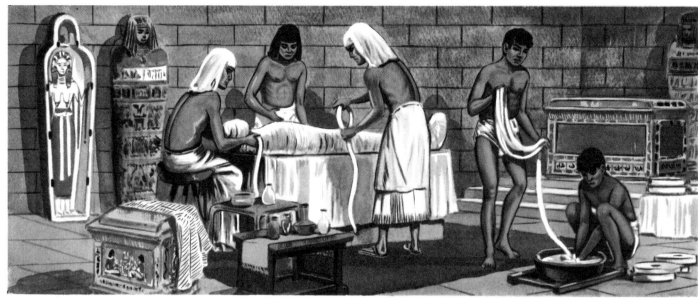

Here in a funeral chamber a body is being embalmed with spices, wrapped in linen and enclosed in a mummy-shaped coffin.

THE DYNASTIC SUCCESSION

Towards the end of the fourth millennium B.C., the first great historical landmark appears. The various communities, or petty States, which occupied the country gradually merged, first into a number of larger States—the whales no doubt often swallowing the minnows—then into the two kingdoms of Upper and Lower Egypt, and finally, perhaps about 3200 B.C., into a single kingdom. Father Nile may have had a say in this unifying process as part of his function of " making Egypt ";. for it is quite probable that the need to co-operate in large-scale irrigation works assisted in drawing the different States together. However that may be, the final outcome was the first of a sequence of thirty-one family groups, or *dynasties*, which, with sundry breaks, were to rule the country for nearly 3,000 years. Egypt's real history, illuminated by the increasing use of written records, had begun. During this epoch the periods of the country's history are distinguished, not by the royal family names (such as our Tudors and Stuarts), but by the number of the dynasty.

The periods of the first three dynasties (perhaps 3200-2680 B.C.), when the new capital city of Memphis was built, marked a time of outstanding importance. They introduced some of the features that were to give Egyptian culture its distinctive character. These were the adoption from abroad of sun-worship and, with it, the practice of *mummification* (the preservation of the bodies of the dead by embalming with spices and other means) and pyramid building.

RELIGION AND THE PHARAOHS

The religion of Egypt in these ancient historic times was a bewilderingly complex medley of local gods, fertility or Nature gods, god-kings and good and evil spirits. In earlier days, each community had had its own local gods, mostly represented in animal forms, and at this time we find such creatures as the crocodile, the jackal and the ibis thus honoured. (Later on they were given a human body with its original animal's head.) When the separate communities united, the local gods of each were commonly adopted into the religion of the new State. The fertility or Nature gods owed their immense influence to the fact that the Egyptians were mainly an agricultural people dependent on the Nile for their crops. The actual worship of the sun-god *Re* was more particularly associated with the royal lines of the kings, or Pharaohs, though his divinity and power were acknowledged by all.

THE OSIRIS MYTH

Egyptian religion is rich in sacred myths that illustrate the people's beliefs. One of the most important of the stories is that of *Osiris*. The tale was woven out of many strands of ancient history and legend. Osiris was believed to be descended from the sun-god. He had been a model king of Egypt who first taught the people agriculture, writing and the other arts of civilisation. His brother *Set*, who hated him, one day tricked him into clambering into a chest, which Set thereupon fastened up and threw into the Nile. Eventually *Isis*, the wife of Osiris, (who came to be worshipped as a goddess of magical power and knowledge), recovered the chest. But Set was bent on his evil purpose. He cut up the body of Osiris and scattered the pieces over Egypt. The devoted Isis, however, was not to be outdone. In the spring, with divine aid and magical spells, the parts were reassembled and the body restored to eternal life. Osiris, accordingly, was worshipped by the Egyptians as a god of Nature who brought forth the springtime crops, of the Nile which watered them and of the sun which ripened them. He was likewise the god of the dead, and his life and death and resurrection were a symbol and a promise of the destiny which all his worshippers hoped to share.

Each reigning Pharaoh was revered as the son of Re. After his death he became one with Osiris and, like him, on the performance of the due rites, entered into everlasting life. He was, in fact, a god-king, and, as such, his authority was all-powerful.

FUNERAL RITES

The ancient Egyptians were a cheerful folk who loved life and hated the thought of its ever coming to an end. They believed that a man's personality survived death, and somehow they acquired the idea that with the aid of magical rites and other performances, it could be made to exist forever by preserving the dead body from decay by mummification. It is to this concern with the after-life, and the resulting burial practices, that we owe so much of our knowledge of their culture. We may, indeed, go further and say that that culture itself—its architecture and sculpture, medicine and music, painting, weaving and jewellers' work—was largely stimulated by the demands of the burial customs.

The preservation of the god-king's body was a matter of national necessity; because it was believed that, if through neglect of the appropriate rites his personality was not brought to life again, all his subjects would suffer the like calamity. The more elaborate burials were originally reserved for the Pharaohs, but in later times, the practice, in less costly forms, spread among the nobles and other superior people. When the body had been embalmed and wrapped in fine linen, it was often enclosed in a mummy-shaped wooden coffin on which the dead man's face was carved or moulded and painted so as to be as lifelike as possible. Usually this coffin was placed inside a second one of wood and sometimes in a third one of stone. These were housed in the tomb-chamber, to the accompaniment of the prescribed prayers and spells, and various items of food and clothing and weapons and other articles, which the resurrected body would need in the next life, were placed in position. Sometimes, too, a life-size painted statue of the dead man was sculptured, before which food offerings and prayers were regularly made.

THE PYRAMIDS

The mummies lead us naturally to the *pyramids*, the tombs of many of the Pharaohs. The Egyptians were the world's first great builders in stone and these monumental masses mark the peak of their constructional achievements. The pyramids of Giza, erected (after some earlier ones) during the 4th dynasty, were counted among the Seven Wonders of the ancient world. Cheops's Great Pyramid, probably the largest structure ever raised by the hand of man, stood 481 feet high when it was built some 4,600 years ago. The stupendous work entailed the labour of dragging some 2,300,000 blocks of stone, averaging 2½ tons in weight, and placing them in position, with beautifully mathematical precision, by sheer muscular power aided only by sledges, rollers, levers and the like.

ERAS OF ANCIENT EGYPTIAN HISTORY

Historians divide the major portion of ancient Egyptian history into the four periods of the *Old*, *Middle* and *New Kingdoms* (interrupted by intervals of civil war and foreign invasion), and the *Late Period*. Egyptian dating is mostly uncertain and the following is only one of the systems in use: the Old Kingdom, 2680-2258 B.C.; the Middle Kingdom, 2134-1786 B.C.; the New Kingdom, 1570-1085 B.C.; the Late Period, 1085-332 B.C.

The New Kingdom saw the country attain the height of its prosperity and glory. No other power could vie with it in culture and wealth. Its armies and navies extended the Pharaohs' dominion into the modern Sudan in the south and over Palestine and Syria up to the River Euphrates in the north-east. Immense irrigation and other engineering works were carried out. Trade and commerce and tribute from the subject kingdoms poured riches into the land. The arts rose to further heights. New wonders of architecture appeared and the magnificent palaces and temples were sumptuously equipped with richly inlaid furniture, beautiful tapestries and the handiwork of accomplished sculptors, painters, goldsmiths, jewellers and glaziers.

The 18th dynasty opened a period which was adorned with some of the finest temples the world has ever seen. The great temple of Karnak (begun earlier), on the site of the new capital city of Thebes, contains a colonnaded hall measuring 338 by 170 feet with sculptured and painted columns 70 feet in height. The temple of Luxor is an imposing monument of massive dignity and beauty. The Valley of the Kings, opposite Thebes, has been richly rewarding in its revelation of the riches and splendours of the times. Here, in the rocky cliffs, the Pharaohs of the New Kingdom excavated their tombs. And it was here that, from 1922 onwards, one of the most sensational of all archaeological finds was made when the English Egyptologist, Howard Carter, opened up the tomb of the eighteen-year-old *Tutankhamen*, a Pharaoh of the 18th dynasty. It was a veritable Aladdin's cave of priceless treasures. Rich furniture and royal attire, chariots and weapons, ornaments and jewellery and carved and inlaid work in ivory and gold and silver, a splendid throne decorated with gold, three mummy-shaped coffins of the dead youth, the innermost of solid inlaid gold—all these riches and more besides spoke their testimony to the abounding wealth and luxury

The fellahin at work on the banks of the Nile, ploughing and sowing seed in the fertile soil.

Wall painting on an ancient tomb depicting young women being entertained by a slave playing on a harp.

and the taste and technical skill of those long past times.

Another famous name is that of the 19th dynasty Pharaoh, Rameses II. His rock-temple at *Abu Simbel* in the Sudan contains four seated figures, carved out of the rock, of a height of 65 feet.

THE ANCIENT ARTS

The arts of Egypt have some unmistakable characteristics. The architects and sculptors worked to a mighty scale. And it is by the sheer magnitude and durability of their productions that they have achieved their effects of awe-inspiring grandeur and timelessness. The paintings and carvings from the walls of the tomb-chapels are apt to set us wondering by their curious style. The figures often seem more like flat and angular cardboard cut-outs than bodies in the round. Their simplicity of outline, and their lack of perspective, remind us of our own first crude efforts in drawing. And, indeed, the Egyptians, as an obstinately conservative race, did in fact, for nearly 3,000 years, remain influenced by the traditions of art practised in the early days of the Old Kingdom. Their aim was to portray their figures, and all their parts, in firm, clear lines (as in a diagram), so that you could never be in doubt about who or what they were. The rest could be left largely to the observer's imagination. None the less, the artists have left us many beautiful paintings and statues executed in a pleasingly natural and graceful style.

The Egyptians excelled in the minor arts. Much of their jewellery and other work in wood, ivory, gold and silver, displays an exquisite taste and a supreme skill in craftsmanship.

GREAT LEARNING

In the fields of science the Egyptians accumulated a good deal of practical knowledge of astronomy, mathematics and engineering and medicine, and they invented the first waterclock for telling the day and night hours in the changing seasons. But they rested unambitiously content with such discoveries as they could put to everyday use. They lacked the eager spirit of curiosity which seeks knowledge for its own sake and leads to new discoveries of natural laws and scientific principles.

Literature was an art which they developed in many directions. In the Pyramid Texts and the Book of the Dead, time had preserved a wondrous collection of magical and ritual writings. Other works of praiseworthy moral maxims and sage sayings are on stone. And there are some pleasing love poems, romantic stories and stage plays and a number of travellers' tales of the wildest adventures among enchanted islands, fabulous serpents and such like excitements.

THE NOBILITY

In the picture of social and political life the nobles occupy a prominent place. They lived in fine brick houses, with pleasant gardens, and luxuriated in rich foods, wines and fruits. Hunting and fishing, music and games, were among their pastimes in the intervals of managing their estates and, in some cases, acting as the Pharaoh's provincial governors. There was a time when these governors encroached on the royal rights and set themselves up as feudal lords. But these presumptions were eventually checked and in time a centralised Civil Service system was created for administering the country's affairs. Another bold feature in the social picture is the priesthood. The priests commanded tremendous power and wealth, and their exclusive knowledge of the rites of mummification and religion generally riveted their influence on the people.

DECLINE

In the time of the 20th dynasty (1197-1085 B.C.), or even earlier, the bright lamps of Egypt's civilisation began to wane. The remainder of her history is largely a tale of decline. A series of alien conquerors set their heels on the kingdom: the Assyrians from 671 B.C., the Persians from 525 B.C., Alexander the Great and his successors, the Ptolemies, from 332 B.C. and finally the Romans in 30 B.C. During these twilight years the last (30th) native dynasty ended in 341 B.C. The splendid city of *Alexandria*, founded by, and named after, the great conqueror, became a renowned centre of learning and commerce. Its famous library housed half a million papyrus rolls containing much of Egypt's ancient learning. And in 48 B.C. the greater part of the building, with its priceless store, was destroyed by fire.

So, with the Roman occupation, the splendour of Egypt's grand old civilisation and culture faded out.

ARCHITECTURE : I
In Ancient Times

Architecture began when men stopped living in caves and started to build homes for themselves and their families. At first they made huts of branches or reeds, and plastered them with mud to help keep out the weather. Although early man had few tools and no machinery to help him, he knew how to raise great stones to make circles, or set them in long lines like avenues. The most famous stone circle is at Stonehenge in Wiltshire. But monuments like Stonehenge are not real architecture. That began in ancient Egypt at least 6,000 years ago. The most famous buildings in Egypt are the Pyramids near Cairo. They are the tombs of Egyptian kings, called the Pharaohs. Thousands of slaves were used to put the great blocks of stone in place, some more than twenty feet long. The largest and oldest is the Pyramid of Cheops (3733 B.C.), which was 482 feet high. Near the Pyramids is an even older monument called the Sphinx. It is a great stone figure of a lioness with the head of a woman.

Most of the Egyptian temples are along the banks of the River Nile. Unlike a church, an Egyptian temple was not a place where ordinary people went to worship. Inside it had a huge hall with a roof of stone slabs supported on round columns, and behind that were many small rooms used by the priests during their religious ceremonies. It was the outside, which would be seen by the people, that was the most impressive part. The Egyptians covered the walls of their temples and tombs with a kind of picture-writing, called hieroglyphics, and also with figures of their gods and Pharaohs. One of the most impressive temples is the Temple of Ammon at Karnak, while another smaller one is at Philae.

HANGING GARDENS OF BABYLON

Only a little less old than Egypt were the kingdoms of Babylonia and Assyria, which existed four thousand years ago in what is now Iraq in the Middle East. Nearly all their cities were close to the great rivers called the Tigris and the Euphrates. Because these rivers often overflowed, flooding the flat plain, the Babylonians and the Assyrians had to build their cities, temples and palaces on huge platforms made of bricks of baked mud. They used mud in Babylonia because there was no stone. The city of Babylon was famous for luxury and for its size. The tops of the great walls were so wide that a four-horse chariot could turn right round, and there were one hundred bronze gates and two hundred and fifty towers. One palace, built by King Nebuchadnezzar, was famous for its " Hanging Gardens "—one of the seven wonders of the ancient world. The gardens were not really hanging, but built on top of arches about seventy-five feet high. The strangest buildings in Babylonia and Assyria were called ziggurats. They were temples shaped like a pyramid but were built with a sloping ramp which went right round the building to the top where there was a shrine to one of their gods.

The palace of the Assyrian King Sargon II (722-705 B.C.) is at Khorsabad, near another ancient Assyrian city called Nineveh. The palace itself was like a small city. It covered twenty-five acres and was built on a platform about fifty feet high. Unlike the Babylonians the Assyrians had some stone to use on their buildings, but because it was scarce they used mud bricks for the inside of their walls, and fronted them with thin blocks of stone. These stones were carved with hunting scenes, while statues of lions with wings were put on either side of the great gateways of King Sargon's palace. Inside, the palace contained about seven hundred rooms, but strangely enough they had no windows. This may have been to keep out the heat in the summer. Also, no columns were

An Egyptian column shaped like a papyrus stem. Right: *the plan of an Egyptian temple.*

A Chaldaic temple, or ziggurat, seven floors high and built in the shape of a square. Note the sloping ramps.

used anywhere in the palace; the walls were so thick that they were not needed.

PERSIA INVADES BABYLON

Babylon was captured by the Persians in 538 B.C., when King Belshazzar was killed. The ancient Persians were a warlike people, and invaded both Egypt and Greece. In Egypt they saw the great temples with their columns, and when they returned home they took the idea with them of using them in their own palaces and buildings at Susa and Persepolis. Because the weather was usually hot and dry the Persians built the halls of the king's palace with open sides to let in the fresh air. A favourite subject of the Persian artists was the bull, and they set up statues of bulls with heads of men on either side of the palace gateways. Also they put bulls' heads on the capitals of their columns (the capital of a column is the top part). One hall in the palace at Persepolis, built by Darius (521-485 B.C.) was called the Hall of a Hundred Columns, but to-day only one column still stands upright and the carved wooden roof has gone.

One of the best known buildings in the ancient world was the Temple of Solomon (1012 B.C.) in Jerusalem, which was destroyed by Nebuchadnezzar. It was built on a huge platform, and it seems that the architects borrowed ideas from both the Egyptians and the Babylonians.

DORIC ORDER

The most important and the most beautiful of the different styles of ancient architecture were the Greek styles. They came to that country from the island of Crete about three thousand five hundred years ago. Some of the oldest buildings in Greece are at Mycenae (about 1400 B.C.), where the Greek hero Agamemnon is supposed to have lived. But the finest Greek temples were built between about 700 B.C. and 150 B.C. There were three different styles, or *orders* as they are called. They are quite easy to tell apart, and the oldest and plainest is called the Doric Order. Doric columns have no base and at the top a very simple capital with no carving. The most famous Doric temple in the world is the Parthenon on the Acropolis in Athens. It was built between 447 and 432 B.C. by two Greek architects called Ictinus and Callicrates, and many people think it is the most perfectly designed building

An approximate reconstruction of King Solomon's temple, the architecture of which showed Egyptian influence.

One of the best preserved temples and a fine example of Doric architecture is the temple of Poseidon in Southern Italy.

in the world. Other famous Greek temples in the Doric style are the Temple of Haephestos (Theseus), also in Athens, and at Paestum in Italy.

IONIC ORDER

The second order of Greek architecture is called the Ionic. Ionic columns are not as thick as Doric columns, and stand on a base. The capitals are more elaborate and are carved at the top so they look rather like sea-shells or rams' horns. A most beautiful Ionic temple is the Erechtheum, begun in 420 B.C. The roof of its porch is not held up by columns, but by six carved figures of young girls, called Caryatids.

CORINTHIAN ORDER

The third order is the Corinthian, and there is a strange story about how it began. In the Greek city of Corinth an old nurse had put a basket which contained offerings on the grave of a dead girl. An acanthus plant, with long leaves, grew round the basket almost hiding it. A craftsman named Callimachus saw it, and it gave him the idea for a new capital, ornamented with carved acanthus leaf designs. The huge temple of the Olympian Zeus (174-131 B.C.) is the finest Corinthian temple in Athens, with columns fifty-six feet high.

GREEK ARCHITECTURE

The Greeks also erected many other kinds of buildings, like the gateway of the Acropolis, called the Propylea. Then there were libraries, and market-places surrounded with colonnades where merchants could meet to discuss business out of the sun or the rain. They also built public baths and stadia for sports events. The most famous stadium is at Olympia, where the Olympic games began. The ancient Greeks loved plays, and because the weather was fine for so much of the year their theatres were in the open. The seats were hollowed out of the hillside and the audience looked down on the round stage, which was rather like a circus arena. These theatres were very large, and the Theatre of Dionysus on the side of the Acropolis could hold thirty thousand people. But the most beautiful theatre is at Epidauros, and it is still used for plays. The Greeks also built beautiful tombs. Most were quite small, but one was very large. It was at Halicarnassos in what is now Turkey. This huge tomb was built for King Mausolos by his widow, and was one of the seven wonders of the ancient world, but to-day there is very little left of it. The king's name, Mausolos, gave us the word mausoleum, which means a large tomb.

ROMAN ARCHITECTURE

If Greek architecture was the most beautiful in the ancient world, Roman was the most impressive. The Romans built many beautiful temples, but they were also great engineers, covering their empire with fine roads from one end to the other. Some of their bridges, like the one over the river Tagus at Alcantara in Spain (A.D. 105), are still in use. In the north of England they built a wall more than seventy miles long to keep out the invading Scottish tribes. It is called Hadrian's Wall, after the emperor who built it. The Romans also erected huge aqueducts to carry water to their cities, in many cases from hills and mountains which were miles away. Ancient Rome had eleven aqueducts. Two very famous ones are at Segovia in Spain, and the Pont du Gard (A.D. 150) near Nîmes in southern France. The Pont du Gard is one of the finest examples of Roman engineering in the world. It is like three bridges built one above the other. The channel for the water is at the top, about one hundred and fifty feet over the river Gard.

What seems rather odd to us to-day is the important part the public baths had in the daily life of the Romans. The baths in Rome were huge, and as many as three thousand people could use one of them at the same time. The baths built by the Emperors Caracalla (A.D. 211-217) and Diocletian (A.D. 302) were bigger than their palaces. The main part of the Baths of Caracalla was about as large as the whole of the Houses of Parliament! A beautiful Roman bath which still has its old lead lining and is filled from a hot spring is at Bath in Somerset. It looks like an open-air swimming pool surrounded with a colonnade. Just as important to the Romans were the circuses and amphitheatres. Circuses were like race-tracks surrounded by tiers of stone seats, while the amphitheatres were smaller, and with an oval arena. The greatest of them is the Colosseum in Rome, begun in the year A.D. 70. It was over one hundred and fifty feet high to the top of the outside wall, and it could hold fifty thousand people who came to watch fights to the death between gladiators and wild animals.

The Romans loved to set up tall columns and triumphal arches to record the victories of their armies. There are three of them in the Forum in Rome, built by the Emperors Titus, Septimius Severus and Constantine. A big difference between Roman and Greek architecture was that the Romans used mortar to hold their stones and brickwork together. None was used in the building of the Parthenon in Athens. Also, the Romans built a great deal with round arches, which the Greeks never did. They used them for windows, archways and for making vaults to cover large halls and rooms in public buildings. There were three Greek orders of architecture, and the Romans added some of their own. One was the " Composite " Order, which was made up of the top part of an Ionic capital and the bottom part of a Corinthian capital. Ruins of their temples can be found all over Europe, North Africa and the Middle East. A temple in Rome that is still complete is the Pantheon. It is round and has a dome and a very beautiful portico with huge Corinthian columns. Another temple which is also intact is the little Maison Carrée at Nîmes in southern France.

POMPEII BURIED

In A.D. 79 the volcano Vesuvius erupted, completely burying the nearby towns of Herculaneum and Pompeii. It all happened so quickly that the towns were buried alive, and when archaeologists started to dig them out again they even found scenes painted on the walls of the houses and the food on the tables. So we have a complete picture of what life was like in a Roman town. Most of their houses were only one storey high with a door but no windows on to the street. Behind was a pleasant courtyard and around it the living-rooms. It is a surprise to find how modern a Roman house could be. It had a real water supply, with taps, and a very clever system of under-floor heating. The floor was warmed by hot air from a furnace which was carried through hollow bricks. So central heating is nothing new!

On the Acropolis stands the Erechtheum. This temple, one of the finest examples of Ionic architecture, was begun by Filocles in 421 B.C. but not completed until 407 B.C. On the right can be seen a corner of the famous Caryatid Porch, named after the six statues of girls of great beauty and perfection which support the porch's roof.

Civilisation and Culture
ANCIENT CHINA

China prides itself on being the oldest surviving civilisation in the world. Its long career has been a strange wavelike succession of rises and falls, but always it has succeeded in marching or staggering on. Many a time the country has been overwhelmed by barbarian invaders, but the conquerors have succumbed to the irresistible spell of the conquered and become as Chinese as their victims.

There are several reasons for these remarkable powers of survival. One is the markedly conservative temperament of the Chinese, which has led them to cling to their time-honoured institutions through every stress and trial. Another is the Chinese written language. Because it is a picture-language its characters have not changed and become unintelligible with the passage of time, as is the case with our language, which uses words to represent the sounds made in speaking. Thus, educated Chinese throughout the centuries have been able to understand their ancient literature and this has forged a lasting link between them.

Another factor is ancestor worship, which is an important part of Chinese religion. From early times the Chinese have believed that the harmonious functioning of the universe was regulated by a supreme law called the *Tao*, " the Way ". Associated with the Tao were the Nature gods, the forces of sun and rain, the winds, the soil and the grain and other elements on which the people's agricultural livelihood depended. Among these forces the sky or " Heaven ", a sort

The Chinese, who possessed the secret of making fine silks, travelled along the Silk Road to trade with other countries.

of Great Spirit, became supreme. To win the favour of the supernatural powers, various strictly prescribed rites and ceremonies were performed. Intimately associated with the worship of the Nature gods was the worship of ancestors, who themselves had become spirits or gods.

Ancestor worship was the crowning feature of Chinese family life. Each household had its own minor gods. The family tie was a bond of steel binding together in harmony, self-sacrifice, courtesy, loyalty and obedience, all the members of the household, which commonly included several generations. The children, especially those of the nobles, were carefully educated in manners and religious rites; for the Chinese are extravagantly courteous and ceremonious and they regard incorrect behaviour as a moral or even religious offence. The great unwritten family law was respect for, and obedience to, the elders. The father's authority actually increased after his death, when he entered the spirit world. The ancestral spirits had to be honoured with regular sacrifices to secure their blessings. The family system became the most influential factor in the people's religious and social life.

THE AGE OF CONFUCIUS

Still looking reverently to the past, the Chinese have always prized the period from the sixth to the third centuries B.C. as the classical age of their philosophy and literature. In that epoch the great sages laid down the principles of good government and wise living and wrestled with the mysteries of the universe. The works of the early sages and moralists, historians and poets have been another unifying element in China's history, for the Chinese cherished them as a treasury of ancient wisdom for the instruction of all future times.

The most famous of the sages was Confucius (551-479 B.C.). In his day a grievous decline had occurred in public morals. Confucius sought to revive and extend the neglected code of family life, stressing the five fundamental virtues of kindness, justice, courtesy, wisdom and good faith. He strove also, as a wholesome discipline, to restore the half-forgotten religious rites and ceremonies. His system is not actually a religious creed but a code of morality, pleasing to Heaven, for practical daily life. The great teacher's endeavours bore little immediate fruit; but his time was to come.

THE THREE RELIGIONS

Confucianism is one of the three " religions " of China, the others being Taoism and Buddhism. Taoism began as a protest against the restless world of action and a passive acceptance of the simple life of Nature as regulated by the Tao. Unfortunately, however, these mystical ideas presently got entangled with popular magic and superstition. In the end a mixed and debased form of the creed became mainly a religion for the ignorant peasants.

Buddhism (which had previously arrived from India) established its hold on China between the third and sixth centuries A.D. Neither Confucianism nor Taoism could

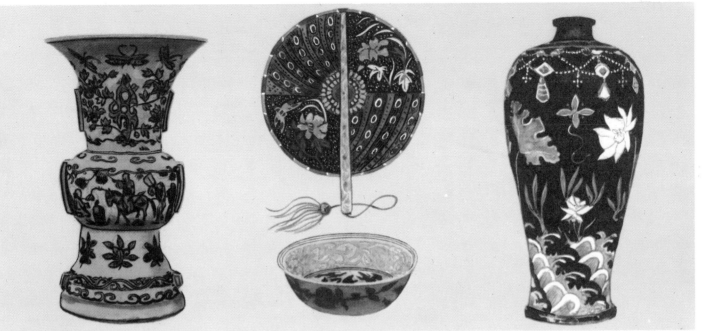

Examples of Chinese pottery. Left to right: *Wang-Li vase, Ming bowl, decorative fan and Ming vase.*

satisfy men's spiritual thirst, and the invading religion with its promise of divine aid and comfort in this world and a heaven of bliss hereafter, was eagerly adopted. But it was placed side by side with the native creeds. The Chinese are blandly accommodating in their attitude to religion, and in practice the three faiths overlapped, each borrowing from the others.

THE GREAT SCHOLAR CLASS

One of the big surprises in Chinese history is the rise of the " scholar class ". It developed in this way. A system of feudalism had early been established, but by the first century B.C. it had expired, and the virtual extinction of the landed nobility followed. In their place a new upper class of gentry, not of noble birth, gradually took shape, and it was through their growing monopoly of classical education that they became a recognised scholar class. It was from this class that the officials who administered the government—the Civil Service—were increasingly recruited. The teachings of Confucius were coming into favour and the ancient classical literature, which was closely associated with his name, furnished—and continued to do so down to recent times— the principal text-books for the Civil Service examinations. The sound moral principles which these taught were valued far more than general knowledge in qualifying students for high office. The scholars became the stronghold of the Confucian learning and the Confucian creed. And that creed (though frequently changing and suffering periods of disfavour) formed the dominant code of the educated classes and, in a measure, became an established State religion for 2,000 years. The scholar-officials, who became the ruling and most honoured class in the State, played a decisive part in preserving the country's traditional culture through the ages. Their great fault was that their limpet-like attachment to the past blocked the path to new and progressive ideas.

CHINESE ART

The Chinese excel in the arts and crafts. Their poetry ranks with the world's great literature and their prose includes monuments of learning. They have produced un- surpassable landscape and figure paintings, and their " writing ", which is commonly done with a brush, is often a work of art in itself. Their work in sculpture, pottery and porcelain, in jade and jewellery, ivory and bronze, is peerless in its technical mastery and artistic taste.

EARLY HISTORY

Our first dim view of the Chinese (who belong to the Mongolian race) goes back to some 4,000-5,000 years ago, when their scattered communities were settled in the Yellow River valley in northern China. They were simple peasants, growing corn and rearing livestock. In time they learned to make wheeled vehicles, boats and pottery, to breed silkworms and to draw the first pictorial characters of their language. We get a clearer view of their progress in the time of the Shang dynasty of priest-kings, say from 1523 to 1027 B.C. Excavations and other discoveries have enabled us to picture the times back to about the fourteenth century B.C. The Shang capital contained many handsome timbered resid- ences. The craftsmen produced richly decorated pottery, superb bronze vessels, carved and inlaid work and beautiful marble sculptures. The nobles fought and hunted in horse- drawn chariots. Among the archaeological finds were the " oracle bones ". They were mostly pieces of animal bone and tortoise-shell, some of them inscribed with questions, written in the current picture-language, addressed to the Shang gods and the ancestors. These " pictograms " threw a flood of light on the life of the times.

CHINA AT THE HEIGHT OF MAGNIFICENCE

The era of the Chou dynasty, perhaps from 1027 to 256 B.C., was one of outstanding development. It witnessed the establishment and subsequent crumbling of feudalism, the beginnings of decline in the prestige of the landed nobility and the growing wealth of traders and merchants. It also embraced the time of Confucius and the classical age of philosophy and literature. The Ch'in line (256-207 B.C.) saw the creation of a strong and immensely expanded empire and the building of the Great Wall of China to keep out the northern barbarians. With the Han dynasty (202 B.C.-

Pai-lou, or memorial gateway, to the sacred tomb area of the emperors of the Ming dynasty. Built in 1541 of white marble, the gateway is about 40 miles from Peking.

A.D. 220), the empire rose to the crest of the wave in one of its most brilliant epochs. Its rule reached out from southern Manchuria to Annam and from the gateways of India and Persia and the Caspian Sea to the eastern ocean. The great Silk Road across Central Asia was opened and along that highway the Chinese—who alone possessed the secret of producing the finest silks—carried on a rich trade with Rome and the West. The arts and crafts flourished. Paper was manufactured, a thousand years in advance of Europe. China's fame spread to all quarters.

The pattern of Chinese customs and institutions by now laid down may be summarised as follows. The community comprised the peasant masses, the artisans, craftsmen and traders, the merchants and manufacturers, the big farmers and the scholars. The nobility of birth had vanished. The Emperor ruled as the sacred " Son of Heaven ". Three religions were practised: Confucianism, Taoism and Buddhism. The family, with its ancestor worship, was the dominating factor in the life of the people. A common culture, based on history, custom, language, literature and religion, distinguished the Chinese from all barbarian races— that is, the rest of the world. It is a very striking fact that this ancient pattern of life remained fundamentally unchanged till modern times.

CHANGING FORTUNES

Unhappily, the empire now took one of its downward plunges. But it rose again in the glories of the T'ang dynasty (618-907). Its dazzling achievements, in war and peace, made China the hub and centre of civilisation. Her poetry and prose, her painting, sculpture and music, her pottery and exquisite porcelain created an age of unparalleled artistic splendour. Then once again came a fall into defeat and anarchy. The Sung dynasty, which rose in 960, held aloft the flag in the south. Painting, scholarly literature and philosophy reached their maturity and printing by movable type was practised, four centuries ahead of Europe. But from this time Chinese civilisation and culture made few noteworthy advances. In the thirteenth century, China suffered the calamity of the Tartar invasion of Jenghiz Khan and his descendants. There were, indeed, compensations,

among them new highways and increased trade. The country was opened up to the outside world, and Marco Polo's famous journey to the magnificent new capital of Peking whetted the appetite of Europe for a taste of China's boundless wealth and commerce.

Liberation arrived with the Ming dynasty (1368-1644). This epoch was notable for the beginnings of continuous contact with Europeans, though the disdainful Emperors tried to slam the door in the faces of the " barbarian " traders. In 1644 the final dynasty, that of the alien Manchus, began. Under their rule Chinese civilisation, with its antiquated outlook and scholar-official government, reached the point of stagnation. The later period is a dismal story of decay and misrule, of blind resistance to Western ideas in science, industry and culture and of the passionate efforts of enlightened reformers to save China by modernising it. The cause of progress finally triumphed. The Manchu dynasty crashed in 1912, and in 1949, the People's Republic of China was proclaimed.

THE NEW COMMUNIST CHINA

The new rulers have undertaken to transform China into a great modern industrialised power based on its own brand of communism. The land has been distributed among the peasants. Agriculture and industry have been modernised and expanded and gigantic public works undertaken. Education has become the right of all. With regard to religion, the Communists frown on all creeds. The three faiths were already in decline, though Confucianism still commanded wide respect among the educated classes. The family system, with its ancestor worship, is being undermined. The younger generation are all for the new movement. The women enjoy new liberties. The condition of the long-suffering peasants, who still form eighty per cent of the population, has been materially improved. Yet the hallowed tradition of the past remains a living influence among them. And a defeated " Nationalist " party, pledged to reform but opposed to Communism, holds out in the island of Formosa. Whether the new China will eventually work out its destiny under the Communist banner is a question which only the future can answer.

THE SCIENCE OF ARCHAEOLOGY

Until a hundred and fifty years ago archaeology (Greek, *archaios*, ancient—*logos*, discourse) interested few people. An archaeologist was often thought of as someone rather odd whose hobby was collecting things which ancient man had left behind him: flint arrow-heads, broken bits of pottery, or even human bones dug from pre-historical burial mounds (tumuli). Little, if anything, was known of the people whose bones they might have been, or of the men who had chipped the arrow-heads, or why.

History was considered to begin with the story of Greece and Rome which was recorded in early histories written in Greek and Latin. Apart from the Bible, lively tales such as those of the Greek traveller and writer, Herodotus (who lived in the fifth century B.C.)—about other people earlier than Greeks or Romans, were suspected of being little more than fables. Facts not already known of men and events in antiquity were thought to be lost for ever. The Renaissance, however, aroused interest in antique art and initiated the rediscovery of " The study of the art of antiquity ", for which the word archaeology was coined in the seventeenth century. Scholars and connoisseurs in the years following began to look actively for ancient monuments to excavate and interpret; and slowly archaeology came to be identified with excavation. Initially, their activities were confined to the classical sites of Italy and Greece. But as interest in the science grew they turned their attention to the East where completely dead and forgotten cultures were waiting to be discovered.

EARLY DISCOVERIES

In Egypt the fine dry climate had left intact on ancient monuments much decorative and painted detail, to say nothing of the majestic and nearly indestructible pyramids, temples, and great stone statues. At the end of the eighteenth century, Napoleon's Egyptian campaign allowed many men to see these splendours and some archaeological work was done on his orders. As a result, for a short time, ancient Egyptian architecture and design took the place in European fashion previously enjoyed by the arts of Greece and Rome.

Egyptian hieroglyphic writing has been known for quite a long time, but it remained an unread mystery until the finding of the Rosetta stone in 1799. On it was an inscription in three languages, including hieroglyphs, which gave scholars the right clue.

Then in 1822 the real excitement began. In the Middle East another form of writing made up of wedge-shaped marks (cuneiform), had been known for many years but all attempts to read it had also failed. At last, on a cliff-face at Behistun, in the wild mountains between Iraq and Persia, a cuneiform inscription was discovered to be in three different languages. This allowed Young and a Frenchman named Champollion, who had worked successfully on the hieroglyphic script, to make the essential comparisons. The first word to be read was the name, Darius, the great king of the Medes and Persians mentioned in the Old Testament. Public interest was caught.

It was not long before Assyrians and Babylonians sprang into life as their letters, state records and documents of all kinds, written in the cuneiform script on tablets of clay or cut into stone, were read and translated. More monuments were soon found. By 1845, Rawlinson and Layard were excavating the site of Nineveh near Mosul in northern Iraq. At much the same time an American, Herzfeld, was at Susa and Persepolis. A French expedition in Southern Iraq uncovered parts of the Sumerian city of Lagash.

GROWTH OF A SCIENCE

With the growth of popular concern in archaeology,

Excavation techniques have developed greatly under the guidance of archaeologists, supplanting the crude methods of earlier days.

museums wished to stock their display cases with more exhibits; money became available to finance expeditions to many areas. A great treasure-hunt began.

By the turn of the century the German, Schliemann, an extremely rich and enthusiastic amateur archaeologist inspired by the tales of Homer, had discovered pre-historic Greece in the successive layers at Troy as well as a different civilisation at Mycenae. Flinders Petrie had excavated the huge site of Lachish in Palestine, which had been left almost uninhabited since the Babylonians sacked the city for the last time in 588 B.C., and Mariette, the great French scholar, had given Egyptology a good start. In Asia Minor, remains of an unknown Hittite civilisation were discovered by Christian Texier. Arthur Evans, excavating in Crete, disinterred the world of the Minoans. What had previously been a trickle of antiquities from Greece, Italy and Egypt into museums and private collections, became streams from many parts of the world.

Gradually, however, it was learnt that the object itself was less valuable than the information which could be obtained from it. Many small things such as fragments of pottery had a hidden message for a trained archaeologist if he knew precisely from where the fragment had come. Unhappily not all seekers of antiquities were either authorised or careful, and not all expeditions were well run. In addition, quantities of such things as beads, seals, pottery, statuettes, coins, tablets, and papyri, many of which were fakes, found their way from the hands of local opportunists on to the market. In any case, it was often impossible later to trace whence an object had originated, and so its hidden message was lost.

Meanwhile, dedicated archaeologists began to evolve truly scientific methods. One of these, stratigraphy, is the dating of objects according to the depth and strata of deposit in which they are found. This and other methods of systematic investigation were used by a German team at Babylon. For years layer by layer, foot by foot they worked over the great mounds which were all that was left of the city.

THE SEARCH FOR NEW SITES

After the Great War of 1914-18, the search began again.

The list of all the sites examined by archaeologists would be a long one. Over and above the work that continued in the " classic " areas of Italy, Greece and the Middle East, there was an urge to look closely at places previously only visited by explorers. For example, in America new studies were undertaken of Pueblo Indian, Aztec, Maya and Inca cultures and antiquities. In Asia, Ankur in Cambodia was explored by archaeologists. From China came very early pre-historic finds at Anyang. Through such studies of ancient remains each continent added to the general story of how men have built literate civilisations and retained their culture, and how sometimes it has been lost.

Some of the new sites soon became famous. For example, in India in 1921 signs were found in the Indus valley of another, and until then quite unknown, civilisation of the Third Millennium B.C. In 1922, an Englishman called Carter discovered the unplundered tomb of one of the Pharoahs of Egypt, Tutankhamen. Fortunately the lessons of the past had been learnt; the priceless treasures of gold were treated as not more worthy of record than the faded, shrivelled flowers, or grains of corn left to nourish the dead king. In Iraq, Leonard Woolley began his long, painstaking examination of the great tel which held the remains of the Sumerian city of Ur. Here, too, treasures were found, many crushed by the weight of earth accumulating above them for more than four thousand years. Such care and skill was now being shown by the excavators that fragile objects, among them musical instruments and delicate head-dresses for Queen Shubad and her attendants, were able to be accurately reconstructed.

MODERN METHODS OF DETECTION

In many countries and by experiment, new ways continued to be invented to help preserve what was found, and to read what the earth itself could also tell; for layers of soil once disturbed are a little different from undisturbed layers, even after thousands of years have gone by. What is more, perishable material such as wood or woven fabric may leave tell-tale traces. At Tara in Ireland, and Stonehenge, careful examination of the ground has allowed the position of postholes to be pin-pointed, although the wood has vanished,

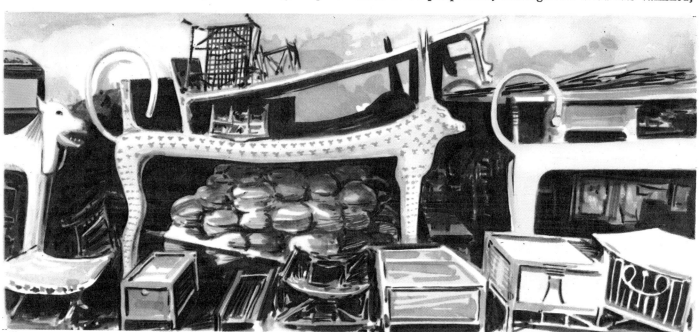

Above is a collection of priceless treasures found in the burial chamber of the tomb of the Pharaoh Tutankhamen.

An aerial view of Maiden Castle, an Iron Age fortress in Dorset.

and all surface marks disappeared. Similarly, at Sutton Hoo in Suffolk, a buried Viking-type ship, eighty-five feet long and containing splendid examples of Saxon art, could be entirely rebuilt.

Nowadays the archaeologist has a battery of powerful means to discover what he wants to know. Aerial photography will disclose, by the slightest shading, bases of hidden walls, roads and earthworks. Especially in clear tropic or Mediterranean waters, skin-diving equipment permits trained men to swim deep to explore drowned cities, buildings or wrecks. Strong beams of artificial light show us pre-historic wall-paintings in pitch-dark caves, such as those found in 1940 at Lascaux in France. By echo-sounding and electrical techniques attempts have been made to locate the crown jewels of King John, traditionally said to have been lost near the Wash in East Anglia. One of the most remarkable and important methods now used to assess the age of any organic (animal or vegetable) material is known as the Carbon-14 test: by measuring the degree of radio-active carbon-14 remaining in the object tested, its age can be estimated to within about 150 years either way.

Such a test is of immense help to archaeologists when studying the remains of people of a pre-historic period. Not all archaeologists are concerned with great civilisations and cultures. In Denmark, Cornwall, Wiltshire, the Orkney Islands, the Americas, Central Africa and Australasia, to mention only a few places, remains of simple, primitive human settlements have been explored. By comparing the characteristics of various settlements in a geographical area, they can be put into relationship one with another, e.g., by plotting sites similar to those of the Hallstatt type Iron Age culture in Austria, it is possible to show how this particular culture spread over most of Europe.

Sometimes the story of great civilisations or cities can be carried back to their humble beginnings. At Jericho in Jordan, within the last few years, the layers of city upon city have been followed down to the first primitive settlement. These Stone Age people built their houses on the virgin rock probably around 8000 B.C. near to the spot where, almost certainly, a spring of water gushed out then as it does to-day.

The work of the archaeologist is not finished when objects

25

have been found and dated, records made and published, and movable things placed in the safe-keeping of museums. Often the site itself has to be preserved in some way, perhaps by covering it up again with soil. Some sites are preserved in the open, such as the streets, houses and shops in the Roman cities of Pompeii and Herculaneum in Italy. Abandoned in A.D. 79 after being buried by ash from the volcano Vesuvius, these sites have been cleared so that anyone may now walk there and see how the inhabitants lived nearly 1,900 years ago. Some discoveries have to be moved to another site; this happened to the Mithraic temple uncovered during post-war rebuilding in London. In the next few years the huge royal statues and temple of Abu Simbel in Egypt must be lifted to the top of the cliff out of which they are carved; if they are left on their original site on the bank of the Nile they will be lost forever as the water rises behind the Aswan High Dam.

Some finds require special methods to preserve them. Water-logged wood, for example, will crumble and warp if allowed to dry under ordinary conditions, so means have had to be devised to impregnate it with preservatives to keep it intact. A Swedish triumph of this kind was the recovery in 1961 of the *Vasa*, a naval vessel of the seventeenth century, which had been lying on the bed of Stockholm harbour for over 300 years. In Denmark, clothed human bodies, remarkably preserved in a bog for hundreds of years, have been found and re-preserved.

ARCHAEOLOGY IN RECENT YEARS

Since 1950 there have been few archaeological discoveries of great treasure to rival those of the preceding hundred years, but work continues all over the world. Modern methods of excavation are slow, often a matter of work with trowel and tiny brush rather than pick and shovel. This is why at Nimrud in Iraq the excavation site has only recently been closed after work lasting twelve years. The finding of the Dead Sea Scrolls has led to many seasons of work at Qumran and neighbouring sites.

The voyage of the raft, Kon Tiki, *proved the possibility of a South American colonisation of the Pacific Islands.*

In the British Isles, every summer sees new sites being explored and old sites enlarged. Schoolboys and girls take part in local excavations such as that at Fishbourne in Sussex, where mosaic floors of a Roman building were found under a field. In London, students have worked on blitzed sites in order to learn before rebuilding started what of Roman, Saxon or medieval London lay beneath the rubble.

Now that travel is easier, archaeology in distant places is no longer just for a few highly trained or wealthy people. To help in the recent excavations at Masada, the Herodian fortress by the Dead Sea in Israel, volunteers have come from many countries to give their labour, if only for a few weeks. Only modern means of transport in the 1950s made feasible the mapping of the Inca road system in Peru— thousands of miles in length, planned and built more than four hundred years ago. The Incas claimed that state messages could be carried along the road from end to end by short stage runners on foot, who ran at a pace equivalent to 246 miles every 24 hours. Such speeds were unimaginable to the first Spanish explorers who explained them in terms of magic, and until a few years ago they were still dismissed as wild exaggerations. Now they are known to have been possible.

In contrast, Thor Heyerdahl chose to experiment with antique transport; within a year or two of the end of the last war he organised the Kon-Tiki raft expedition. As well as a first class adventure, his journey was really a kind of practical archaeological study: he wanted to find out if people from South America, with the means known to have been at their disposal centuries ago, would have been able to drift westwards on rafts over the vast Pacific Ocean to reach and inhabit remote islands. If this was so, it would be one solution for various archaeological puzzles.

Some archaeological sites of particular interest have also been further investigated within recent years. Among them are several at Jerusalem, and below St. Peter's basilica in Rome. Tantalising though it may be to archaeologists, work on such sites is often, of necessity, limited. In many instances the existence of remains of great interest is suspected, or even known of, but they cannot be reached without endangering, or perhaps desecrating, precious and venerated buildings now covering the site.

Every year and in all parts of the world the work goes on of discovering more about the great and small achievements of our ancestors upon the earth, their arts, buildings, thoughts, skills, and every detail of the way they lived, both in those periods for which we have at least a thread of connected written records, and those of pre-history. Every year some of the once lost pieces of the jig-saw are detected and put into their proper place. Occasionally, when more pieces come to be fitted into the whole, the position of fragments placed earlier has to be adjusted. Sometimes what is found cannot be understood. Despite the efforts of scholars, it was over forty years between the discovery of a mysterious script on tablets in the palace of Knossos in Crete, and its identification in the 1950s as a primitive form of Greek. The script has been called Linear B, and was first read by two young men, Michael Ventris and John Chadwick, working together. They were not even born when the script was found.

There are always problems waiting to be solved.

It is amusing to speculate which of the objects that surround us in our day-to-day lives, which of our buildings and treasures, books and pictures, will puzzle or delight archaeologists of future centuries.

CERAMICS

Ceramics is a general term for articles made in fired clay, and for the study of the art of the potter. Famous collections include rare and beautiful specimens of figurines, vases, and table china; but in every home there are many examples of ceramic products. The house, itself, is probably built of brick and roofed with tiles; fireplaces and bathrooms are tiled; the electrical equipment made safe for use by ceramic insulators; and drain pipes, wash basins, lavatory pans, and baths manufactured from ceramic materials. From the humble origin of the Greek word *keramos*, meaning earthenware, the word ceramic is now applied to articles as diverse as teacups and missile nose-cones.

EARLY HISTORY

Although it has flourished most spectacularly in certain countries, and their products have influenced others, the art of the potter appears to have been indigenous to all civilisations and countries from the earliest time when man left his cave to build shelter for himself, and tired of cold raw food. The Egyptians and Babylonians used fired brick as a building material ten thousand years ago, and the first known example of Egyptian red and black pottery dates from about 4000 B.C.

From Egypt, knowledge of methods of modelling and decorating spread through Cyprus and Crete to Greece and Rome, and thus to Europe.

In China the art made swift progress from the crude efforts of the Chou dynasty (1122-206 B.C.) to those of the Sung dynasty (A.D. 960-1279)—some of the finest pieces ever made anywhere in the world.

MATERIALS

The majority of the materials used in the production of pottery are the products of oxidisation: the three most important being clay, flint, and feldspar. Clay which comes from the weathering of feldspathic rock, gives the body its plasticity; flint (pulverised silicon dioxide, usually from quartzite sand or rock) adds whiteness and is used as a " filler " to prevent the collapse of shapes in firing; feldspar acts as a flux—the material in a composition with the lowest melting point which serves as a cementing element for the others, gives the body its strength, and governs its porosity. To these, other materials may be added, most notably pulverised animal bone for the production of bone china, an English invention still unrivalled for whiteness, strength, and translucency.

MANUFACTURE

These basic materials in modern pottery-making are ground, purified, filtered, kneaded and mixed with water to provide the plastic clay body for the potter to work. The simplest pots of ancient times were shaped by hand or built up in coils of clay. The invention of the potter's wheel, a rotating circular platform, provided the means for shaping symmetrically curved pieces and, apart from the introduction of electricity to power the wheel, this method, known as throwing, has altered little from biblical times to the present day. Next in importance is the process of casting, which is particularly suitable for ornamented pieces or those of a shape which it would be difficult or impossible to make on a wheel. Liquid clay is poured into a plaster mould cut to the profile of the piece required. Water is absorbed by the porous mould, leaving a thin coating of clay in the profile. Excess liquid is poured away and the clay coating allowed to dry and contract away from the profile before being finished and fired (baked) in the kiln (oven). These two methods—or modern developments of them—are those most commonly employed in the production of domestic pottery to-day.

Left: *a Cretan vase of 1600 B.C. decorated with polyps, seaweed and an octopus.* Right: *a Cretan vase of the Minoan age.*

This pitcher with a griffon's head and the chalice with the decorated base are of ancient Greek origin.

27

Examples of Persian pottery. The star tile at the bottom left is thirteenth-century.

The words China and Pottery are often loosely used to describe any ceramic tableware, and it is therefore essential to define the difference between these two important domestic products. Pottery, or earthenware, is made from ball clay, china clay, and feldspar. It is opaque, and porous. China, or porcelain, is made principally from china clay and feldspar: the fired body is translucent, whiter than earthenware, and extremely strong. Bone china, stronger, whiter, and more translucent than feldspathic china, is made of china stone, china clay, and a high percentage of calcined animal bone. It is fired at about 1300° Centigrade—about 200° higher than earthenware.

China and earthenware for domestic use are normally protected by a covering of translucent glaze. Prepared to a chemical formula, glaze is a form of liquid glass used originally to seal porous ceramic bodies, but developed, tinted and coloured, as an important form of decoration. Coloured glaze is only one of many types of decoration for pots. The clay body itself may be coloured, ornamented, or decorated in coloured clay; the fired biscuit (unglazed) or glazed body may be printed, painted free-hand, enamelled (printed and then filled in by hand) or lithographed (transfer-printed in several colours) and enriched with gold or platinum. The earliest pottery decoration relied upon the colours of the clay body and glazes, or simple designs in slip (liquid clay).

DEVELOPMENT

The earliest known Chinese pottery dates from about 2500 B.C., but the production of porcelain is not recorded until the beginning of the T'ang dynasty (A.D. 618-906). The finest of all Chinese porcelain belongs to the Sung dynasty (960-1279), a period unique in ceramic history. The wares of this period depend entirely upon beauty of form and the colours of the glazes, which are unsurpassed in modern times. The later development of a brilliant white porcelain encouraged the use of painted decoration which, although often superbly handled, does not bear comparison with the rich purity of the Sung wares. Blue and white decoration was introduced in the Yüan dynasty (1280-1368), and enamelling in colour followed in the period of the Ming dynasty (1368-1644). The wares of the Ch'ing dynasty (1644-1912) are chiefly remarkable for their variety, much of which was

introduced with a form of mass production to satisfy an enormous export trade to Europe through the East India companies; but the porcelain of the eighteenth century was rightly prized for the excellence of its polychrome enamelling and, in particular, it is to this period that we owe the forms of decoration now known as *famille verte* and *famille rose*. Chinese porcelain of the nineteenth century showed a marked decline in artistry and quality, being generally inferior reproductions of earlier styles, or over-meticulous and fussy in decoration.

EUROPE

Chinese porcelain was exported in quantity to Europe in the sixteenth century, and many experiments were made in attempts to discover the secret of its manufacture.

The importance of German ceramics derives from the collaboration between Johann Friedrich Böttger and Ehrenfried Walther von Tschirnhaus at the beginning of the eighteenth century, when they discovered the nature of Chinese porcelain and methods of imitating it. The great Meissen factory was founded in 1710. The formulae for the porcelain and glaze were closely guarded, but in spite of every precaution they found their way to Vienna, where du Paquier established a factory in 1719, and a year later to Venice. The first Meissen porcelain was decorated in enamel colours, and for a full century the factory continued to produce beautifully decorated china in a wide variety of styles. In 1731 Johann Joachim Kändler joined the factory and created in Europe a new art—that of modelling figures. He is estimated to have modelled more than one thousand figures for Meissen and remains one of the most important influences in European ceramic history. Other factories of particular importance in Germany in the second half of the eighteenth century included Berlin, Fürstenberg, Höchst, Nymphenburg (where the great Bustelli was modeller), Ludwigsburg, and Frankenthal.

The contribution of Greece, Italy, Spain, and Holland lies in their earthenwares. Examples of vases and ewers made in Crete about 1500 B.C., magnificently decorated with human and animal motifs in black on a reddish-brown body, give us much information about the habits and customs of the people. Italian and Spanish pottery of the fifteenth and

Left: *the Alhambra Palace in Granada.* Right: *a small part of the interior showing the terra-cotta ornamentation and enamelled bricks.*

sixteenth centuries, known as *maiolica* or *faience*, was gaily coloured and often decorated with classical, mythological, or biblical scenes. Dutch *delft* earthenware, named after the town where Chinese porcelain was copied for the European market, owed much to Italian influence, an influence which extended through Holland to England. The name is most generally associated with wares decorated in dark blue on a white ground.

In France, the faience of the sixteenth and seventeenth centuries was inspired by Italian maiolica, and it was not until the establishment of a factory in Rouen in 1650 by Edme Poterat that a new national tradition of decoration, making use of scrolls, lacework, and draped motifs, was evolved. Even more important was the founding, early in the eighteenth century, of the royal Sèvres factory to make porcelain. The chemical formula of the body differed substantially from those of the Chinese and German porcelains, but it was light and translucent and lent itself admirably to fine decorations of landscape, flowers, birds, and figure subjects after the paintings of such fashionable artists as Boucher and Watteau, which made the Sèvres factory the leader of taste in European ceramics for many years.

English porcelain of the eighteenth century imitated the styles of Sèvres and Meissen, both in tableware and figures, and some beautiful work—highly derivative in design, but with a certain freedom, simplicity and charm which many people find lacking in the greater perfection of the originals—was carried out at the Chelsea, Bow, Derby, and Worcester factories. English delft derived variously from the styles of Holland, China, and Italy, and provided little of originality until the establishment, in 1759, of the Wedgwood factory. Fairly described as the "Father of English Pottery", Josiah Wedgwood laid the foundations for modern systems of mass production and thus of the important British pottery industry. Of all his original inventions and productions, his firm was then and is now probably most famous for the blue and white jasper, a stoneware decorated with classical reliefs copied from Greek and Roman antiquities; but his outstanding achievement was the introduction of an improved creamware, a domestic earthenware so fine that it was ordered

In Italy, famed for its ceramics, the most highly esteemed ceramic-producing centre was at Faenza. Established early in the fifteenth century, the craft of the Faenza potters attained such a high standard that the name faience *was adopted in French and other languages for enamelled earthenware.*

Copying the classical styles which were then enjoying a return to favour, Josiah Wedgwood designed his famous jasper ware.

for the richest houses (huge sets were commissioned for the Empress Catherine of Russia, and for Queen Charlotte, consort of George III), and yet cheap enough to be afforded by all but the poorest families. This creamware, later named, with Queen Charlotte's permission, Queensware, revolutionised not only the industry but also the eating habits of Europe, whose people had until then eaten off silver, Chinese porcelain, pewter, or wooden plates. With the introduction in 1810 by Josiah Spode of bone china, now accepted as the finest tableware product in the modern world, English ceramics took a lead in the domestic field which has never been lost.

SCIENCE AND CERAMICS

Perhaps the most remarkable aspect of ceramics is the wealth of early examples of the potter's art—some made as much as five thousand or more years ago and which are still in existence. Oxygen, the very air we breathe, destroys most of the materials commonly used by man: iron and steel rust; paper becomes yellow and brittle with age; oxygen supports the combustion of organic materials such as wood. Ceramic materials are, however, unaffected by oxygen and are therefore among the most durable of all. They are also extremely hard, having a compressive strength of up to 100,000 pounds per square inch, and are thus resistant to abrasion. Lastly they have exceptional thermal durability, easily withstanding very high temperatures. These properties of chemical, mechanical, and thermal strength make ceramics suitable for widely varied uses including flooring, heat-containing equipment (such as ceramic refractories used in the construction of kilns for the ceramics industry, furnaces for the metal industry, inner linings of fireplaces, and home-heating furnaces), electrical insulators, and most recently for the nose-cones of missiles.

Much of what we know about past civilisations comes from the ability of ceramics—tiles, bricks, and domestic pottery—to withstand the chemical effects of age; much of the comfort of our present civilisation depends upon the use of ceramics in building, heating, lighting, and industry; future civilisations may be founded upon the development of ceramics for space travel and exploration.

EGYPT

The story of the rise and fall of Egypt is one of the most fabulous in ancient history. Egypt owed its extremes of splendour and poverty to the great river Nile which flows through it. The annual floods, caused by the melting of the mountain snows at the source of the river, made all the difference between bread and hunger to those who cultivated the arid, narrow land between the desert and the Red Sea.

We owe the preservation of the records of Egypt's majestic past to its hot, dry climate. When the desert sands drifted over cities and temples, the carvings, wall paintings and inscriptions which glorified her dead kings were perpetuated in dry storage for hundreds, even thousands of years. Because of their custom of burying their dead rulers in gorgeously furnished tombs, surrounded by members of their household, their animals, and all the food, weapons and clothes they might need for their journey into the other world, other indications of how the ancient Egyptians lived were preserved.

Heavy clothes were out of the question owing to the extreme heat and dry atmosphere. For men, the basic garment was a loin-cloth. The many thousands of slaves who did the manual work in Egypt merely twisted this long strip of white, or coloured material round their waists. They wore only this and a head-cloth for protection against the hot rays of the sun.

KINGS' APPAREL

The earliest records of Egypt's past go back beyond 4,000 B.C. Then, even the king, his courtiers, statesmen and commanders, often wore not more than a loin-cloth and head covering. However, the king's loin-cloth was finely pleated and woven from exquisite gold thread; in front of the loin-cloth was a stiffened triangle of linen, with its point fastened to the girdle and its base half-way to the knees. On this panel

hung the royal insignia, ornaments of gold and precious stones, threaded together to give the general effect of a sporran on the front of a kilt. The upper part of his body was usually bare, except for a splendid collar of concentric rings of gold and precious stones, and he wore a specially splendid striped head-cloth, cut in the fashion we associate with pictures of the Sphinx. It was cut across the forehead, then folded or stitched to fall in a sort of lappet on either side of the face and across the shoulders at the back. Round the king's head-cloth was clasped the royal diadem, in jewel-studded gold. This was surmounted by the uraeus, the sacred serpent which was the symbol of regal power.

On ceremonial occasions, the king carried the two sceptres of Egypt, the crook and the flail. These were probably ancient symbols of the two sorts of husbandry, the care of flocks and the harvesting of grain. In the earliest recorded times, he also wore a symbolic lion's tail attached to the back of his girdle, which suggests a still remoter past as leader of the wild nomadic tribes of North Africa.

Sometimes the king and his officials are shown wearing cloaks or a type of wrap-around skirt. In the New Kingdom (about 1350 B.C.), we find a shirt-like garment called *kalasiris*, with or without sleeves, which was worn ankle-length, by men of wealth and position. Over this, the king still wore the sporran-like insignia of royalty hanging from his girdle. Incidentally, the name " Pharaoh " for the ruler of Egypt seems to be used only by the compilers of the Bible and writings derived from it, not by his own people.

Because of the heat, many men shaved their heads, and then wore elaborately curled wigs when they went out of doors. For ceremonial occasions they also put on short, square-cut artificial beards, which they fastened round their ears with loops. It was essential that the king's beard should be slightly longer than that of any other member of his court. Both men and women went barefoot, or wore the lightest of

The Pharaoh, his soldiers and servants in procession—this picture shows the varied costumes of Ancient Egypt.

Assyrian costumes c. *1500* B.C. Left to right: *a monarch, noble, priest, satrap, young priest and scribe.*

rush-woven sandals. Slave girls wore nothing but a girdle and a filmy, almost transparent cloak. Wealthy women also wore fine, filmy materials; their long, ungirdled tunics fitted closely to their bodies and were supported by braces which were sometimes wide enough to cover the breasts and sometimes not. The really elegant wore wigs, wide, jewelled collars and wrist and ankle bracelets.

An ostrich-feather fan, consisting of a single plume mounted on a long handle, was given as a special honour to princes, important officials and army leaders. These fans were carried on state occasions. It is assumed that Egyptian kings led their people in sport and war, for wall paintings show such rulers as Rameses II (1332 B.C.) riding out in his one-man war chariot. He is wearing a helmet surmounted by the sacred serpent, his jewelled collar, and a linen loin-cloth. The absence of protective armour suggests he may have been hunting rather than fighting. The problem of how to use a bow and arrow while driving a chariot seems to have been daringly solved by fastening the reins to the girdle while the king took aim with his horses at full gallop. Other pictures show the king equipped for war in helmet and armoured jacket. Over all he wore a surcoat embroidered with the design of the sacred vulture, its wings spread as if in protection across the wearer's breast.

YOUTHFUL FASHION

An odd fashion for youths seems to have come in during the latter centuries of the New Kingdom. Princes shaved all their heads except for a single, long lock. The lock was tied with ribbon to fall forward on to the left shoulder. The ordinary soldiers wore body armour of leather covered with pieces of metal, which either covered the whole coat or were sewn to long strips of leather and wound spirally round the body. They also wore the typical, square-cut, sphinx-like head-cloth and their loin-cloths usually had a triangular or leaf-shaped panel in front. They were armed with spears, swords, clubs or bows and arrows; their shields were long and rectangular and made of wood covered with skin. These shields had the unusual feature of quite large eye-holes near the top.

ASSYRIA

"The Assyrian came down like the wolf on the fold, and his cohorts were gleaming in purple and gold". Byron's poem caught two of the dominant characteristics of this ancient hill empire of Mesopotamia. For the Assyrians were both aggressive and gorgeous. Their culture was not as old as that of Egypt, for it was not till about 2,000 B.C. that they emerged from the hill country, through which the Tigris ran, to conquer Nineveh and make it their capital. After the fall of Babylon, in 1280 B.C. and with Egypt in decline, Assyria became a great power in the Middle East.

UNIVERSAL GARMENT

As a people, the Assyrians seem to have cared more for magnificence than elegance. The clothes of the Assyrian rulers were made of the richest available materials, in brilliant colours, with lavishly ornate trimmings. Basically, the universal garment worn by both men and women was a sort of shirt, rather like the Egyptian *kalasiris*. It had short, tight sleeves and came down to the ankles of the members of the ruling classes, but only to the knees of working men, who seem, throughout history, to have dressed much more sensibly than their rulers. This short shirt was the only garment of the many slaves, but for people of rank and importance it was merely a foundation for the gorgeously fringed and tasselled mantles, girdles and sashes with which they loaded themselves. These mantles varied a good deal in style as time went on, but at the height of Assyrian splendour they practically covered the wearer, coming down the arms as far as the elbow, with only a few inches of heavily fringed shirt showing below.

OFFICIAL ROBES

Court and state officials also wore long, fringed stoles, and their importance was indicated by such details as the length of the fringe, the way the stole was worn, and the richness of the material. Priests had a rich and most distinctive dress, based on the short-sleeved shirt, over which a sort of long, narrow mantle was spirally draped round the body from the feet to the shoulders. Their fringed and embroidered breast and back covering was made rather like a sleeveless pullover, open at the sides, with a central hole through which the priest put his head. Then he girdled the drapery into place. Kings, priests and nobles, all seem to have worn high, conical hats, lavishly ornamented, and both men and women loaded

31

An Assyrian general in his war chariot before a fortified city. The Assyrian chariot was of heavier structure than the Egyptian war chariot and its wheels could be fitted with scythes. The breast-plate and helmet of the Assyrian general were made of leather, reinforced with metal bands and plates.

themselves with bracelets, jewelled collars, and ear-rings. The king and his nobles wore swords, even on peaceful occasions, and they either went barefoot or wore sandals. Women draped long—or short—fringed mantles over their ankle-length, fringed shirts.

ARMY UNIFORM

The Assyrian soldier was a very striking figure, in his high, pointed, metal helmet, shirt of mail, which sometimes reached to his ankles, and he was girded with a broad, leather belt to which the sword was slung almost horizontally. He wore long hose, gartered at the knee, and high, laced boots and fought with a spear and a powerful short bow. The Assyrian shield was round, coming to a point at the centre, and the war horses were ridden in rather modern-looking snaffle bridles, but with only a padded skin knotted under the belly instead of a saddle. Their riders, who used no stirrups, were the terror of the Middle East till they were conquered by Alexander the Great in 332 B.C.

CRETE

The island civilisation of Crete in the Eastern Mediterranean is one of the most tantalising mysteries of the ancient world. It was in full flower about the same time as the Middle Kingdom of Egypt, and was the legendary home of the Minotaur in his labyrinth. The people of Crete left no written records. We can only piece together a picture of their costume from such things as the beautiful seals, ornamented goblets or pieces of statuary which have been unearthed from the ruins of some of her cities.

The Cretans, apparently, had none of the barbaric love of ornamentation found in Assyria. Both men and women seemed to have worn short loin-cloths; the men are shown wearing little else as they drove their teams of horses in the arena, wrestled with each other, or fought bulls or wild animals. In war, however, they are shown with plumed helmets, body armour, and calf-high boots. But the dress of the women was unique. They wore bell-shaped skirts almost like crinolines, either flounced or beautifully pleated in layers up to the rolled girdles encircling the tiny waists. Women of the upper classes wore an apron-type garment over the

skirts and little short jackets with sleeves. Other women wore the skirt alone. We cannot, unfortunately, do more than guess what materials were used for the elaborate skirts, short swinging jackets and turban-like head-dresses, but the pleating and the flouncing and the bright colours of the porcelain figures stress the beauty of the Cretan costume without telling us nearly all we want to know.

GREECE

The beginnings of ancient Greece, veiled in some of the most enchanting legends of ancient history, give glimpses of this great people as far back as 2,000 B.C. The great period of Greece was between the sixth and the fourth centuries B.C. By 146 B.C., she was steam-rollered into the Roman Empire. Yet, during her splendid centuries, she made a far greater and more lasting contribution to world culture than any other civilisation in the ancient world.

The Greeks were originally a pastoral people, who wove their clothes from the fleeces of their own sheep. It was not until they discovered the possibilities of linen that their dress gained the flowing lines which are typically Grecian. With their characteristic restraint, they avoided the barbaric and the over-decorated. Basically, they had only three garments, though these could be varied in many ways. The pleated linen shirt or *chiton*, might be long or short, either sleeveless or short-sleeved, and was worn by either men or women. The *peplos* was a type of shawl or plaid which was worn by women only. The *chlamys* was a woollen cloak which both men and women wore when necessary. The chiton might be worn with a girdle or without one. Sometimes the girdle was worn round the waist, crossed on the back and brought over the shoulders to the waist again. Its short sleeves were sometimes not continuously stitched from shoulder to elbow, but caught at intervals with stitching or ribbons. In earlier times, the chiton was bordered with designs of checks, lines, stripes or flowers. Then, for a time, patterns disappeared, to return again at the end of the fifth century B.C. Both linen and woollen garments were often dyed in rich and lovely colours. It is quite a mistake to suppose that the Greeks went about in sheet-like draperies, though skill must have been needed to drape the various forms of cloak securely, since the chlamys

Left: *Cretan woman.* Centre: *noble adorned with peacock feathers and fleur-de-lis.* Right: *serpent priestess.*

A bull-ring scene from a Knossos fresco showing young men performing acrobatic tricks over a charging bull.

was often the only garment a man wore. But the chiton or tunic was more convenient for active youths, and it was the typical garment of gymnasts and athletes.

PROTECTIVE WEAR FOR THE ARMY

Soldiers, too, wore the chiton under their armour. Their armour was a fitting coat of mail made up of metal scales stitched on to leather. The mail coat was clasped round the waist, and had a short, protective skirt built up in layers of metal and leather to protect the hips, and reached nearly to the hem of the chiton. The thighs were bare; the front of the legs were protected by metal greaves, rather like hockey pads, and the feet were sometimes bare and sometimes sandalled. The helmet had adjustable cheek guards and a semi-lunar plume of dyed horse hair. The Greek soldier fought with spear and sword and carried a smallish round shield.

GREEK FOOTWEAR

Footwear varied a great deal. Both men and women often went barefoot at home, and preferred the lightest sort of sandals whenever possible. Men wore stouter footgear for heavy work or when on campaign. The simplest form of ancient shoe was simply a circular piece of hide, cut rather larger than the foot and pierced with holes all round the edge. A thong was run in and out of the holes and the wearer stood on the leather and drew it up round his ankles. This elementary shoe was the blue-print for all the elaborate varieties of sandals and high-lacing boots worn by both Greeks and Romans.

HAIR STYLES

Hair styles were varied. In earlier times men wore long hair, which might be curled, left shaggy, or plaited. From the fifth century on, men's hair was cropped short. Women piled their hair high, let it hang in curls, or drew it into a soft knot at the back of the neck. They used hot irons, fillets, kerchiefs and jewels to get the effects they wanted. It was as if they felt the need to balance the simplicity of their dress by the elaboration of their hair. They do not seem to have

The Greeks represented here are from the Classical period.   Left to right: a trumpeter, a spearman, a king dressed after the fashion in which Zeus was depicted, a heavily-armed foot soldier, a young man arming himself, and a Phrygian archer.

33

Roman costume. Left to right: *A tragedian with mask, mantle and high buskins; a citizen wearing a toga; a provincial wearing a tunic and mantle; a general; a general wearing a breast-plate and helmet; and an emperor crowned with a laurel wreath.*

worn any definite form of head-dress. When it rained, they merely pulled a fold of their cloak over their head. Men, on the other hand, who travelled more, wore soft, peaked caps, or straw hats with either wide or narrow brims. The Greek travelling hat, called *petasos*, was a wide-brimmed, modern-looking straw hat which, when not in use, could hang from its long ribbons, down the wearer's back.

ROME

The *toga* is perhaps the one garment of antiquity about which nearly everybody knows. It was the most significant part of a Roman citizen's dress, indicating his rank and calling by means of the variously coloured stripes, or *clavi*, which bordered it. These stripes also bordered the *tunica*, or under-garment, which the Roman man might or might not wear with the toga, in much the same way as Greek men wore the cloak-like chlamys with or without the chiton underneath. But the toga was a voluminous garment, a tremendous oval of fine woollen material, measuring three times the wearer's height from end to end and twice his height across. Like the chlamys, it had no fastenings and required skilful draping.

The tunica, which was not so elegantly pleated as the chiton, might reach just to the knees, or come down to the ankles. The longer form was called the *tunica talaris*, and men wore it on formal occasions. A tunica might have short sleeves or long, but long sleeves were considered rather affected, except for priests and actors. Only working men walked out of doors in the tunica alone. Those who wished to claim rank or privilege wore it in their own homes, and draped themselves in the toga in public.

FASHION FOR WOMEN

Women wore an inner garment, or *tunica intima*, next to the skin. This was plain and tube-like, with short sleeves. In early times it was made of wool, then later of linen. Sometimes it was worn with a girdle and sometimes not. In the latter days of the Roman Empire, the garment became more elaborate and had a train. A hole was left in the tunica intima to allow the wearer's head to go through and the surplus material was then caught up with a brooch or ribbon on the shoulder.

Over the tunica, women wore the *stola*, a garment very

like the one underneath, except that it had elbow-length sleeves. This was often edged with material of a contrasting colour, which was braided or trimmed with jewels. Over this was draped the *palla*, or mantle. In earlier times this was nearly as voluminous as the toga, but was later modified. The Roman ladies wore the palla when they went out, and in wet weather draped a fold of the palla over their elaborately dressed heads. The Roman hair-do was such a tremendous affair that rich women often kept specially skilled slave-girls to curl, frizz, pin, adorn and dye it.

Men entitled to wear the toga also drew a fold of it over their heads for protection in wet weather. However, the workers had a very sensible hooded cloak called *cucullus*, and men who lived in the country wore hats rather like those of the Greeks.

In the centuries immediately before and after the birth of Christ, the uniform of the Roman army must have been a glorious sight. The officers were splendidly equipped with body armour consisting of metal scales attached to a cuirass of leather which was specially moulded to fit each officer. Their short kilt of metal strips on leather was an improved version of the Greek, and so was the *abolla*, the splendid helmet with an upstanding semi-circular plume of dyed horsehair, worn with a scarlet military cloak. Footwear had to be solid; the legions covered great distances along the roads they themselves had made. The men wore hob-nailed sandals and the officers a variety of ornamented, calf-high boots. Later, the Romans took to wearing breeches, copying the trousers, or breeches, of the barbarians they had conquered. On their conquering progress, the Romans carried spears, short stabbing swords, and round or oblong shields.

They were confirmed law-makers. They laid down rules for almost everything. The exact make of soldiers' sandals; the footwear considered correct for members of the Senate; the width and colour of the stripes on toga and tunic, all were exactly ordained. The Empire, in fact, was a great, but also a rigid organisation. In times of stress it could not adapt. So when the stress became too great, it broke, and left the world it had ruled at the mercy of the barbarians it had despised. And, in the so-called Dark Ages which followed the fall of Rome, many things, costume among them, became entirely different.

34

Civilisation and Culture
ASSYRIA AND BABYLONIA

Assyrians were people whose way of life for about 1,500 years centred upon the city of Ashur in the northern part of what is now Iraq. Assyrian culture was, in many ways, shared with and even based upon that of people living farther south in the plains of Babylon, or Sumer and Akkad as it was originally called.

Iraq is roughly bordered by mountains to the north and east, and by the Arabian Desert to the west. There are two great rivers, the Euphrates and the Tigris. In their lower courses they run somewhat parallel through a wide plain and marshes before they join together to reach the sea at the head of the Persian Gulf.

The founders of Assyrian culture are believed to have first built their small towns and villages on the edge of the southern marshes. They probably arrived from the mountains to the east at some time early in the fourth millenium B.C. or before. They were not a primitive people; they grew good harvests of wheat and barley, and gathered the fruit of the date palms. The marshes and rivers provided plentiful fish and wild fowl. Their flocks of sheep, goats and cattle prospered, so they had meat, butter, leather and wool. Clay for bricks and pottery filled most of their other needs.

Gradually these Sumerians spread upriver, building towns whose names and ancient sites we know as Ur, Lagash, Umma, Nippur. But the towns of Sumer constantly quarrelled and fought among themselves. It was not difficult for desert tribesmen from the west to come sweeping into the northern part of the plain. These invaders were Semites, a different people from the Sumerians, with a quite different language. Their king, Sargon, soon united his own new kingdom of Akkad with the older, southern towns. From now on Sumer and Akkad formed one kingdom.

The Sumerians used a cuneiform script which they had developed. This was a complicated system of writing which entailed the use of a stylus to impress small, wedge-shaped marks on to soft clay. The clay was probably dried and hardened in the sun, thus preserving the writing. The Akkadians, who apparently had not writing of their own, adapted the Sumerian script to their own language.

The Akkadians did not long retain power. Various cities struggled for the leadership of the kingdom. One of the most successful at the end of the third millenium B.C. was a Neo-Sumerian dynasty at Ur (Ur III). In their turn they were defeated by another wave of Semitic invaders (Amorites), who ruled from two cities, Isin and Larsa. It was not until the eighteenth century B.C. that the supreme kingship was seized by Babylon (Babylon I), a relatively young but enterprising town. King Hammurabi expanded his rule in all directions. He enforced law and order, and created a great code of laws which he probably chose from older laws existing in other cities.

It was at this period that the Assyrians entered the political scene. Some centuries before, into the wide valley of the upper Tigris had come another Amorite tribe. They settled down and built a capital city on the west bank of the Tigris. It was called Ashur, after their particular and patron god. These Assyrians spread mainly northwards along the Tigris until, under King Shamshi-Adad I, they controlled the whole of the upper Tigris area and as far west as the Habur River, a tributary of the middle Euphrates. But as soon as Shamshi-Adad I died, the Babylonians under King Hammurabi made their first successful, if temporary, bid to impose their sovereignty over the Assyrians.

For several centuries, sometimes Babylonia (the enlarged Sumer and Akkad) and sometimes Assyria, was dominant. Their neighbours, such as the Hittites, Mitanni and Urartu, played off the rivals one against the other. The most famous periods of both states came to each in their last dynasties.

Taken from a relief in the palace of Nineveh, this scene shows King Ashurbanipal hunting lions.

In 1722 B.C. another Sargon seized power in Assyria. He founded an empire that stretched from the borders of Persia to the Mediterranean Sea and Egypt. Sargon was followed on the throne by Sennacherib, Esarhaddon and Ashurbanipal. Their capital city was Nineveh, a city largely rebuilt by slave labour from the subject people of the empire and one which was intended to be impregnable. However, in 612 B.C. and after a long siege, an alliance of Medes, Scyths and Babylonians succeeded in breaking into the city. The walls and buildings were razed, the accumulated treasures destroyed or carried away. Assyria ceased to exist.

Now Babylon had a last taste of glory. A new empire was gathered together by King Nebuchadrezzar (spelled Nebuchadnezzar in the Bible). He had been present at the fall of Nineveh. To make sure that a similar fate never overwhelmed Babylon, the city was rebuilt on such a massive scale and adorned so magnificently that it has remained legendary for size, beauty and wealth.

But the long history of the civilisation that Babylon represented was nearing its end. In 538 B.C. the empire and Babylon itself were conquered by Cyrus of Persia, although it is said that the city was only surrendered through treachery. After the Persians, Babylonia came under the rule of Alexander the Great and his Hellenistic successors, then Romans and Parthians. New cultures grew over the old. New languages, new gods, new alphabetic scripts, a foreign aristocracy, and finally a new capital city, first Ctesiphon and later Baghdad, helped to fade the memory and traditions of three or four thousand years of Sumerian, Babylonian and Assyrian history. Soon all that was left of the old cities were vast ruin mounds of crumbling mud brick. These ruins, which have been rediscovered during the last hundred years, tell the story of the people who once lived there.

WORSHIP OF THE GODS

We now know that the way of life of Sumerians, Babylonians and Assyrians was founded upon polytheism, kingship and slavery, but there were slight differences between their social customs and laws. Polytheism means the worship of many gods and kingship that the kings were the earthly vice-regents of their divine masters, the gods.

The Sumerians set the pattern for accepting gods as masters. The people worshipped many gods and each city had its special patron god. Nannar was the patron god of Ur, and was also associated with the moon. Marduk of Babylon and Ashur of the Assyrians were praised as warrior gods, and so was Ishtar. She was a popular goddess also of arts and fertility, with many sanctuaries dedicated to her. At Lagash, fertility was a favourite aspect of the goddess Babu, while Ninhursag was " lady of the mountains ", mother of gods. These were great gods, but there were one or two even greater, such as Anu, whose power was almost infinite. Besides these great, distant and often terrible gods, there were many lesser gods and kindly spirits. Most families had a small family god or spirit who, in response to proper devotion and care, might be expected to protect the family from attack by demons and evil spirits. These were believed to cause all misfortune and illness, including that which any aggrieved god might command to be inflicted as punishment.

The Sumerians, Babylonians and Assyrians gave their divine lords the greatest attention and many offerings. They built the gods earthly homes complete with human officials and domestic servants. In an inner sanctuary stood images of the gods. When a new image of a god was made, magic rituals took place in order to induce some of the divine power of the older image to enter the new. At festivals these images might be taken in procession through the city or countryside. Sometimes they were carried into battle to fortify " their " army.

Kings were considered to be divinely chosen to rule over the earthly realm of the gods. If a king was successful, it was taken as a sign of divine favour and approval. If he or his city or country suffered unusual misfortune, someone else might soon be king. At all points the will of the gods was consulted through their special officials by means of omens, and other secret processes.

As the areas to be governed became greater, officials were appointed to act for the king. They had salaries or the reward of grants of land or enjoyment of taxes. The great wealth of Babylonians and Assyrians was based on agriculture. The particularly rich crops of Babylonia, where rainfall was very low, depended on irrigation. In times of war

Assyrian gods. Centre: *an early type of sculpture, cruder in construction than the later models flanking it.*

Moving a man-headed winged bull of the type later to be discovered by archaeologist, Austen Henry Layard.

or weak government the canals were liable to neglect, and land quickly lapsed into desert. Assyria had more rain, but the land was not so exceptionally fertile.

SLAVE LABOUR

Most of the work of the land was done by small tenant farmers who paid a proportion of their harvest to their landlord. If harvests were poor they might not survive from harvest to harvest without borrowing. Often the debt could only be repaid, if ever, by the farmer or one of his family working it off through a period of slavery. Prisoners of war were also used for such work as public or royal building and canal digging. Unless they were lucky there was little hope of freedom for slaves or their children.

Slaves were the main supply of domestic and commercial labour in town and country and, normally, these slaves were valuable and reasonably well cared for. They could own property, and their status was defined and protected by laws. It was not until the time of the later Assyrian and Babylonian empires that vast numbers of foreigners were brought as slaves from conquered lands to live and work in gangs in harsh conditions.

WRITTEN RECORDS

Although cuneiform writing was so difficult that only trained scribes could read or write, the Assyrians, like the Babylonians, made a common use of it for letters, including the kings who regularly sent written instructions to officials and governors. Contracts, receipts, wage lists, and all kinds of business records were kept. Nothing was legal unless it was adequately witnessed and dated. Sometimes these documents, mostly in the form of clay tablets, were kiln-baked to preserve them permanently; sometimes they were simply dried in the sun. Some of these tablets have been found in the ruin mounds of Iraq, and they have been read and translated.

The chief building material available was mud brick. Houses had solid walls, and heavy, flat roofs made of wooden beams and covered with wattle and clay. Palaces and temples were built on the same basic design as private houses, but on a grander scale: rooms surrounding one or more open courtyards. In old cities space within the en-circling city walls was limited, so from Sumerian times some houses had two or even three storeys. Temple areas had only one special feature, a stepped, four-sided pyramid of brick called a ziggurat. Its precise purpose and function is not quite understood, but each was probably crowned by a small sanctuary or room.

The ziggurat at Babylon was so enormous that trees grew on its terraces, and perhaps helped to create the marvel of the Hanging Gardens.

No coinage as such existed, but fragments of gold and silver and small bars of bronze were carefully weighed to serve the purpose, although the ordinary standard of exchange was barley. Many Assyrians and Babylonians had a high stand-ard of living. They imported luxuries from distant places, including timber from the Lebanon. Babylonians and Sumerians were obliged to import stone. It was used only for important statues and valued objects. The Assyrians lived nearer to quarries, so they were able to decorate their palaces with lavish bas-reliefs showing the triumphs of the kings in war and hunting, and with huge guardian images of bull-like genii. From early Sumerian times, pottery, gold and silver work and bronze objects, as well as weaving, were produced by men and women skilled in the crafts.

We still use the mathematical methods devised by the Sumerians. For example, they divided the day into twelve periods, or double hours, and 360 shorter periods; their year of 360 days had twelve months, with an occasional extra month to adjust to the correct solar year. They divided the circle into the 360 degrees still used. Helped by the clear skies of Iraq, astronomy and astrology were keenly studied. Sumerian, Babylonian and Assyrian records of the move-ments of planets and stars are sufficiently accurate and reliable to be consulted in modern studies of such subjects as stellar cycles.

Civilisation and Culture
GREECE

Greece is renowned as the home of one of the greatest civilisations the world has seen. Geographically it is a predominantly mountainous country. It has, however, very fertile valleys and coastal plains; it was there that the early Greeks established themselves.

The first settlers to populate Greece were peoples from Asia who migrated westwards not later than 3000 B.C. and brought their culture with them. They settled on Crete, the Cyclades, on some of the other island groups, and on the east coast mainland itself. They were subsequently reinforced by further settlers from the East around 2600 B.C. Newcomers infiltrated during the period 1900-1600 B.C. and probably entered from the western side of Greece. It is generally agreed that these newcomers were the first Greek-speaking peoples to reach the central part of Greece and the Peloponnese; they were probably descended from the early settlers of Macedonia.

By about the eighth or ninth centuries B.C., after various migrations of the preceding centuries, the Greek race was divided by dialect into three main groups—the Ionians, the Aeolians, and the Dorians. The division probably existed from about 2600 B.C. and may have begun in Macedonia, Epirus or other adjacent areas since the peoples who made up these groups had come from different places at different times.

This is a simplified picture of the settlement of Greece which began about 3000 B.C. and continued sporadically for approximately two thousand years until about 1000 B.C. Writings which have been handed down in plenty from the fifth century B.C., and a smaller amount from about the eighth century tell us something of the early history of Greece. Archaeology is the other main source, and is more and more important the farther back into history we go.

Greek history falls into five main periods, called Minoan-Mycenaean, Early Iron Age, Archaic, Classical, and Hellenistic. There is no clear break between these periods.

MINOAN-MYCENAEAN PERIOD (2500 B.C.-1000 B.C.)

Crete is the island which was the first home of Greek culture. Though the earliest inhabitants may not have spoken Greek, Greek was certainly the language of the later Minoan (or Cretan) court, which was destroyed either in the fifteenth or thirteenth century B.C., thus bringing to an end a culture which had developed without a serious break for fifteen hundred years. Our knowledge of this culture comes from archaeology, and is now helped by the deciphering of the Linear B writing which was used towards the end of the Minoan period for a primitive dialect of the Greek language. The early Cretans were rich and prosperous, and probably controlled the sea with a navy. They built palaces and ruled as local kings over people partly free, partly slave.

As their power grew, they built large palaces, some of them three storeys high, with many courts and corridors. They decorated the palaces with bright paintings: pottery covered with intricate designs of sea-creatures, and statuettes of human beings and animals were carved and moulded.

Greek colonists from the mainland came to Crete and the Aegean islands about 1500 B.C. We cannot be sure whether they sacked the main Minoan towns about 1400 B.C., or whether the disaster which befell them at this time was due to natural causes, but political power shifted and became centred on the mainland, in the cities of Pylos, Mycenae, Tisyns, Argos, and others. The legendary rulers are the Homeric heroes—Agamemnon, Menelaus and Nestor—but we can say very little about the history of the towns. The civilisation was rich and powerful. Magnificent armour, and many ornaments and objects of gold have been found in the ruins of the great fortress towns. Elaborate graves were built, either in the shape of beehives, or as simple deep shafts in the ground.

The Trojan war is a historical fact surrounded by a cloud of myth and legend. We can be sure that the town of Troy was destroyed at one point by fire. But we do not know who destroyed it: it may have been a local war, or part of the great Dorian invasion which swept away the Mycenaean and Minoan civilisations, and began the Dark Age, in which Classical Greece was born.

THE EARLY IRON AGE (1000 B.C.-700 B.C.)

Most of the movements of Greek peoples had finished by the eleventh century, and the Greeks had spread from the mainland to colonise the islands and the coast of Asia Minor (modern Turkey). The cities usually remained separate, and were ruled by a king and nobles. The king led his city in the frequent raids and wars on neighbours and was often the chief priest as well. People were still conscious of their old tribes and families, which often tore cities apart in civil war. The people were mostly farmers of corn, wine and olives, herdsmen, or fishermen. There was little trade between cities, except in luxuries which at that time included iron. Money had not been invented, so trade was carried on by barter. Women played an important and respected role in the house, spinning, weaving, caring for the household, while the men produced food, followed a trade, and went to war.

Religion was very local. A few gods and goddesses—Zeus, his wife Hera, Apollo, Artemis and others—were worshipped over most of Greece, but the enormous number of local deities were no less important. There were spirits of nature—of springs, woods, winds, seasons—and animal gods like the satyrs and centaurs, but most of them had a human shape. There was no tidy plan of their relations or functions but a jumble of worship and rituals to cater for all tastes and situations. The Greeks at this period spent little time wondering about death and life after death, but Fate was present behind the other gods and goddesses, ordering men's destiny.

Buildings in this period were usually of mud-brick or rubble: the important ones had a stone base. Roofs were of timber or thatch. Temples were little more than a simple, single room and the statues inside were rough wood carvings or, occasionally, small figures of iron or bronze. Pottery was made in a large variety of shapes, and decorated with simple line and curve patterns, though later, human beings and animals were portrayed.

The surviving literature of this period is the work of Homer and Hesiod. Whoever Homer may have been, the Iliad and the Odyssey were written in the latter part of the eighth century. The poems contain many traditional elements which go back to Mycenaean times: the Iliad tells the story of the siege and fall of Troy, while the Odyssey recounts the adventures and safe return of Odysseus after the fall of the city. Hesiod was a farmer in Boeotia, who, at the end of the eighth century, composed two famous poems. The " Works and Days " describes the farmer's life, while the " Theogony " is a collection of myths about the gods and goddesses.

Our knowledge of this period is hazy and incomplete. It is the dawn of Greek civilisation. The sun begins to shine clearly in the Archaic period.

THE ARCHAIC PERIOD (700 B.C.-480 B.C.)

The quiet conditions after the movement of peoples led to an increase of population in the eighth century. There was not enough land for the people, so they emigrated to found new towns overseas, particularly around the Black Sea, Southern Italy and Sicily. This brought them in contact with the culture of other people, started trade, and sparked off the growth of Greek culture—a culture in which the individual played an important part for the first time.

The history of this period is one of continual wars and raids between cities. A few cities—Athens, Sicyon, Corinth, Megara—began to control their neighbours, and win more than local power. Warriors were mounted or on foot. The " hoplite " became the chief infantry force: he was too heavily armed to move fast, but formed a solid mass or " phalanx " normally eight ranks deep, which was supported by the cavalry. Battles were formal affairs, often preceded by long negotiations between heralds, and conducted according to very elaborate rules, like a game of chess. Religious ritual was an important part of military campaigns. The history of this period ends with the two famous Persian invasions of Greece in 490 and 480, which resulted in the battles of Thermopylae, Marathon, Salamis, and Plataea. The Greeks

for the first time formed a rough league, and were victorious: for the first time they realised that they were all Greeks, and not just a collection of separate cities or tribes.

Colonisation brought with it trade. This resulted in a new class of merchants, who gradually won power in the cities from the nobles who, with the king, had been supreme until then. The change was often accompanied by civil war, and the reign of a " tyrant ". A tyrant was not necessarily a civil dictator, but a person with enough power to change traditions and redistribute power. Solon and Pisistratus at Athens, Polycrates of Samos, Cyprelus of Corinth, and many others, were leaders who reorganised their cities and paved the way for rich development. They often promoted trade, built temples, fortifications, and aqueducts and encouraged art at their courts.

With the increase of trade across the sea, ships developed. The penteconter, or fifty-oared ship gave way to the bireme and then the trireme, a low warship about one hundred and forty feet in length, and twenty in beam. We are still uncertain precisely how the three banks of oars were arranged. Merchants used smaller ships which combined oars and sail: often the merchant was no more than a farmer who sold his spare produce abroad on one or two brief summer voyages.

Trade increased the number of luxuries to be acquired, and the Greeks were especially proud of jewellery and personal ornaments. Other arts also developed. The Greek lyric poets—Archilocus, Sappho, and Tyrtaeus—developed a new type of short poem quite unlike the epics of Homer, though both were accompanied by music. Painted decoration on pottery became more frequent and more skilled—especially human or animal figures outlined in black. New shapes of pottery were invented. Sculpture in stone spread, and although the human figures may look stiff and unnatural, their colouring was vivid and fresh. Temples of stone, with tiled roofs, were built: they usually consisted of a sanctuary or closed room surrounded by a row of pillars.

In this period, games in honour of the gods became popular—The Olympian, Zethmian, Nemean, and others. Physical training was a large part of ordinary education, together with poetry, singing and playing the lyre, reading,

A burial party about to enter a beehive tomb of the later Mycaenean period (1400-1200 B.C.).

39

writing, arithmetic, and religious instruction. Religion changed little; Dionysus became more popular, and cults concerned with life after death (" mystery cults ") sprang up, but the basic beliefs remained the same. This period marks the beginning of " philosophy ", when Thales, Anaximander, Anaximines, Pythagoras, and Heraclitus began to investigate science, mathematics, religion, and ethics.

This period marks the beginnings of a culture which we can call Greek. It burst into flower in the fifth century.

THE CLASSICAL PERIOD (480 B.C.-338 B.C.)

This is the age of the blossoming of Greek culture under the leadership of Athens, and is bounded by the Persian invasions at its beginning and the conquest of Greece by Philip of Macedon at its end. It is the age of the famous dramatists and philosophers, sculptors and architects, generals and statesmen, who produced the Golden Age of Greece.

Up till the year 404, the main political event was the growth of the Athenian empire. A long series of wars and treaties gave the Athenian navy control of the Aegean sea and Athens became immensely rich and powerful through trade with and tribute from her subjects. On land, Athens created a short-lived empire which was lost by 445. In 431 began the series of wars in which Sparta, Athens's greatest enemy was eventually victorious. There were sea and land battles throughout Greece, a great campaign in Sicily, many treaties and leagues, until Sparta, helped by Persia, captured Athens in 404. The Athenian empire was destroyed: many soldiers who saw no prospects at home marched with Xenophon to the Persian empire, to free the Greek cities there.

It is often said that Greece invented democracy during this period. But in fact many of the cities were still ruled by oligarchs or kings. Democracy occurred more by chance than by design, and was often short-lived. Greek cities were very unstable, and many of them changed from democracy to oligarchy and back again about as often as we have elections.

The towns grew in size, and money was spent on large public buildings and temples such as the Parthenon at Athens. The state paid for defence, water-supply, religious festivals and services and wages for the people who served it—public officials, the army, the navy, the police, and public slaves. Corinth had about 90,000 inhabitants, Athens rather more. Trade increased, but was considered degrading by the old noble classes. Sailors ventured farther afield, both north and west, but the basic peasant life remained the same in most of Greece. Ploughing, sowing, reaping, dyeing, spinning and all the normal household occupations underwent little change.

Athens was the cultural centre of Greece during this period. The age of Pericles, the leader of Athens for thirty years until 429 and the designer of her empire, is the age in which most of the famous artists lived. Aeschylus, Sophocles, Euripides and Aristophanes wrote their plays; Thucydides wrote his History of the Peloponnesian War, Herodotus his histories. Myron and Polyclitus produced statues, architects produced new towns, theatres, temples and other buildings whose ruins can still be seen to-day.

Philosophy advanced everywhere through thinkers such as Parmenides and Leucippus, Democritus and Zeno, but Athens became the centre of progress. Socrates and his pupil Plato were only two of many thinkers who questioned the old ideas and religious traditions, and whose influence is felt even to-day.

The fourth century also produced great artists and thinkers, although Athens's political power was not so great. Xenophon, Isocrates and Demosthenes wrote their works, Aristotle developed philosophy, Praxiteles produced his sculpture. But it is to the fifth century, and to Athens in particular, that we must look for evidence of the finest Greek culture.

We can say that the Greeks produced the first modern civilisation—where men are individuals. It is difficult to point to one, or even a few, reasons for this achievement: perhaps it is more a combination of accidents than any particular " genius of the Greek race ". The Greek type of city state certainly had much to do with it, but otherwise it is better to benefit from what Greece has given us, than to spend time wondering why Greece was able to do so.

HELLENISTIC PERIOD (380 B.C.-100 B.C.)

Leagues and wars followed each other at short intervals: sometimes Persian influence was strong, sometimes Spartan. Thebes, under Epaminondas, after his victory at Leuctra in 371, was for a short time the most powerful city in Greece. This disunity continued until Philip II of Macedon, who became king in 359, developed the military strength of backward northern Greece. He was able to defeat or buy the southern cities, one by one, because of their inability to band together and resist him. A last minute league was defeated by Philip at Chaeronea in 338. In 336 Philip was murdered, and succeeded by his son Alexander the Great.

Between 336 and 323 Alexander the Great made his enormous conquests over the Persian empire in the East, and reached India. Greece became just one province in this empire, and the centre of culture and influence moved to Alexandria, in Egypt. Nevertheless, it was Alexander's conquests and those of his generals among whom were Seleucus, Antiochus, and Ptolemy, which spread Greek culture over most of the Eastern Mediterranean and the nearby lands. Greek remained the language of the various Eastern empires, especially of Byzantium, for nearly two thousand years more. But the creative life of Greece itself was over by the end of the fourth century B.C. The cultures which blossomed in the following centuries were not truly Greek.

The Parthenon on the Acropolis at Athens.

MOSAIC ART

Mosaic is the art of decorating a surface by means of small pieces of marble, tile or glass cemented into position close together. These small units, which are usually square, are called tesserae.

EARLY MOSAICS

The earliest known mosaics decorated small objects, such as carvings in wood or stone. An example over five thousand years old was discovered in Mesopotamia (Iraq); it is decorated with small pieces of lapis lazuli and pink sandstone, and may have been a military standard. Very early mosaics have also been found in Egypt and Greece.

The Romans used this form of decoration a great deal, mainly for paving floors, but sometimes on walls and roof vaults also. Floors demand a bold, simple patterning and this is what we usually find. The colours are mostly subdued greys, yellows, and brick red, for tesserae of marble or tile were most frequently used.

In Britain, far from Rome itself, many Roman " villas " had mosaic pavements. Most of the walls of the villas have long since fallen, but their rich floor mosaics have lain, often for centuries, protected by a layer of turf, only to be rediscovered in recent years.

PICTURE MOSAICS

Their designs are mainly geometric patterns, though they sometimes contain pictures formed by the different coloured tesserae. These occasionally serve a useful purpose, like a representation of a dog in the flooring at the entrance of a house, with the added warning in Latin, *Cave canem* (Beware of the dog).

Usually, however, the pictures which form part of these designs are mere decoration, the head of a sea-god, perhaps, or some scene from a Roman myth. Hunting and fishing scenes were popular and animal subjects such as dolphins or peacocks. But there are a few designs in which the picture occupies almost the whole area; most famous of these is the " Battle of Issus ", from Pompeii, depicting Alexander the Great capturing Darius the Persian.

After the collapse of the Roman Empire, poverty descended on Italy and those buildings that were erected—mostly churches—were simple and severe, without the lavish carved ornament of Imperial times. The broad, plain wall surfaces of these buildings were a perfect setting for mosaic decoration.

Away to the east the Byzantine empire continued, with Constantinople as its capital. There, too, the buildings had broad, simple expanses of wall, but for a different reason. For lack of better building material near at hand, the construction there was of brick, and brick needs surfacing. Marble could be used for this in such buildings as churches, but it had to be imported from a distance, so what better than to use mosaics.

MOSAIC MURALS

Thus, both in Italy and Byzantium, conditions favoured the development of mosaic decorations on walls, vaults and domes, and there the craft was refined and elaborated far beyond the limited floor mosaics of Roman times. On walls it was possible to use materials that would be too fragile for floors—substances such as bone, mother-of-pearl and glass, and these gave a much wider range of colours. Blues, greens, reds, purples and yellows could be used, with black and white and all the subdued tones of earlier work. By means of encasing gold leaf between two layers of glass, gold, too, was brought into use and, in time, came to be the dominant colour.

The technique of mosaics set strict limitations on the designers, and from the fourth to the twelfth century A.D., they made no attempt to imitate paintings. Figures and landscapes were symbolic, not pictorial, and were designed in terms of mosaic and nothing else.

Those were the early, growing days of the Christian church, and most of the mosaic work that has survived is to be found in churches. There the mosaic decorations produce an effect of serene and reverent grandeur.

PLACING OF TESSERAE

The tesserae were then cut fairly large and not exactly square. The craftsmen had to work extremely fast to get an area covered before their cement set fast. Consequently, the joints were allowed to show and each separate tessera was set at a slightly different angle. This gives a lively, broken surface and as the eye moves the light glints now from one tessera, now from the next. A vibrant, flickering effect is produced, especially where many gold tesserae are used. The buildings which these mosaics adorn are usually rather dark, and many candles must have been used to light them. Thus in the old days there would have been many tiny points

In Greece and later in Rome, the floor mosaics were of high artistic quality. During the Hellenistic period of the Greek civilisation, tesserae of coloured stone, or tile, replaced the pebble formerly used. This method was improved upon by the Romans who decorated their buildings with mosaics.

CONSTANTINVS MAIOR IMPERATOR
HERACLII ET TIBERII IMPERATOR

AR
CIOP
VS

PRIVILEGIA

HIS IGITVR SOCIVS MERITIS REPARATVS VT ESSET
AVLA NOVOS HABITVS FECIT FLAGRARE PER AEVVM

The Indians of Mexico and the Andes created decorative feather mosaics. The feathers, chosen for their colours, were fixed on to textiles or tanned skins on which the design had been traced. The finished result gave the impression of being an oil painting. Unfortunately, there are very few examples of these mosaics remaining to-day.

of light to reflect from the broken surface of the mosaic-covered walls and domes.

SPREAD OF BYZANTINE STYLE

The two main centres of mosaic work in early Christian times were Rome and Byzantium. The Byzantine style later spread far and wide, to Greece, to the neighbourhood of Venice and Ravenna in the north of Italy, and to Palermo in Sicily, and, in time, even influenced the style in Rome.

In the earliest Christian mosaics in Rome, Christ is depicted as youthful and beardless, and the figure drawing shows something of the fore-shortening and realism of the Imperial Roman style. In Byzantine work, on the other hand, Christ is bearded and very majestic, and the drawing is stiff and two-dimensional.

FINE EXAMPLES OF CHURCH MOSAICS

Some of the earliest examples of Christian mosaics are those in the church of Santa Maria Maggiore, in Rome, which date from about A.D. 435 and show scenes from the Old Testament and the life of the Virgin. A little more than a century later, the church of St. Appollinari Nuovo in Ravenna was adorned with a procession of martyr virgins down one side of the nave. Facing them on the other side of the nave was a similar procession of martyr saints. The simple shapes, nearly repeated, and the colours—white, gold, soft turquoise, black and a little red—produce an effect of unequalled dignity and richness. Nearby, in the church of St. Vitali, there are also mosaics of unsurpassed beauty.

Of about the same date as the Ravenna mosaics are those in the cathedral of St. Sophia in Constantinople. Those that can still be seen suggest that these must have been unrivalled

in their solemn richness. None of the figures, however, can be judged because the city was captured by the Turks in 1543 and the cathedral became a Moslem mosque. The representation of human figures is forbidden in that religion; so all the figure work in these mosaics has been obliterated.

The decorations in St. Sophia set the fashion for all others in the neighbouring countries, notably in the lavish use of gold backgrounds.

After the fall of the Byzantine Empire much fine mosaic work was still produced under Mohammedan rule. As pictorial decoration was not permitted these Moslem mosaics are restricted to geometric patterns, but none-the-less are often of a very high order. This tradition was carried eastwards into Persia and other Mohammedan countries.

A LOST ART

In Europe, with the coming of the Renaissance, there was a great development in fresco painting as wall decoration. As the fresco painters gained skill and confidence, so the mosaic designers began to neglect the special demand of their own art and tried to imitate the work of the painters. Tesserae were then cut very evenly and fitted so closely that the joints were scarcely visible. They were also set so evenly that the whole surface no longer had the glinting vitality of the earlier, rough-set work. In fact, skill tended to take the place of art, and mosaic work from the thirteenth century onwards lost its charm and character.

There have since been many attempts to revive the art of mosaic, but none has equalled the work of the early designers. Among the recent examples are those in the Houses of Parliament, Westminster Cathedral and the new Coventry Cathedral.

← *Sixth-century mosaic at Ravenna, depicting Constantine IV granting privileges to the Christian church.*

Civilisation and Culture
INDIA

India's ancient civilisation has been largely conditioned by geography. The sub-continent itself is built on a mighty scale, its extreme measurements being some 2,000 miles in length and breadth. The Himalaya mountains bar it from Central Asia, save for the high passes of the north-west. Its peoples number over 500 millions and speak more than 150 different languages and dialects. There are many different religious creeds: Hindu, Moslem, Sikh, Jain, Christian (claiming nearly eleven million followers) and others.

The north-western passes have played a decisive part in India's history. Through those gateways a succession of invaders has descended on to the rich alluvial plains of the north. The plains are watered by the three great river systems of the Indus, the Ganges and the Brahmaputra, and the vast fertile expanse has ever been the main setting in India's story. Two-thirds of her population are massed there to-day. Southern India—the Deccan—has played a far less formative part; though it can boast many powerful kingdoms and splendid cities and rich contributions to Indian architecture, literature and other arts. Nearly three-quarters of the Indian people draw their livelihood from the soil.

The story of India's civilisation can best be told by following the course of her history, beginning with the surprise discoveries in the Indus valley. These revealed that, about 2500 B.C. a people of advanced culture, perhaps related to that of Sumeria in Mesopotamia, were settled in the region. They had handsome cities with well-drained streets, a royal palace, burnt-brick houses and public baths. They were a wealthy and highly artistic people and they used a picture-language. Fate eventually overwhelmed these gifted folk. A new dark-skinned people, called the Dasyus, about whom little is known, succeeded them. Then, from about 1500 B.C., or earlier, lighter-skinned Aryan tribes came trooping down

the passes in a long succession and put their stamp on India's history.

One feature of these tribes is of particular interest. Their Sanskrit language shows certain similarities to those of the European peoples, including English, which strongly suggest that somewhere in the past, they sprang from a common source. Philologists, therefore, group them together as belonging to the Aryan or Indo-European stock. Sanskrit became the basis of most of the languages of present-day India, except in the South.

The Aryans' tribal hymns, the Vedas, which are one of the oldest collections of the world's literature, tell us a great deal about the invaders' customs. The first of the collections, the Rig Veda, begun perhaps about 1200 B.C., comprises 1,028 hymns, mostly in praise of different gods. They were considered too sacred to be committed to writing and were passed verbally from father to son. Family groups, we learn, formed separate self-contained villages, each under a headman. The villagers raised cattle and sheep and cultivated various corn crops. Potters, weavers, carpenters and smiths practised their hereditary crafts. The nobles wore armour and fought from horse-drawn chariots. Hunting, chariot-racing, dancing, music and gambling were favourite amusements. The community was divided into four classes; the Brahmins or priests, the warriors, the common people and the serfs. The Aryan religion was a form of Nature worship in which the sky, sun, moon, fire and other objects were personified. Besides these powers there were numerous minor gods and undesirable demons.

During the course of many centuries the Aryans gradually conquered or fused with the native population and, perhaps by the sixth century B.C., extended their range over most of northern India. It was through the contacts and commingling of the two races, in which the conquered ultimately absorbed their conquerors, that the religious and social system of the Hindus (who to-day form the vast majority of India's population) was broadly shaped.

HINDUISM

The system of Hinduism, as then and afterwards developed, is much more than a religion. It is also a code of everyday conduct. And it is an extraordinarily mixed code, comprising conflicting beliefs and practices from the most primitive superstitions to the loftiest philosophical principles. The old Vedic gods have sunk into the background and the foremost deities now worshipped are the Hindu Vishnu the Preserver and Siva the Destroyer, who are different forms of Brahma the Creator. In addition, every village has its minor gods and spirits. Yet there are Hindus who believe, either in many gods, or in any one god, and even in one supreme god. Certain animals, trees and rivers are held sacred by many and the cow by all. The dominating figures in Hinduism are the Brahmin priests. They are learned in the Vedas and other sacred lore and they alone are privileged to conduct the religious rites which are indispensable to the people's salva-

The famous statue of Buddha in the Ajanta caves.

Left: *Vishnu in one of his human forms as Rama.* Centre: *Shiva the destroyer, represented with three faces—as a man, the impersonal absolute and a woman.* Right: *Shiva dancing.*

tion. For these reasons they are held in the utmost awe and veneration.

The doctrine of reincarnation, or rebirth, is an outstanding feature of the system. Man dies only to be born again. And the character of each rebirth depends on how he behaved himself in his previous life. A wrong-doer may be reborn as an insect, a worm, even a vile pig. In time—but commonly almost an eternity of time—he may attain the state of eternal bliss.

THE CASTE SYSTEM

Hindu society is dominated by the caste system, which itself claims a religious origin. Every individual is born into a particular group with fixed rules of daily life. He may not marry into another caste. His food and drink, his company at table and, usually, his occupation are strictly determined. The four Aryan classes have become split up into over 3,000 castes. They are mostly based on a man's calling or occupation, but they are also associated with distinctions of race, tribe or religion. Present-day conditions are tending to relax caste distinctions.

In the sixth century B.C., religious reformers were getting active. A profound discontent with the old system of gods and sacrifices and the presumptions of the Brahmin priests had spread among the educated classes. Thoughtful minds were seeking a truer illumination of the mysteries of man's life and destiny. As a result, two reformed creeds arose—Jainism and Buddhism. Both ignored the Vedic gods, the Brahmins' exclusive claims and all caste distinctions.

BUDDHISM

Buddhism was founded by the most famous of India's ancient philosophers, Gautama Buddha. Gautama was much concerned with the problem of rebirth. Like many other sages, he found life a dubious blessing, with more sufferings than joys. Reincarnation, therefore, became a nightmare prospect and Gautama taught a way to escape it. Men must renounce all the natural desires of life, even for existence as separate individuals. Instead, they must devote themselves to helping others along life's troubled way. Thus, freed from self and purified, they would at last avoid reincarnation and attain *nirvana*. This mystical creed, in various forms, spread far and wide over Asia and still holds sway in Japan, Burma, Ceylon and other countries. But in India it had lost its popular hold by the eleventh century. Jainism (which numbers two million believers) sets up a very strict code of conduct and its followers hold the most extreme views about the wrongfulness of killing any living creature. You must not even swallow a gnat.

The sixth and third centuries B.C. brought two invasions of the Punjab, the first by Persia, the second by no less a personage than Alexander the Great. They passed away, but one result of them was that India came into contact with the culture of Greece and the Western world. Her progress during these times and right on to the seventh century A.D. was made against a background of fresh foreign intrusions and the rise and fall of various Hindu kingdoms which had come into being. Of these latter the Maurya empire (321-185 B.C.) was made illustrious for all time by the noblest and best-loved of India's rulers. The great Asoka (about 264-228 B.C.) reigned over all India save the south. But he was great, not because of his empire, but because he hated war and strove to put the humane teachings of Buddhism into practice. Unhappily his good work died with him.

THE ARTS FLOURISH

The Gupta empire, founded in A.D. 320, has other claims to

The Republic of India came into being after the passing of the Indian Independence Act of 1947.

fame. The Gupta period, extending to the seventh century, embraces the classical age of ancient Hindu civilisation. In its finest years the empire won widespread political power and glory. Sanskrit literature reached its Golden Age. Music flourished. Astronomy and mathematics advanced. What remains of the architecture and sculpture of the times is sufficient to testify to the fine qualities of its lavishly sculptured temples and monasteries, many of them hewn out of the solid rock.

THE MOSLEM INVASION

In the ensuing centuries the Hindu peoples reeled before a staggering blow. A sequence of invasions by fierce Turkish, Afghan and Mongol tribes, bringing with them the Moslem creed of Allah and his prophet Mohammed, burst on the unhappy land. The final phase set in with the arrival of the Moghuls in 1525. By the seventeenth century that renowned dynasty bestrode practically the entire peninsula. The Moslem conquest reduced the Hindus to the condition of a subject people and India became a country of two sharply divided creeds.

The Moghul emperor, Akbar the Great (1542-1605), tried to close the breach between Hindu and Moslem by treating them as equals. But his successors ignored his example. None-the-less, the Moslems have made valuable contributions to every branch of Indian life. Delhi, for long their capital, and other cities became luxurious centres of refined culture. Their splendid palaces and pavilions, their lovely mosques and minarets, are superb creations of dreamlike grace and beauty. Literature and paintings were patronised. The handicraftsmen produced exquisite jewellery and inlaid and enamelled work, gorgeously coloured carpets and lustrous silks.

A mixed Moslem-Hindu language, called Urdu, is used among Mohammedans and their Hindu associates. The Sikh religion, counting now nearly eight million devotees, was founded in the fifteenth century in an attempt to combine the best of the Moslem and Hindu faiths. It has the character of a military Order, like that of the Knights Templars of Europe.

EUROPEAN INFLUENCE

At length there came another change of masters, this time from the sea. From the early sixteenth century, various European countries had been planting trading stations along the Indian coasts. By the mid-eighteenth century the Moghul empire was dissolving and India had fallen into anarchy. The European scramble for trade became a struggle for empire between Britain and France—and Britain finished on top. By the mid-nineteenth century she had become the paramount power in the peninsula.

British Imperial rule gave the country peace, settled government and equal justice for all. The benefits of Western science and technology—roads, railways, electricity and other services—were introduced. Western education came in, and Western ideas, political, social and cultural, were eagerly absorbed. In the surge of national consciousness and racial pride that followed, India clamoured for independence. But it was a divided people that won it. The country was partitioned into two separate states: Hindu " India " and Moslem " Pakistan ".

Modern India is in the throes of change. The old religions still prevail among the masses, but their hold is weakening with the more educated. The European system of free parliamentary government is as yet in its infancy. Much has been done to improve the condition of the peasants, and trade and industry have been immensely expanded to pay for a higher standard of living. India is an Oriental country, wedded to Oriental ways and rich in her native philosophy and art and literature. To-day she is seeking to blend the more acceptable of the teachings of Western civilisation with her own cherished cultural heritage.

THE HISTORY OF THE DOLL

Taking into account the perishable materials of which dolls were made, and the " love " bestowed upon them by little girls of bygone days, no wonder we have very little to go on to discover the earliest dolls of the pre-historic times. Although toy dolls must have existed amongst the earliest inhabitants of our world, it is difficult to prove it historically. The only evidence of dolls we have is from the excavations of tombs and buried civilisations, and most of those dolls were connected with religious rites and superstitious beliefs.

The " magic " dolls found during these excavations were probably the forerunners of our lucky mascots; and the " harvest " dolls, which are still made in some areas, were made of straw and carried at the head of processions to bring rich harvests for the coming year. Later, in the Middle Ages, " bread " dolls, representing saints, were made. These dolls were eaten on feast days to inspire people with some of the good qualities of these holy men.

It is from Egypt, already a civilised society in 2000 B.C., that our first traces of toy dolls originate. Egyptian dolls had flat, wooden bodies and were decorated with typical Egyptian ornaments of squares and triangles, coloured black, red and yellow, and they had human or animal hair, or hair made of small, mud beads. (British Museum exhibit 6459). Although several wooden dolls have been discovered—there is only one rag-doll which has survived to our time. This doll, dating from about the same period as her wooden companions, was made of coarse woven material. Her face, which must have been pretty, is now completely faded and only a few stitches remain outlining her features. (British Museum exhibit 1905.)

In the Far East, the Chinese were the leaders of an ancient civilisation and about 500 B.C. their beautiful dolls, with papier-mâché heads, were magnificently dressed in rich and colourful silks.

In Japan, the ancient Doll Festival, held on the 3rd of March every year, is known as Hinamatsuri. It is on this day that little Japanese girls bring out their lovely collections of dolls to be admired and played with in public.

The Indian dolls of antiquity were very elaborate and it is difficult to say whether they were used as toys or had religious significance. The Asiatic people and the various tribes of Africa had crude, wooden dolls, some of which may have been toys and others offerings to their gods. These dolls have not changed much in appearance through the ages.

The dolls of the Americas have not changed much either, and these also may have been toys or offerings to gods. For certain we can say that only the people of Peru had toy dolls; both dolls and dolls' clothes were found there during excavations. These dolls were either carved out of dark wood or made of woven material fixed over a string frame. (British Museum, Ethnographical section.)

EUROPEAN DOLLS

But the real development of dolls belongs to the European countries with their use of more and more advanced materials. It started in Egypt and was followed up by the Greeks, who made exquisite terra-cotta dolls with movable arms and legs. These dolls were often preoccupied with such homely tasks as kneading the dough (British Museum, Greek Department exhibit 234), or rolling out the pastry (British Museum exhibit 233). Greece, in fact, was the centre of the doll trade, and in the fifth and fourth centuries B.C. they made furniture and tiny cooking utensils for dolls.

The Romans continued this trade and dolls were taken all over their vast empire until, eventually, they arrived as far away as Sandy in Bedfordshire. There, during excavations, a small doll was found, obviously a plaything and without arms or legs.

Left to right: *a Coptic doll, an American Indian doll, an Egyptian doll and a Chinese doll.   The antiquity of the doll is attested by remains found in ancient graves, especially those of children.   Some dolls were not merely playthings for children, but had a religious significance.*

THE MIDDLE AGES

References to dolls of the Middle Ages are very scarce and we know even less about them than we do of those of antiquity. The education of children in the Middle Ages was rough and there was a total absence of comfort. In the many burnings and plunderings of towns and settlements, little objects such as dolls must have been completely destroyed.

Only a few remains of clay dolls have been found in graves in old German and French towns. These were simple dolls with a circular depression in the breast to hold a piece of money. It is believed that the depression contained a christening coin, perhaps a present from god-parents at baptism.

Glass toys, also, must have been made. Although none has been found, there is a reference made to them in a charming legend concerning St. Elisabeth. Apparently, she bought at Eisenach all kinds of glass toys for the children of Wartburg. Returning there on her palfrey, these fragile objects fell from her lap over a high cliff but not one was broken!

FASHION DOLLS

A further mention of dolls is in 1391, when we read in chronicles that the Queen of England received fashion dolls from France. These expensively-dressed models were introduced to the French Court by the Queen of Bavaria, and, as " charming and beautiful " models, they spread to the various courts of Europe. It is assumed that once the fashions were copied, the dolls found their way to the nursery to amuse little princesses. These wooden dolls were hand-carved by the workers in the Nuremberg area of South Germany, and imported to France to be dressed in the latest fashions.

In 1413 and 1465, " Dockenmachers " are specifically mentioned as living in Nuremberg and " Docke ", even to-day, is the usual word for doll in that part of the world. It has been suggested that the English word " doll " might have stemmed from the German word *Docke*. The doll-makers, together with other toymakers, organised themselves into Guilds, and Nuremberg soon became the centre of the toy industry—a distinction which it was to maintain up to the start of the twentieth century.

In Japan, a doll festival is held each year on the 3rd of March. Ceremonial dolls symbolising the Imperial court are then displayed to the public by Japanese girls.

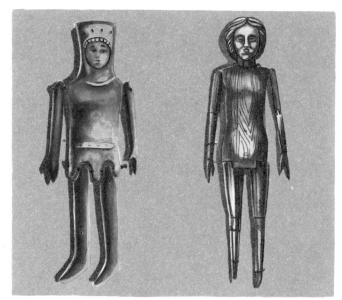

Ancient Roman terra-cotta and wooden dolls. These were gifted to children towards the end of the festival of Saturn.

HOUSES FOR DOLLS

With the advent of the sixteenth century, a new importance was put upon dolls and toys. People on the whole had more time and money and they became more interested in their children and their homes. All this led to a new fashion of forming collections of little objects, which, as might be expected, stimulated the toy industry. Cabinet-makers in Augsburg and Ulm were renowned for their wonderful doll's-houses, which came complete with kitchen utensils made by tin and copper founders, and dolls supplied by the doll-makers.

In 1572, the Prince of Saxony gave his little daughter a doll's kitchen with 71 dishes, 40 meat plates, 100 other plates, 36 spoons and 28 egg cups and several wooden dolls to do the cooking. But not only royal children were so privileged. The new trend spread amongst all levels of society, and the doll-making industry grew steadily in strength.

The dolls of the sixteenth and seventeenth centuries were carved out of wood and had arms and legs which moved in simple joints, or were attached by string after the manner of the jointed terra-cotta dolls of antiquity. Then the bodies were improved and given a life-like " feel "; instead of wood, they were made of leather and stuffed with rags, bran or sawdust.

NEW MATERIALS FOR DOLLS

In the seventeenth and eighteenth centuries, the doll-makers experimented with different materials for the head of the doll. From the early wooden dolls with painted faces and a few human hairs gummed in position, they progressed to beautifully moulded and delicately painted wax heads, and later to alabaster heads. However, alabaster was soon abandoned because it broke too easily when the doll suffered a fall. As early as 1750, some dolls had enamel or blown-glass eyes. Later, another material, much lighter and more durable than wax, was used for the heads of dolls. This material was papier-mâché, which was known to the ancient Chinese and to the early German doll-makers who had discontinued it in favour of wood. With great success, Evans and Cartwright, an English firm in Wolverhampton, started producing papier-mâché heads. Then, towards the end of the eighteenth and the beginning of the nineteenth century, porcelain, stone china and bone china were used. Lovely Dresden china heads were exported all over the world by Germany. In Britain, in 1805, the firm of Spode made the first stone china heads for dolls. Copelands of Stoke-on-Trent followed Spode's lead and they, too, made china heads. Eventually, arms, hands, legs and feet were made of china, thus giving the doll a delicate finish.

Hair and hair-styles became important too. There were wigs made of goat's hair, silk, flax or human hair. Human hair was inserted with hot needles singly, or in small clumps, to look natural. At the Crystal Palace Exhibition of 1851, the dolls on display had long, flowing locks, which sometimes fell well below the waist.

The body, too, had undergone further changes. Fine kid and muslin replaced the leather, and stiff wooden joints acquired certain flexibility with jointed elbows, knees and wrists.

With the arrival of rubber imports from Malaya, a composition material was found. This composition material enabled the doll-makers to produce a hollow body and limbs in which wires were inserted to give the doll a more natural movement. The dolls were then able to turn their heads and sit as well as stand. By 1826, they could even close their eyes. Four years later, a German inventor, Maelzel, devised a speaking device. The sound was produced by the passage of air across a horn. The movement of the doll's arms operated a small bellows; a right arm movement operated " Mama " and a left arm movement, " Papa ". Much later, Edison invented the singing doll.

ROYAL DOLLS

Whilst mentioning the dolls of the early nineteenth century, reference must be made to Queen Victoria's famous collection, of which some are on show in the London Museum, London. She had 132 dolls, many of them wooden dolls and marketed in England under the name of " Dutch " dolls. These dolls were clad in costumes made to represent the ladies-in-waiting, famous actresses and singers of the day, and the clothes were made by the young princess and her companion, Baroness Lehzen. These dolls were catalogued by the princess with names and proper description of the clothing.

In Nuremberg in the nineteenth century, many dolls' accessories such as little wooden houses, complete with furniture, were made.

Italian and French dolls of the Renaissance.

At this period of history, English dolls were almost always made with blue eyes as a compliment to Her Majesty.

So far, dolls were made in the form of grown-up young ladies, but in 1850 the first baby doll was introduced. At about the same time, America flooded the European market with their first black doll, dressed in the fashion of an American Negress, with a jolly Golliwog—not exactly a doll—escorting her. Both were a huge success.

What we now take for granted in our modern doll, had its beginnings some 100 years ago. No end of time, money and thought was spent on the perfection of the head, the body and life-like movement of limbs. Richard Brooman invented a new process for making dolls. He first made a metal mould in the shape of a doll. He then put a ball of caoutchouc (rubber) into the mould which he plunged into a hot vulcanising compound. The caoutchouc expanded to fill the mould and the completed doll was then removed. In fact the doll was made in two parts, a top half and a bottom half, the join being hidden by a belt. This process has been adapted to the manufacture of our popular plastic doll.

MECHANICAL DOLLS

Many mechanical dolls came in during the 1860s. William Clark invented a walking doll, Clivell patented a moving doll, and Rudolph Steiner of Germany made the first feeding doll.

Now not only Germany had the privilege of exporting and making dolls, but England, America and France competed for the market. To keep the lead in the international field, many clever brains were put to invent more exciting dolls, and many factories were set to mass-produce them. The prices were very low. Dressed dolls were bought for as little as eightpence a dozen and undressed dolls were sold for twopence halfpenny a dozen.

The best-known English doll-makers at that time were the Pierottis—Madam Montanari, Charles March, and H. J. Meech (doll-maker to the Royal Family). The Pierotti family all seem to have lived and worked in London, most of them near and around Oxford Circus. Unfortunately, not one of the Pierotti firms survived the blow of the First World War, and their splendid craftsmanship disappeared along with their firms. However, they were soon replaced by others and the story of the doll continues, with new materials, new methods and new faces to give pleasure to many little girls.

MUSICAL INSTRUMENTS : I
From early times to seventeenth century

The excavations of archaeologists have brought to light musical instruments from early civilisations which are so fragile that the sound they once produced must now necessarily remain unheard. Curved trumpets from the Bronze Age (c.1800-900 B.C.), dug up in Ireland, now lie silent in museum cases beside Egyptian clappers, made of ivory and wood about 1600 B.C.

We can only guess how the first musical instruments came to be. Perhaps a hunter accidentally twanged his bow, repeated the noise because he liked the sound, then made it deliberately, and experimented until the first string instrument was made. Certainly, we can see counterparts of these in the present African musical bow and Chinese beggar's fiddle.

In essence, we take a musical instrument to be any object used to make sounds which are musically satisfying to a player. There are two main groups: those which make a noise, like rattles, and those which have differing tones, like recorders. The player may make his sounds by beating, striking, shaking, scraping, plucking, sucking or blowing.

The first wind instrument after man's own voice was a primitive tube of some kind, made first perhaps by blowing into hollow bones, or whistles from sticks of wood, or across the tops of reeds, just as you can blow across a fountain-pen top.

Noise makers were probably invented in self-defence: a man living in a cave might make a rattle from clay shapes with little stones inside, or rasp sticks and stones together to frighten wild animals away.

As well as from the instruments themselves, and from similar ones which are still in use, we have found out a great deal about early musical instruments from ancient records.

You will remember that the Old Testament refers to David playing the harp, and to King Nebuchadnezzar's musicians playing the " cornet, flute, harp, sackbut, psaltery, dulcimer and all kinds of music." Early pictures, from cave paintings onwards, show us what old instruments used to look like. Greek vases, Egyptian pottery, medieval sculpture and stained glass reveal instruments, which have long been replaced or forgotten, and their players.

Looking back on the developing musical instruments, we have grouped them into families according to the way in which the musical sound is produced. The range is enormous. This can only be a brief outline.

STRINGED INSTRUMENTS

In this family, sound is produced from the vibration of stretched strings. This may be done by rubbing or plucking the strings. Then the sound is amplified by the strings being attached to a resonator, as, for example, the violin's body, which enlarges the sound. The note a string sounds is altered by shortening its vibrating length; for example, by pressing it on to a violin's finger board near the head of the instrument. The strings of the violin play higher notes than the long-stringed double bass. Thick strings can make a lower note, because they vibrate more slowly. Many stringed instruments developed all over the world from the early musical bows, shaped like hunting bows. As early as the sixth century, simple fiddles were found in Africa and Asia, made from such material as coconut shells, and played with bows. Gradually, a four-stringed instrument came into being; experiments to make it easier for the player to bow each string separately changed its shape from that of a spade to a pear; then a waist was added. The rebec was originally

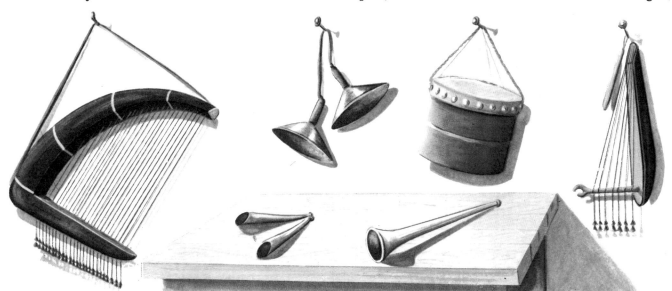

Early musical instruments from the ancient civilisations of Babylon and Assyria. Hanging on the wall can be seen (from left to right) a standing harp, small cymbals, a drum and a shoulder harp (that is, a harp slung from the shoulder). On the table are a pair of small horns and a trumpet.

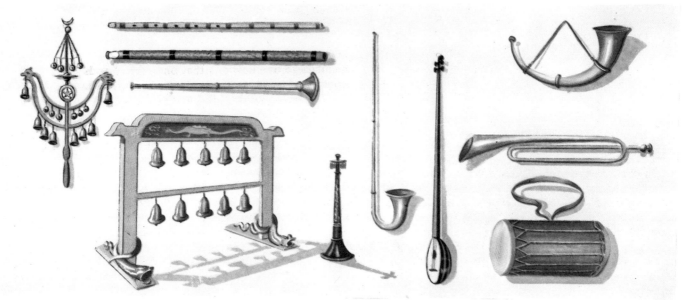

The instruments shown above are all from China or India. The first five on the left are Chinese while the last four on the right are Indian. The flute and trumpet in the centre are Indo-Chinese.

a Greek type of fiddle, which reached the west during the eleventh century.

The *lira da braccio*, or " arm lyre ", as well as the rebec probably influenced the development of the violin, because it had a similar body shape, though was larger, with seven strings.

Viols, treble, tenor and bass of varying sizes, as illustrated, were old string instruments played with bows, deriving from the fifteenth century Spanish guitar. They had six strings, and the finger board, where the player pressed the string to alter its sounding length, was fretted, or marked out with pieces of gut. Eventually, the viols were superseded by the violin family.

The hurdy-gurdy was an old instrument looking a little like a violin, but played with finger keys for the left hand, and a wheel to rub the strings with the right hand. Besides using a bow to vibrate the strings some instruments of this family were played by plucking with the fingers or a plectrum, a plucking blade or quill. Of these, the harp was known in the Middle East by 3000 B.C., and later was an instrument played by the Greeks and Romans. It consisted of a frame across which a number of strings of various lengths were stretched. The lyre was really a small kind of harp, a favourite instrument of the Greeks, played with fingers or a plectrum. The psaltery was a box form, made in different shapes to be held against the chest or on the knees. Fourteenth and fifteenth century pictures witness its popularity in Europe.

Lutes, with small, pear-shaped bodies and long necks, were played 2,000 years before Christ was born. By the fifteenth century, players used their fingers instead of a plectrum. The peak of popularity came late in the sixteenth and early seventeenth centuries, when John Dowland composed and played his famous " Ayres ". The sturdier guitar was also an old instrument; by the sixteenth century, a five stringed version had established itself as the national instrument of Spain.

A few stringed instruments were struck by hammers. The dulcimer was a box across which strings were stretched then tapped with wooden hammers. It is about a thousand years old, and survives to-day in a Hungarian version, called a cimbalom.

PERCUSSION INSTRUMENTS

The sound of percussion instruments is produced by striking one object against another. Probably they are the oldest family, and were first used to emphasise rhythm in dancing. The audience, as well as the dancers might beat the ground, clap their hands or bodies, shake rattles or strings of bones and teeth, shells and other things. Primitive tribes still associate such instruments with magical powers. Ancient rock gongs have been discovered in Africa and Europe: they were slabs of stone beaten to produce ringing notes and had a part in religious ceremonies.

China was the home of the earliest bells, which were made of tortoise shells and many other fabrics. Early drums were like flat tambourines, without the jingles. Arab drums came into Europe during the Crusades, first as small shallow ones, then later, in the fifteenth century, egg-shaped ones, played in pairs, mounted on a camel or horse.

WIND INSTRUMENTS

We now divide the instruments which are sounded by blowing into two main families, brass and woodwind.

" Brass " includes all those instruments which used to be made of brass, even though other metals are now used. They have mouth-pieces which are cup or funnel-shaped, on to which the player presses his lips. The vibration of his lips is passed down the air column in the tube of the instrument, and sound is produced, then checked by the movement of the player's tongue.

One kind of brass instrument is based on the animal horn, with a conical shape. Curved models were used for hunting signals.

The second, trumpet type, probably came from experiments in blowing down hollow bones or canes, and at first was used to make rhythmic blaring noises in temples and in battle. Four hundred years before the birth of Christ, Greeks played trumpets at the Olympic Games. The Romans made their own variants.

In the Middle Ages, trumpets were also made in the shape of a long " S ", then given telescopic mouthpieces, so that by 1500, they looked like our modern trombone, though they carried the name sackbut.

51

The clavichord was a fore-runner of the pianoforte and differed in action from the earlier harpsichord. The harpsichord strings were sounded by being plucked by a quill while the clavichord was sounded by striking the strings with a metal blade (or tangent). The instrument shown here is unusual in not being oblong-shaped.

WOODWIND INSTRUMENTS

The flute is the best-known instrument of this family. The earliest form is probably the shepherd's pipe, blown at the end, like the recorder. This is open at each end, and has a plug, or fipple, making a whistle mouthpiece. Two or more tuned pipes, joined together and stopped at the bottom, made an old folk instrument, the Pan-pipes. Early flutes with three holes, have been found in Egyptian tombs. Flutes are not always tubes: for instance, ancient Peruvian ones, in clay, were shaped like eggs. During the Middle Ages in Europe, a small pipe was often played with the left hand to the accompaniment of a small drum or tabor, beaten with the right.

FREE REED INSTRUMENTS

The earliest is the Chinese mouth organ, or cheng, about three thousand years old. A number of pipes are set into a mouthpiece which also acts as a resonator. The reed is a metal tongue fastened at one end, which vibrates when the player sucks in or blows.

ORGAN.

The organ, of course, is a wind instrument which is now played by means of a keyboard. The earliest organs, however, were manipulated by push and pull slides which opened and shut the pipes to the air blowing through them, thus making them sound. Basically it is " a box of whistles with bellows ".

An Egyptian invented the earliest kind we know, in about 300 B.C., called a *hydraulis*, or water organ, working by pressure of water. Developed by the Romans, it was forgotten in the Middle Ages, when smaller ones, portative organs, were carried by the player in processions, one hand working a bellows and the other playing the keys. Larger ones were supported by poles. Positive organs were not moved, and developed from the early wind organs with sliders. A keyboard operated by levers, needing the pressure of a clenched fist, came next, and this keyboard was gradually refined and improved into the simple finger keyboard of the

chamber organs. By the fifteenth century, German organs added pedals for the feet, which also sounded notes.

KEYBOARD INSTRUMENTS

The advantage of the keyboard is that one player's hands can control a large number of strings, pipes or reeds at once. The keyboard most familiar to you will be that of a modern piano. A simple keyboard was developed during the thirteenth and fourteenth centuries and by 1450, the organ had a small keyboard similar to a modern one.

Although there were primitive earlier forms, the harpsichord became the most important keyboard stringed instrument during the sixteenth and seventeenth centuries. It is the largest of a group of three, harpsichord, virginal and spinet. The harpsichord has the shape of a grand piano, the virginal an oblong, and the spinet a leg-of-mutton. In each of these three, the sound is produced by a plectrum, a small wedge of leather or quill, which plucks the string when the keys are pressed down.

As early as the fifteenth century, the clavichord had established itself, deriving from the monochord, a single string stretched between two bridge pieces resting on a sound box. In time, a keyboard was added and improved. The clavichord strings were sounded by being struck by a brass blade called a tangent, which rose to tap the string when the key was pressed down. This instrument was made in an oblong wooden case. Sometimes the lids and cases of these instruments were highly decorated.

By the end of the sixteenth century, there was an enormous variety of instruments, many already highly developed, but often used to accompany the human voice rather than to shine alone. But the consorts or groups of viols, and the loose bands of assorted instruments, harps, lutes, viols and harpsichords, were to point the way to the perfecting of chamber and orchestral music which followed. The popular Fitzwilliam Virginal Book of keyboard pieces was written before the development of the pianoforte, which was to replace the harpsichord family and the clavichord as the favourite keyboard instrument in the home.

The organ is one of the oldest keyboard instruments. A primitive form of organ was known to the Byzantines. The organ we see here with its fourteen pipes is medieval. Observe that the keyboard does not have the familiar "black and white" keys, which were a much later invention.

THE STORY OF JOSEPH

The story of Joseph, who came to Egypt to be sold as a slave and later rose to become Prime Minister of the country, is one of the most romantic that the Old Testament records.

Joseph was the eleventh son of Jacob and he lived probably in the seventeenth century B.C., although we cannot tell exactly. We know little of Joseph's life until he was seventeen years of age, except that he was a bit of a tale-bearer and seemed to his older brothers a bit of a boaster as well. This annoyed them, but what annoyed them even more was that Joseph was their father's favourite.

The ten older brothers had grown quite resentful of Joseph by the time he was seventeen and when the opportunity came, they took revenge. One day, Jacob sent Joseph to join his brothers as they tended their flocks. They had been with their flocks at Shechem, but, when Joseph arrived there, he found they had moved northwards to Dothan. So he followed them.

COAT OF MANY COLOURS

When the brothers saw him approaching, they reckoned that here in the remoteness of Dothan they had a fine opportunity of dealing with this young brother whom they had come to resent so much. So they laid hold of him and kept him prisoner in a pit in the ground until a caravan of Ishmaelites passed by and then they sold Joseph to them. After this they smeared with goat's blood Joseph's well-known coat of many colours, a present from his father, and took back a report to Jacob that Joseph had been torn to pieces by wild animals.

Joseph, meanwhile, was taken to Egypt and sold as a slave. He was purchased by Potiphar, an official at the Court of the Pharaoh, or king, of Egypt. Joseph did so well in Potiphar's service and proved himself so intelligent and so reliable that, very soon, he was entrusted with the management of the whole house.

JOSEPH IN PRISON

Things were prospering for Joseph, but through no fault of his own he fell foul of Potiphar's wife. Out of spite, she made a false charge against him and he was put in prison.

Even in prison, Joseph's qualities were recognised and very soon the jailer made him overseer of the other prisoners. Some time later there came under Joseph's care in the prison two of Pharaoh's staff, his chief butler and his chief baker, both of whom had offended Pharaoh in some way.

During their period of custody, both of these men had strange dreams which puzzled and worried them. Joseph interpreted their dreams for them as meaning speedy release for the butler and speedy execution for the baker. Things worked out just as Joseph had said and his interpretation of the dreams proved exactly true.

PHARAOH'S DREAMS

The chief butler, however, when restored to favour, forgot all about Joseph and the promises he had made to help him when he was released from prison. But, two years later, Pharaoh had two dreams, one about fat and thin cows and another about full and thin ears of grain, and he was distressed because he could not find anyone who could interpret his dreams for him.

Then the butler remembered Joseph and how successful he had been earlier in interpreting dreams. He told his master about Joseph and the Pharaoh sent for him at once. He told Joseph his dreams and asked if he could tell what they meant. Joseph said that they were a forecast of seven years of plenty which were to be followed by seven years of famine and that

Joseph is summoned before Pharaoh on the chief butler's advice. Joseph interprets the meaning of Pharaoh's dreams of the fat cows and the thin cows, the full ears of grain and the lean ones.

the dreams were a warning to make provision in the good years for the bad years that were to come after.

Pharaoh was so pleased by Joseph's skill and wisdom that he appointed him to be his Prime Minister and to attend in particular to the reorganisation required to deal with the approaching years of famine. Joseph was at this time thirty years of age.

He made an enormous success of his job. During the first seven years, when there were plentiful harvests, Joseph saw to it that the surplus was carefully gathered up and safely stored. Then, when the famine years came, Joseph had grain enough at his disposal to sell to the Egyptians in their need.

SEVEN YEARS OF FAMINE

The famine which struck Egypt during these seven years struck other countries, too. It was a terrible famine, long-drawn-out and widespread. The surrounding countries, not having had the benefit of Joseph's wisdom and foresight, were in great trouble when the famine came. The result was that people came from far beyond the borders of Egypt in order to buy grain from Egypt's store-houses.

Among the other countries affected by the famine was Canaan, the land from which Joseph had come and where his family still lived. When Jacob learned that grain was to be bought in Egypt, he sent all his sons there with the exception of Benjamin, the youngest, to buy food to tide them over.

When they came to Egypt, it was with Joseph that they had to deal. But, while Joseph recognised them at once, they failed to detect in him any connection with the brother they had so long ago sold into slavery. Joseph, of course, would be much more changed than they were. He had been a boy and was now a man. He would be dressed in Egyptian clothes and would be clean shaven as was the Egyptian custom.

Joseph decided to have some sport with his brothers and he accused them of being spies, come to spy out possible weaknesses in the Egyptian defences. This they vehemently denied. Joseph renewed his accusations and said that he was going to keep them prisoner until one of them should go back to Canaan and, as a token of good faith, return with the youngest brother whom they had told him about.

Joseph kept them in prison for three days, adding to their fears. Then, keeping Simeon behind as a hostage against the coming of Benjamin, he allowed them to return home. Unknown to his brothers, however, he had the money they had paid for their sacks of grain put into the top of the sacks before they departed. When this was discovered on the homeward journey, their fears increased all the more.

When they told their tale to Jacob, he shared their fears and he absolutely refused to let them take Benjamin down to Egypt, even to obtain the return of Simeon. "I am taking no chances," he said, "that I may lose Benjamin, my youngest and most beloved son. I could not bear it."

But the famine continued and, indeed, grew more severe. Jacob held out as long as he could but, in the end, the threat of starvation forced him to give in. So the brothers went back once more to Egypt to buy food, this time taking Benjamin with them.

On their arrival in Egypt, they were well received and were invited to a banquet in Joseph's house. They offered back the money they had found in their sacks on the previous occasion, but Joseph's steward waved it aside and said that payment had already been received for the grain. Much was made of them, especially Benjamin, at the banquet.

So it was that they left for home in the best of spirits, Simeon now being with them. Little did they know that Joseph had again arranged for their money to be placed in their sacks of grain and, in addition, that his own silver divining cup should be secreted in Benjamin's sack. Joseph

It was Joseph's foresight that ensured that Pharaoh's people had grain to spare during the famine. Here Joseph speaks with his brothers who have come to Egypt to buy food for their starving family in Canaan.

Joseph reveals himself to his brothers.   At first they fear he will take his revenge, but he soon reassures them.

let them go a little distance on their way and then sent a messenger after them to accuse them of the theft of the cup.

They denied the charge indignantly and invited the messenger to search them.   He did so and brought to light the silver cup concealed in Benjamin's sack.

The whole party trooped back to Joseph, who declared that as punishment he would keep hold of Benjamin as his slave but would let the others go free.   It was at this point that Judah made such a moving speech about the sorrow this would cause their aged father and the utter impossibility of their returning home minus Benjamin.   At this Joseph could no longer keep up his pretence.

IDENTITY REVEALED

Deeply touched, he had everyone else leave the room so that only he and his brothers were left.   Then he told them who he was.   At first, they would hardly believe him and, when they did, they were afraid that he was going to take revenge for the shameful way they had treated him all those years ago.   But Joseph soon set their minds at rest.   He believed, he said, that God had been using them in this way so that he, Joseph, would be able to come to this position and thus be the means of saving many lives.

He then invited them to make their home in Egypt.   "Go back," he said, " and get our father Jacob and fetch him down here."   And when the Pharaoh heard of the matter, he approved of what Joseph was suggesting and told him to make arrangements to transport his brothers and their families to Egypt and to settle them in the best of the land.   So off they went home to Canaan to carry the news to Jacob.   Jacob could not believe that what they told him was true, but, eventually, he was persuaded to accept Joseph's invitation to go and settle in Egypt.

FAMILY RE-UNITED

Hoshen was the district chosen for the settlement of the family of Jacob.   There they made their home happily and prosperously.   And Jacob, although an old man when he arrived in Egypt, enjoyed a further seventeen years of contentment before he finally died.

Meanwhile, Joseph continued to administer the affairs of the Pharaoh very successfully.   There were still five years of famine to come when Jacob and his family settled in Egypt, but the wise and careful provision that Joseph had made during the plentiful years proved sufficient to see the country through these difficult years.

JOSEPH IS MERCIFUL

But, even to the Egyptians, Joseph did not just give away the food he had gathered.   It belonged to Pharaoh and Joseph was the Pharaoh's Prime Minister.   So Joseph sold the food on Pharaoh's behalf.   As time went by and the famine continued, the people became short of money.   When this happened, Joseph took their animals in exchange for grain.   As the famine persisted, he then began to accept their land in exchange for food.   In this way, Joseph increased the power and wealth and authority of the Pharaoh.   By so doing, it may seem to us that Joseph acted rather harshly.   He was, after all, taking advantage of the people's needs in order to build up his master's house.   But Joseph was gentle by nature, too.   For example, this was obvious in his attitude towards his brothers.   He never took revenge on them for the way they had treated him.   When Jacob died, they were afraid that Joseph might seek some vengeance on them.   But Joseph assured them that they need have no fear and he continued to look after them as before.

Joseph was one of the great men of Israel and his loyalty and uprightness were outstanding features of his character. He may have been less pleasant as a boy, as his brothers at least seemed to find, but as a grown man he was most likeable and he was much mourned in Egypt when he died at the age of 110 years.

THE ILIAD

In Greek mythology, Paris, also known as Alexander, was the son of King Priam of Troy. His mother, Hecuba, had had bad dreams about him before he was born, so at his birth he was exposed to die on Mount Ida. However he was rescued by shepherds, and grew up under their care. When he was a young man, he went back to Troy, and took part in various contests in which he defeated all his brothers. His sister Cassandra, a prophetess, recognised him, and he was re-united with his family.

One day Peleus and the goddess Thetis celebrated their wedding, and all the kings and queens, princes and princesses from neighbouring lands gathered for the great feast. The goddess of strife, Eris, threw down among them a golden apple, on which was written " To the most beautiful ". Three goddesses, Hera, wife of Zeus, Athena, goddess of wisdom, and Aphrodite, goddess of love, all laid claim to the apple. Zeus, the king of the gods, chose Paris to award the apple, as he was the most handsome of men.

The god Hermes took the three goddesses and Paris to Mount Ida, near Troy, and there the judgment of Paris took place. All three goddesses tried to bribe Paris: Hera offered him power, Athena victory in war, and Aphrodite promised him the most beautiful woman in the world for his wife. Paris chose Aphrodite, and awarded her the golden apple. So, while he won the favour of Aphrodite, he incurred the perpetual hatred of Hera and Athena. Aphrodite fulfilled her promise by sending Paris to Sparta, in Greece, where he met Helen. He fell in love with her, took her back to Troy, while her husband Menelaus was absent, and so began the war of the Greeks against Troy.

WAR AGAINST TROY

King Agamemnon of Mycenae, who was Menelaus's elder brother, summoned the Greek kings and chiefs to sail to Troy, bring back Helen, and punish Paris.

At first, the Greeks tried to parley with the Trojans, but Paris refused to give back either Helen or the treasure which she had taken with her. So the Greeks prepared to sail to Troy. They all met at Aulis, a town on the Greek mainland, by the straits of Euboea. Contrary winds stopped the expedition from sailing through the straits, and when Agamemnon prayed to the gods for a fair wind, he was told by the prophet Calchas that he must sacrifice his daughter Iphigenia to satisfy the anger of the goddess Artemis. He did so, and with a fair wind the ships sailed through the straits, and reached the eastern shore of the Aegean Sea.

The Greeks landed first in Mysia, and then sailed northwards to Troy, which lies about two miles from the sea, on the plain by the entrance to the straits called the Dardanelles. The army landed, built a camp, and the siege of Troy, which was to last ten years, began. The besiegers did not surround the whole city, and so cut it off completely and conquer it by starvation. Instead, they waited for the Trojans to come out from behind their walls, and then fought man against man. Sometimes they staged battles according to very elaborate rules on which both sides had agreed. The Greeks got a firm foothold in the land of Troy by cutting off the Trojans from the sea, and by capturing the smaller towns and villages which lay close at hand on the plain.

Agamemnon and Menelaus were the supreme commanders of the Greeks, but many other kings commanded their own armies under these two leaders. There was Achilles and his army of Myrmidons. He was the son of Peleus and Thetis, a brave and ferocious warrior whose anger is the main theme of the poem, the *Iliad*. There were also leaders called Ajax, Palamedes, Diomedes, Nestor, Odysseus, and others. Odysseus himself was less warlike than the other chiefs, but much more cunning in his advice and his plans.

The Trojan king was Priam, but the *Iliad* tells us more about two of his sons, Paris and Hector. Hector was the hero of the Trojan side; he saw that he would be defeated, but still fought bravely and hopefully, until he was killed

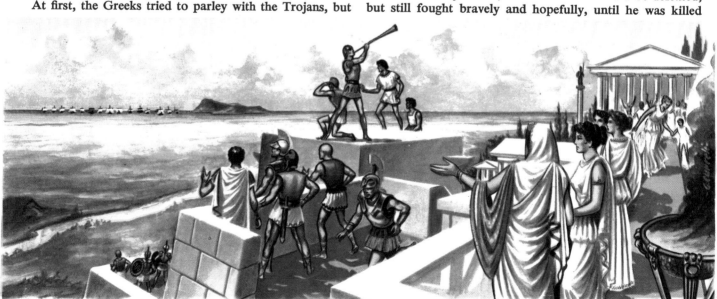

The trumpeter on the walls of Troy sounds the alarm as the invading Greek fleet sails into view.

56

Menelaus, the Greek champion, wounds Paris in the side and would have killed him but for Aphrodite's intervention.

by Achilles. Paris was a cunning archer, who preferred being with Helen to fighting in battle. Another royal warrior was Aeneas, the son of Anchises and the goddess Aphrodite. He survived the sack of Troy and became the legendary founder of the Julian family in Italy, and an important figure to the Romans. Not all the Trojans were warriors: the old counsellor Antenor wanted to hand over Helen to the Greeks, and end the long siege. But the other Trojans defended Helen.

The story which the poet Homer tells in the *Iliad* starts in the tenth year of the siege. Although he recounts adventures which have happened in the first nine years, he gives no details of how the Greek army arrived, set up camp, and won their foothold on the land around Troy. He started at the point in the tenth year of the siege where King Agamemnon had divided up the booty, and taken for himself the captive girl, Chryseis, daughter of Chryses, a priest of Apollo. Chryses came to ransom his daughter, but Agamemnon refused to hand her back. So Chryses prayed to Apollo for vengeance. Apollo sent a plague on the Greek army which forced Agamemnon to hand over Chryseis to her father, and to make sacrifice to the offended god, Apollo.

But Agamemnon insisted on his share of the booty, and took for himself Briseis, a captive girl who had been awarded to Achilles. Achilles was furious: he and his men refused to fight for Agamemnon, and his mother Thetis persuaded Zeus, the king of the gods, to let the Trojans win until her son was fully avenged. Zeus sent a false dream to Agamemnon, persuading him to attack Troy. Agamemnon did so, but he was met by Hector, who suggested that the war should be settled by a duel between Paris and Menelaus, while the armies kept a truce. Paris was defeated by Menelaus in the duel, but was saved from harm by the goddess Aphrodite. The goddess Athena, who was determined to see Troy destroyed, decided to break the truce, and made a Trojan warrior called Pandarus shoot at Menelaus. Menelaus was wounded, and fighting began, which led to a full-scale battle. The Greek Diomedes defeated Aeneas, and even managed to wound Aphrodite and Ares, the god of war himself. There was a fierce duel between Hector and Ajax, the son of Telamon. But the great battle was not a clear victory for either side, and Agamemnon was bitterly disappointed that his dream of conquering Troy had not been fulfilled. He decided to build a strong fort around the Greek ships and huts which were scattered along the beach by the sea.

The Greeks held a council of war, and Nestor, the wise old king of Pylos, persuaded Agamemnon to win back Achilles to help the Greek army. So Agamemnon sent men to Achilles's tent, and offered to give back Briseis: he also promised many fine gifts to satisfy Achilles's wounded pride. But Achilles refused Agamemnon's offers; his anger got the better of him, and now put him in the wrong, because Agamemnon had acted generously and honourably in offering to give back Briseis. When the men returned from Achilles, Agamemnon was so angry and disappointed that he made plans to put the army on board their ships and sail back to Greece, leaving Troy unconquered.

ACHILLES AND HECTOR

But that night Odysseus and Diomedes made a raid on a small band of Thracians, who had recently come to help King Priam. They stole the magnificent horses of the Thracian king, Rhesus, and brought them back to the Greek

Hector embraces his wife, Andromeda, for the last time.

Patroclus, resplendent in his borrowed armour, is no match for Hector, who slays him with his lance.

camp. This piece of luck encouraged Agamemnon to fight the Trojans again next day. But the gods were against him: he was wounded and the whole Greek army was driven back within the walls of their camp. Just as the Trojans, led by Hector and Sarpedon, were about to storm the Greek wall, Achilles, who had been sulking in his tent, gave in to the request of his dearest friend Patroclus, that he might dress in Achilles's own armour and lead his men to the aid of the hard-pressed Greeks. Patroclus was at first successful, and drove off the Trojans: but he advanced too far, was driven back from the walls of Troy, and killed by Hector, who stripped him of Achilles's armour and put it on himself.

Achilles was grief-stricken at the death of Patroclus. In a furious desire to avenge his friend, he made up his quarrel with Agamemnon over the captive Briseis, and two days later came into battle against the Trojans. His mother Thetis had asked Hephaestus, the god of fire and metal-working, to forge him a magnificent new suit of armour, for she had been told that her son would die soon after Hector. Wearing this armour, Achilles led the Greeks into battle, and chased the Trojans over the open plain back into the city of Troy. Hector himself was ashamed to retreat inside the city and waited for Achilles outside the city gate, although he knew well that he was doomed to die by the hand of Achilles. But at the last moment his courage failed, and he ran away from him. He was chased three times round the city, strengthened by Apollo, and only stopped when he thought he saw his brother Deiphobus coming to help him. Too late he realised that this was not his brother, but his enemy, the goddess Athena, in disguise. With a last burst of courage, he turned and faced Achilles. They fought at close quarters, and Hector was mortally wounded. Before he died, he asked Achilles not to maltreat his body in revenge for the death of Patroclus. Achilles refused to make such a promise, and Hector summoned enough breath to foretell to Achilles his doom, before he died. Achilles tied Hector's body to his chariot, and dragged it back over the plain to the Greek camp. There he mourned Patroclus, and held games in his honour, as was the Greek custom. For twelve days he dragged Hector's body round the tomb of Patroclus. But the gods preserved Hector's body from decay, and one night his father, King Priam, was secretly guided by the god Hermes to the Greek camp, where he ransomed his son's body. It was taken back to Troy and given a ceremonial burial. Here Homer ended the story of Achilles—the brave warrior whose own anger led him from chivalry to sin and impiety.

Greek mythology carried the story further. Achilles fought against two Trojan allies, Queen Penthesilea the Amazon, and King Memnon the Ethiopian. He killed both of them, but was then wounded in the heel by Paris, who shot an arrow at him with the guidance of Apollo. The arrow was poisoned, and the dying Achilles was carried back by Ajax to the Greek camp. He died, lamented by his mother Thetis, the sea-nymphs who were her followers, and all the Greek army.

The armour of Achilles, which had been made by the god Hephaestus, became the object of a bitter struggle between the Greek chiefs. Ajax and Odysseus both claimed it, so the problem was put before the leaders of the army. They decided that Odysseus deserved the armour because their Trojan prisoners were more afraid of him than of Ajax. Ajax went mad with grief, and started to murder sheep, supposing in his madness that they were the Greek chiefs. When his madness left him, he committed suicide because he was so ashamed of what he had done.

The Greek army was now reunited in a last effort to capture Troy. First, Odysseus and Diomedes managed to enter Troy secretly and stole the Palladium, an ancient statue of Athena which protected Troy and kept her walls safe during siege. Then the Greek Epeius built an enormous wooden horse in which the bravest warriors were hidden. The rest of the Greek army sailed away just out of sight, and the Trojans thinking that the Greeks had abandoned the siege after ten long years, pulled the wooden horse into the city as a gift for the gods. That very night, the Greek army sailed back from the island of Tenedos where they had been hiding. The men inside the wooden horse came out secretly and opened the gates of Troy to them. There was a desperate fight in the streets, but the Greeks managed to set fire to the city. King Priam, Paris, Deiphobus, and many other Trojan leaders were killed, but others (such as Aeneas) escaped the fire and slaughter.

So after ten years of siege the Greeks captured Troy. They plundered the city, divided the booty among themselves, and sailed back to their homes in Greece.

Civilisation and Culture
POLYNESIA

The Polynesians who inhabit the coral atolls and volcanic islands of the south-eastern Pacific Ocean and who are known as Maoris in New Zealand appear to be of one stock and speak dialects of a common Malayo-Polynesian language. Brown-skinned, their hair is dark brown or black, smooth and curly, and their features are similar to those of Europeans, except for the characteristic oriental eye-fold. According to anthropologists the Polynesians derive from the mixing of three distinct racial stocks over a long period of time, a caucasoid people resembling the Ainu of Japan, a mongoloid people from the steppes of central Asia who absorbed them, and oceanic Negroes who once inhabited southern Asia. They are usually tall, broad-limbed, and well rounded, with wide noses and high cheekbones. Polynesia, the ethno-geographical term used to describe the " many islands " in which they live can be shown on a map of the Pacific by drawing a triangle joining the points at Hawaii, New Zealand and Easter Island. This includes all of Polynesia except the Lau islands of Fiji, Rotuma, the Ellice Islands and several pockets of Polynesian influence such as Tikopia within Melanesia and Kapingamarangi within Micronesia.

It is quite evident that there has been intermarriage and cultural contact with other peoples, in some instances with darker Melanesian or Papuan peoples, in some instances with more oriental peoples from the Asian archipelagos, and it has also been suggested, though with less probability, that there has been contact with the Indians of both American continents. However, the principal migrations of man which peopled the islands, either by planned voyage or accidental drift, gradually evolved a number of island civilisations of basic type, though with marked regional differences.

There are many theories to account for the peopling of Polynesia. Traces of the basic culture can be found on the south-east Asian mainland and in some of the islands *en route* to the eastern Pacific inhabited to-day by other racial groups. It is now assumed, mainly from the archaeological evidence, that the ancestral Polynesians were Neolithic fishermen living on the South China coast who were driven to seek new homes as the result of population movements caused by political expansion in North China, about two thousand years before the birth of Christ. Tools and implements excavated in South Asia, are essentially the same as those found on the earliest Polynesian sites. Villages have been excavated in Fiji and New Caledonia, and evidence was found to indicate that these people had reached the islands of Melanesia some time before 1000 B.C. The dates of these sites are determined by testing carbon deposits.

Although there is evidence of remarkable drift voyages, it is also certain that the ancestral Polynesians had gifted navigational skill. Their large outrigger and double canoes were well equipped to transport sizeable family groups, with live provisions, over thousands of miles of ocean often against prevailing winds and currents. In these canoes they took live pigs, dogs, jungle fowl (for plumage) and even rats, as well as root plants such as *taro* and yams. They also took coconuts, breadfruit and other tropical plants. Their knowledge of astronomy was of great assistance in determining courses. However the success of these voyages depended mainly on the combination of sail and hull design, the triangular sail being so utilised that the canoes could actually sail the most difficult seas in all conditions, thus anticipating modern research in aerodynamics.

Tonga and Samoa were presumably the first islands to be

This type of canoe with its stabilising outrigger is widely used by the fishing people of Polynesia.

permanently settled by the Polynesians, probably as early as 1500 B.C. Indeed, in Samoa, the myth of their being the original inhabitants of the land was very strongly held, suggesting a very long period of residence, whilst the myths of the sailing gods are more evident in eastern Polynesia. Of the eastern islands the Marquesas seem to have had the first settlers, about 700 B.C., probably from Tonga. Tahiti was also peopled from the western islands of this early period, language and traditions suggesting Samoa and Rotuma as early homelands, though the first settlers may have come via the Marquesas. The first settlers of Hawaii evidently came from the Marquesas about A.D. 100 though the Hawaiian culture was considerably influenced by contact with Tahiti in later years. The remote Easter Island was settled from the Marquesas about A.D. 300 while New Zealand was first settled from Tahiti about A.D. 1000.

RELIGION

Although animism, or the endowing of all objects with a spirit, was an essential feature of Polynesian religion, more sophisticated religious beliefs had been developed by the priests. These beliefs appear to have been related either to certain fertility aspects of religion or to a basic philosophy of man's place in the universe. Their claimed skills in divination and the manipulation of psychic phenomena were carefully cultivated with other more obvious conjuring skills. The *kahunas* in Hawaii and the *tohunga* in New Zealand taught their secret lore to a chosen few. The mythology of the Polynesians may have preserved a certain amount of history, but much of it was an attempt to explain natural phenomena and to define man's relations with the universe. Often the original point of a story may have been sacrificed to the literary embellishments of the story-teller more interested in humorous incident or the delineation of character. Tangaroa was the god with the most widespread influence, and in western Polynesia had several manifestations. In the eastern Pacific, Tangaroa's influence was shared by other gods, who were possibly established firmly by earlier migrations and who were mostly connected with strong fertility cults, such as Tane, the " god of beauty " in Tahiti. In addition, there were

great navigational gods such as Maui, who is said to have pulled up islands out of the sea, and Hiro of Raiatea, who were perhaps deified leaders of early expeditions. The links between mythology and astronomy were very close, and possibly the stars were used as a great cosmic abacus for teaching by repetition. Some gods had fairly localised fame such as Pele, the volcano goddess in Hawaii.

In parts of eastern Polynesia the *marae* or sacred stone ancestral shrine was the centre of all religious and social observances. In Tahiti the bodies of human sacrifices were often hung about these *maraes* for long periods. Some of these *maraes* were built on grand proportions and resembled the pyramids of other civilisations. However, most large stone structures in Polynesia belong to comparatively recent times, and are usually associated with the development of more autocratic forms of chieftainship. The upright stone monuments, or trilithons, of Tonga probably belong to the twelfth century. The *maraes* of Tahiti and the stone plazas of the Marquesas probably achieved their greatest proportions by the eighteenth century and the giant statues of Easter Island belong to the two centuries preceding the coming of the European, and not to some " lost civilisation " as was once thought by early explorers.

RITUAL CANNIBALISM

Legends and traditions suggest that most of the Polynesian peoples had at one time been acquainted with ritual cannibalism. However when Europeans first reached the islands only the Marquesans, Cook Islanders, and Maoris of New Zealand practised cannibalism to any large extent. Tahitians, though they went through the motions of eating the eyes of human sacrifices, showed revulsion for cannibalism.

ART AND ARCHITECTURE

The art of the Polynesians was considerably advanced, particularly in wood-carving. Maori architecture, especially, displays the Polynesian talent for harmony of design and the stylisation of the human form. The motifs and patterns on the bark cloth or *tapa* manufactured by most Polynesian

On Easter Island stand these famous and mysterious statues, gazing like watchful giants across the Pacific.

Queen Salote, ruler of the island kingdom of Tonga (1900-65).

peoples also displayed this talent. Tattoo designs, which were particularly detailed in the Marquesas, were considered a particularly beautiful form of adornment, and certainly displayed great ingenuity and skill. In New Zealand, the Polynesian women were forced to abandon the making of *tapa* but found an admirable substitute for clothing in the native flax. Also in New Zealand, the rich supplies of timber and the cooler climate meant that more wood could be used in the construction of buildings thus giving greater scope for artistic decoration. Also the potentials of green stone were quickly realised by the Maori carvers. On the whole, stone figures in Polynesia tended to be more crude in concept, though they admirably fulfilled the purpose of inspiring awe.

Of the social arts oratory was a highly developed skill in most Polynesian communities. Traditions were also carefully memorised in chants of artistic composition. Though writing was unknown the Polynesians had developed many aids to memory. Besides using the stars, they also depended on the mythographic representation of myths in carving, tattoo designs and the embellishments on sacred objects. More abstract ideas were conveyed by string figures (cat's cradles), and on Easter Island, hieroglyphs had actually been devised and were in use until the beginning of the nineteenth century. The large wooden figures of gods often contained the images of lesser gods. Each had a name and linked together provided the characters for an ancient story. The use of sennit, or native cordage, was also used to preserve traditions. Its colour and shape were significant and it was used in the manufacture and adornment of sacred objects. Traditions were also retained because each craft had its own rules and ritual.

POLYNESIAN RITUALS·

The ritual of the dance also helped to preserve the folk memory as well as serve a religious function either in promoting fertility or in placating spirits. Everywhere in Polynesia the dance was developed to a remarkable extent. As with the sacred Indian dancers, the Polynesians had to learn the ritual movements at a very early age. In Tahiti many of the privileged members of society (mainly priests and chiefs

of both sexes) belonged to a semi-religious order, known as the *arioi* society, which gave itself up to the organisation of ritual pleasure. They were rather like travelling players as they provided entertainment wherever they visited. No great occasion was complete without their presence. Games were also well developed in Polynesia, as for instance, one similar to draughts. Ball games and surfing sports were also widely played.

Warriors had a place of high esteem in the Polynesian community and warfare had an elaborate ritual and literature of its own. Social status in Polynesia depended on the possession of *mana*, a mysterious power or mystical quality usually transmitted by birth. Chiefs and priests were said to possess considerable *mana* while the common people possessed it in small degrees, usually according to their position in the family where the principle of primogeniture (firstborn) was carefully observed. Closely connected with the possession of *mana* was the *tapu* system, a code of sanctions which were rigorously observed, infringements being punished by death or fear of supernatural action. Anyone who touched a sacred (or *tapu*) person or object could expect to die immediately.

SOCIAL CLASSES

In most islands the common people were regarded as being mere food-getters by those of high lineage, and in Tonga, for instance, it was presumed that they did not share the immortality of the chiefs. However in the Marquesas and some other groups, social distinctions were far less apparent; even the highest chiefs did not stand out conspicuously from the people. The Polynesians had a highly developed political consciousness and though absolute rule was known and developed considerably as in the islands of Hawaii, the principle of the balance of power had widespread acceptance, and a tyrant could expect to be overthrown by a combination of other chiefs. In some islands a system of dual chieftainship existed whereby paramountcy depended on a number of factors distinct from heredity. In Samoa, where there were more eligible candidates for the highest title than elsewhere, generations might elapse before an acceptable claimant was given the highest rank, which was social rather than political. It was expected that the *Tupu o Samoa* could speak for at least the four principal families of the group. Salamasina was such a queen of Samoa in the sixteenth century and was celebrated in the chants for the peace and prosperity associated with her rule.

Ceremonial played a large part in the life of the Polynesian peoples especially through the medium of oratory. *Kava* drinking, or the ceremonial connected with a beverage made from the root of a plant cultivated by the Polynesians, was a distinct feature of ancient Polynesian society though, like a number of other customs, it could not be maintained in New Zealand. Where it is found to-day in Fiji and the more western parts of Melanesia it can be traced to Polynesian origin. The use of *tapa* cloth and sennit also had a fixed place in the highly complex social system. Some ceremonial rites intimately connected with the ancient way of life were afterwards discouraged because they appeared crude and shocking by European standards.

Cultivation of crops, besides fishing, provided for the basic wants of the people. In the coral atolls it was often difficult to cultivate the plants which the Polynesians brought with them, and *taro* had to be grown in large pits. In the more fertile islands certain crops developed better than others and

The Maoris of to-day have not forgotten their warrior past. These men are dancing a traditional war-dance.

tended to become the staple diet, as breadfruit in the Marquesas. Although the pig may have been introduced into New Zealand at some time, the presence of large edible birds (including the now extinct *moa*), may have discouraged the Polynesian pioneers from keeping their pigs for breeding purposes. Dogs, of course, were useful for hunting the *moa* as well as being edible.

ARRIVAL OF THE EUROPEANS

With the discovery of the Polynesian islands in the sixteenth century by Europeans the traditional way of life was gradually affected. The cultural change was accelerated after the discovery of Tahiti by Wallis in 1767 and the " rediscovery " of Hawaii by Cook in 1778 (Hawaii may have been discovered by a Spanish expedition, as Hawaiian traditions affirm an earlier European visit than Cook's). Fascinated by the noble dignity of the Polynesian, his typical classical physique, and the social refinements of Polynesian society as distinct from the more savage appearance of the Melanesians, the European explorers believed that they had found the noble savage, then the popular ideal of the humanist philosophers. The old civilisations of the islands fast disintegrated, first through internal discord accentuated by the breakdown of the balance of power, helped by the introduction of European firearms, and also by disease, demoralisation and disillusion with the old religion which seemed powerless against the new forces. New skills, European clothing, a literate religion and general culture all seemed superior to the traditional way of life and led to the reformation of Polynesian society. Unfortunately much that was of aesthetic and cultural value was sacrificed to European influence. On the other hand, despite early ravages of disease, there were compensations. The Europeans introduced cures for some of the local tropical ailments, and missionaries in particular introduced a positive way of life to replace the disintegrating traditional way, and so helped them adjust to the dominant European civilisation. Often, however, the missionaries were not sufficiently appreciative of the virtues of the old culture. In many of the islands, powerful or paramount chiefs were encouraged or influenced to set themselves up as kings of a European type. The Hawaiian mon-

archy lasted till 1893; the Tahitian monarchy till 1880; and monarchical experiments were tried in Samoa and Fiji, and some of the other groups. The Tongan monarchy is the only one which survived with full sovereign status into the twentieth century.

In New Zealand the Maori people have provided a number of distinguished writers and leaders. It would be difficult to say which of the Polynesian civilisations was the most advanced. Certainly the Samoans were beyond competition in political diplomacy and social etiquette. However it was the islands which possessed the more dominant cult centres which played an important role in enriching the literature and philosophy of the people. Thus, in eastern Polynesia, the *marae* of Taputaputea on the island of Raiatea was the centre of an influential semi-priestly movement with an influence extending to other islands. In western Polynesia the sacred chiefs of Tonga had gradually assumed a position of superior social status and much of this prestige survives to-day in the position of H.M. King Tanfa'ahau Tupou IV.

LITERATURE TO READ

There are many books to read about the Polynesians. Robert C. Suggs, the American archaeologist, has written a very readable account of the story of Polynesia called *Lords of the Blue Pacific*. Another book by him, *The Island Civilisations of Polynesia*, is more detailed. Many of the stories of this ancient seafaring people are told in Johannes C. Andersen's *Myths and Legends of the Polynesians*. Andrew Sharp has also discussed the great problem of Polynesian navigation in his book, *Ancient Voyages in the Pacific*.

Captain Cook's book, *Voyages*, contains much information about the Polynesians as they were when virtually untouched by European civilisation. Thor Heyerdahl's story of the *Kon-Tiki* raft expedition is still a good adventure story even if the theories he was trying to prove have little scientific foundation.

The Polynesians have also been immortalised in European literature. Herman Melville's great stories of *Typee* and *Omoo* are classics everyone should read. Robert Louis Stevenson's *In the South Seas* and other works reveal the novelist's love for the Polynesians.

The first king that Israel ever had was a mighty warrior named Saul. But Saul, although a first-class ruler to begin with, as the years went by became much less satisfactory and in the end, and long before his death, a successor was marked out. Guided by God, the Prophet Samuel made his way to the house and family of Jesse in Bethlehem and there Samuel took anointing oil and consecrated as the future king of Israel the youngest of Jesse's eight sons. The lad was very young and very handsome and his name was David.

It was not very long after this that a great battle was in prospect between the Israelites on the one hand, and the Philistines, their long standing and bitter enemies, on the other hand. The opposing armies were drawn up facing each other on either side of a valley. But, before the battle could begin, the champion of the Philistines, a giant of a man called Goliath, stepped forward and issued a challenge to the Israelites. "There is no need", he said, "for these two armies to engage in bloody battle. Let the matter be decided in single combat. Choose a champion for yourselves and send him out to meet me. He and I shall fight to the death. If I win, you will accept us as your masters. If your champion should win, we will accept you as our masters."

Saul and his company were appalled. Who was there on their side who would have the slightest chance against such an enormous man and one so heavily armoured as Goliath? The challenge, therefore, was not accepted, but day after day, both morning and evening, Goliath stepped out in front of the Philistine army and bellowed his challenge to the Israelites.

This went on for weeks until, one day, David happened to be there when Goliath made his challenge and heard what he said. David himself was a shepherd boy but he had three brothers serving in Saul's army and from time to time he visited them and brought them delicacies. On this particular occasion he heard Goliath speak and when he heard what was going on David was ashamed. He regarded it as a great insult to Israel that this challenge should be flung at the army day after day without ever being taken up. So David offered to be Israel's champion.

At first Saul refused to take this offer seriously. After all David was not even in the army whilst Goliath was a soldier with many years of experience behind him. And then, in addition, Goliath was a much bigger and a much stronger man than David. It would be folly to send out David as Israel's champion. This would be suicide for David and it would also be disaster for Israel.

But David's eagerness and confidence finally overcame Saul's hesitation and he gave his consent. He dressed David for the battle in his own armour. But Saul's armour did not fit David and he could scarcely move in it. So David put off the armour and went out to do battle as he was, without armour and carrying only his staff, his sling and, in his wallet, five smooth stones which he had taken from the brook.

The two champions left their armies and moved towards each other while the soldiers on both sides watched eagerly. Goliath was scornful of David because he was only a lad and was so poorly armed. But David had no fear and he ran quickly forward to meet his opponent. When he judged that the range was right he put a stone in his sling and hurled it at Goliath. The stone hit Goliath right in the centre of his forehead and knocked him out. David then ran to Goliath's side as he lay prone, drew the Philistine's sword from its sheath and cut off his head.

The Philistines were shocked and dismayed. Their unbeatable champion was dead. But the Israelites were jubilant and, as their enemies turned and fled, they pursued them relentlessly and made the victory complete.

SAUL'S JEALOUSY

This remarkable exploit earned David immediate fame as a

The old prophet, Samuel, anoints the young David, thus establishing him as the future king of Israel.

Goliath, the gigantic champion of the Philistines, hurls his challenge at the Israelites who are too fearful to respond.

The young David, apparently too small and puny to be of any consequence to Goliath, confronts him.

For the second time David refuses to revenge himself on the defenceless Saul, merely stealing his spear and water jar.

warrior and Saul made him a general in his army. But this great achievement also marked the start of jealousy on the part of Saul towards David, because David's killing of Goliath had gained him so much popularity.

David proved very successful as a general and won many famous victories. Saul, however, was growing steadily more jealous of David's increasing success and popularity and, in the end, he began to plot against his life. David, however, was warned of Saul's intention, first by Jonathan, Saul's son, who was David's closest friend, and then by Michal, Saul's daughter, whom David had married.

Because of the warnings, David was able to escape from his house before Saul's men came to kill him. But Saul had now come to hate David so much that he was determined that he should be put to death. By this time Saul had become more than a little mad and in his madness he turned even upon Jonathan, his own son, because he had befriended David.

It was clear that there was no hope of Saul and David ever being reconciled. It was equally clear that it would be very

dangerous for David to venture back to the king's palace. So David now became an outlaw, moving from place to place, snatching shelter and finding food as and where he could.

As time went by he gathered a band of followers to his side, a band that grew into a small army. These were fighting men, who fought for their existence, raiding and plundering under the leadership of David.

All this time David continued to be under the constant threat of death at the hands of Saul. He was rarely given any peace as Saul hunted and harried him continually. David was driven from one refuge to another and always the danger of making a mistake or being caught off guard hung over his head.

And yet there were two remarkable incidents during this time when David could have killed Saul but on each occasion spared his life. He knew that Saul meant to kill him. He knew that he would be safer if Saul were dead. But, at the same time, he held the kingship in such reverence that he could not bring himself to do any harm to the person who occupied the throne. Saul, he believed, had been appointed by God and David was unwilling to raise a finger against a servant of God.

The first of these incidents occurred when Saul had organised a large scale search for David in the wilderness of Engedi. Saul took 3,000 picked men in order to conduct this search but, in the course of it, he happened to go by himself into a cave in whose recesses David and his men were hidden.

David could easily have killed Saul then and his men wanted him to do so. But David refused. Instead he crept up stealthily behind the unsuspecting king and cut a piece from the border of his robe. When Saul had left the cave and was at a safe distance, David called after him, showed him the piece of cloth and told him what had happened. Saul, realising that his life had been at David's mercy, broke down and wept and vowed that he would bear no further enmity towards David.

But Saul did not keep this resolution and soon he was hunting David as savagely as ever. And it was while he was hunting David in Ziph that the second instance occurred when David had his enemy's life in his hand and let him go free.

David's successes began to make his King so jealous that he eventually had to fly for his life from him.

From the safety of a hill, David rouses Saul.

During the night when Saul and his army were encamped, David and Abishai penetrated unobserved into the very heart of the encampment and made their way to the side of the sleeping king. Abishai wanted to kill Saul on the spot but once again David would not permit it.

He contented himself with taking away the spear and the jar of water that stood at Saul's head. David and Abishai then retreated as quietly and as unobserved as they had come, made their way down the hillside, across the valley and up the opposite hill. From the safety of the hill top across the valley, David then called over to the camp and told Saul what he had done. Once more the king expressed his regret for his treatment of David and promised that he would no longer seek his death.

But David was sadly aware that he could place no reliance on this promise and he realised that he could not hope to go on escaping Saul indefinitely. If he stayed on in Israel, sooner or later Saul was bound to catch up with him and that would be the end. Reluctantly he decided that the only thing for him to do was to leave the country.

So David made up his mind to cross the border into the land of the Philistines. No sooner had he made his decision than he acted upon it. He and his band, now grown to 600 men, made their way to Gath, one of the Philistine territories, and there King Achish gave them residence, reckoning that he was thus going to gain valuable allies.

David and his men spent a year and four months in that country and they were highly regarded by King Achish. So much so that when war threatened once again between the Philistines and the Israelites, Achish invited David and his men to fight with him and David agreed. He and his men had been driven out from Israel, while Achish had given them a home. David therefore reckoned that the King of Gath was the man who deserved his loyalty now.

So David and his men went with Achish and his army to Aphek which was the place where the Philistine forces were assembling together. But when they got there they ran into difficulties. A number of the Philistine commanders objected to the presence of David and his men in the Philistine ranks. "These men", they said, "have deserted from Israel. How can we be sure that they will remain loyal to us in the heat of battle?" Achish argued that David had already been with him for sixteen months and that his loyalty had been above suspicion all that time. But the commanders were adamant and, in the end, Achish was forced to send David and his men back home.

KING DAVID

So David missed the battle. As he and his men left the Philistine assembly point and began to make their way back to Ziklag, their adopted home, the Philistine army moved forward to join battle with the assembled Israelites. The result was a decisive victory in favour of the Philistines and as the routed Israelites fled before the victorious Philistines, Saul and three of his sons lost their lives. Jonathan, David's faithful and constant friend, was slain by the enemy and so were his brothers, Abinadab and Malchishua. Saul was badly wounded by an arrow and, knowing that all was lost, he ran himself through with his own sword. His death left the throne of Israel vacant and while it was occupied for a time by Saul's son Ish-Bosheth, it was not very long before it came to be occupied by that same David whom Saul had long feared and harried.

David laments the deaths of Saul and Jonathan.

Abner installs Saul's son, Ish-bosheth, as king on Saul's death.

THE STORY OF DAVID : II

Shortly after the death of Saul, David was anointed King of Judah, the Southern part of Palestine. Not long after this he entered into warfare with Ish-Bosheth, that son of Saul who had succeeded to the throne of Israel. This was a long drawn out affair, but David slowly and surely gained the upper hand and in the end he acquired the throne of Israel, too. This was two years after he had been appointed King of Judah and he reigned over the whole land, Israel and Judah together, for a further thirty-eight years, the first five of these from Hebron and the remaining thirty-three from Jerusalem.

But David was not immediately the undisputed ruler of the newly united land. Although he had overcome all opposition from the House of Saul, he had still to contend with the ancient enemies of the Israelites, the Philistines. Since their defeat of Saul, the Philistines had been much stronger than the Israelites. So long as the people of Palestine were divided into two kingdoms, Israel in the north and Judah in the south, the Philistines do not seem to have minded their having their own kings. But as soon as David took over both thrones and joined the countries into one kingdom, the position changed dramatically. This was likely to create a kingdom that would be too strong for their comfort and so the Philistines decided to wage war.

But David was a great soldier. Although his responsibilities were new and his resources limited, it was David who won the war. He defeated the Philistine army in two engagements in the Valley of Rephaim, the second of which was decisive.

Not only did David gain a complete victory over the Philistines in the Valley of Rephaim, he managed to capture the city of Jerusalem, lying on the border between Israel and Judah and occupied by the Jebusites. This accomplishment was a feat which few would even have attempted, for Jerusalem, set on a hill as it was and heavily fortified, appeared to be beyond any hope of capture. Nevertheless, David not only launched an assault against it, he actually took it.

This was the beginning of the greatness of Jerusalem. David made it his capital and, as the kingdom flourished under his wise and strong rule, both the size and reputation of Jerusalem increased.

THE ARK OF GOD

One thing David did which more than anything else helped to make Jerusalem a city of great and undying importance was to bring to it the Ark of God. This was the chest in which were housed the Tables of the Covenant, the two stone tablets on which were inscribed that Covenant which God had given to Moses for the people of Israel.

The bringing of this very holy object into Jerusalem was what began to make Jerusalem the very holy city it ultimately became. For by this action David made Jerusalem not only the political and military capital of his kingdom but also its religious centre. And that was a position it never lost.

David was an excellent ruler. This was due to a number of things. For one thing, he was a first-rate soldier. For another, he was a splendid organiser. In addition, he was a man of great personal charm. As a result of all this, his long reign was a very successful one and it built Israel up into a strong and powerful nation.

This does not mean, however, that David had no troubles in his reign and no faults in his character. He had plenty of both.

Firstly, during his reign there was much warfare. He was sometimes attacked but sometimes he was the attacker. For David was bent on building up his kingdom and he was anxious to extend it. And so part of his work as king was a work of conquest. The territory he possessed as ruler of the joint kingdoms of Israel and Judah was still quite small. David, therefore, set about systematically extending it, first

Abner climbs to the top of a hill to shout to Joab that he is willing to surrender and to end the pursuit.

David throws his whole army into the assault of Jerusalem and is initially repulsed by the Jebusites.

After the death of Uriah, David summons his widow Bathsheba to the palace and marries her.

Through the mouth of the prophet, Nathan, David is promised a long reign and that he will be succeeded by his son.

of all by bringing within his dominion all who properly belonged to the Israelite nation and religion, but also by extending beyond the borders of Israel proper.

And so we find David conquering Edom and Moab and Ammon and Syria.

BATH-SHEBA

It was during the war with the Ammonites that David performed one of the most shameful acts of his life. He happened one afternoon when taking a stroll on the flat roof of his house, to see a woman bathing and was so greatly attracted by her beauty that he decided he wanted her for his wife. The woman, however, whose name was Bath-sheba was already married—to Uriah the Hittite.

Now, Uriah was a soldier in Joab's army, Joab being David's commander-in-chief and presently engaged in the Ammonite war. This gave David an idea. He sent a note to Joab, carried by Uriah's own hand, in which he instructed Joab to put Uriah right in the front line and to expose him as much as possible so that he might be shot down and killed.

Joab did as he was ordered. Uriah was placed in the most dangerous position and in the very next battle was killed. David's plan had been successful and the way was now open for him to marry Bath-Sheba, which he did. But Nathan, a Prophet of God, came to David soon afterwards and told him a story. " There were two men," he said, " one rich, with many flocks and herds, and one poor who possessed only one ewe lamb, of which he grew very fond. One day a traveller came to visit the rich man and, unwilling to take one of his own animals to provide a meal for his visitor, the rich man took the poor man's single ewe away from him and served it up to the traveller. What do you think of that action ? " Nathan asked. David was furiously angry when he heard this story. " The man must surely be punished," he cried. " Tell me who he is ".

Nathan said, " You are the man ", and David felt as if someone had struck him a blow.

This was an unsavoury episode in David's life for which he had no one to blame but himself. But he had other troubles which were not of his making. One of these was the rebellion of Absalom, his own son and one whom he loved very dearly.

Absalom was an ambitious young man and for long had been of the opinion that he would make a better king than his father, who was now growing old. For a time Absalom worked in secret to win the affection of the people to himself and to turn it away from David. At last, when he judged the time was ripe, he came out into the open and called for support to establish him as king. He raised the standard of revolt at Hebron and so well had he made his preparations that it seemed as if practically the whole country was ready to support him. So much so, that when the news was brought to David at Jerusalem he thought it prudent to flee from the city.

David had a Philistine personal bodyguard of some hundreds of men. These, along with a few Israelite soldiers and Joab his general, were all that accompanied him on his flight from the city. His friend Hushai, the Archite, wanted to come with him too, but David left him in Jerusalem to act as a spy for him and to work on his behalf there. For David had not abandoned hope. He was convinced that, if it were God's

After David's flight, Absalom and Ahitophel entered Jerusalem with Hushai, a spy of David's.

67

David crosses the Jordan and prepares for battle.

will, the rebellion would be overthrown and he would find himself back once more in his capital city.

That, indeed, is how it turned out, although not at once. At first everything seemed to be going Absalom's way. Support came to him from all quarters. Even Ahithophel, David's chief adviser, attached himself to Absalom's side. Absalom took up residence in Jerusalem and was hailed as king.

But Ahithophel knew that, so long as David was alive, Absalom's kingship was far from safe. He therefore advised Absalom to take immediately 12,000 men and to pursue David to the death, before he had time to recover and begin to re-organise his forces. But Absalom hesitated and sought additional advice from Hushai the Archite, that friend whom David had left behind as his spy. Hushai had already won his way into Absalom's confidence. He knew that David needed a breathing space and so he advised Absalom not to pursue David right away, but to wait until he could gather a mighty army. He would then be able to administer a crushing defeat upon David and his men. Absalom decided to take Hushai's advice rather than Ahitho-

phel's and Ahithophel went off and hanged himself. Meanwhile, Hushai sent a messenger to David telling him to get away as far and as quickly as he could.

On receiving Hushai's message, David withdrew across the Jordan where he was among friends and found help and assistance. He made his headquarters at Manahaim and there he marshalled his forces under the leadership of his faithful general, Joab. Then at Manahaim David and his army waited for the coming of Absalom and his troops. A decisive battle followed, in which David's army gained a complete victory.

David was in many ways a ruthless man but he was also a man of many tender sympathies, as was shown by his reaction to the death of Absalom. After his defeat at Manahaim, Absalom was fleeing, when his hair caught in the low hanging branches of an oak tree so that he was pulled from his horse. There he was left suspended until the pursuing Joab found and killed him.

ABSALOM—MY SON!

Joab sent a messenger to tell the news to David that victory had been won and won convincingly and that his rebellious son had been slain. You would have thought that David could scarcely have received better news. But all he could think of was that Absalom, his beloved son, was dead. Rebel he might have been but David had loved him. David was so moved that he went away to the privacy of his room and there wept for Absalom, uttering as he went words that have become immortal. " Oh my son, Absalom, my son, my son Absalom! Would God I had died for thee, O Absalom, my son, my son! "

There was another but less serious rebellion against David, this time under a man called Sheba. But it was quelled without any great difficulty and there was never any other serious questioning of the supremacy of David the King. So it was that after 40 years of monarchy, 7 spent at Hebron and 33 at Jerusalem, during which he was engaged in much warfare and many battles, King David in the end died in his bed. But he left behind a glorious reputation and, despite his faults and his weaknesses, that reputation had been well earned and was thoroughly deserved. David was a truly great king and no one did more for his nation than did he.

Victorious over Absalom, David re-enters Jerusalem in triumph.

David declares to his advisers that Solomon shall be king.

THE GOLDEN FLEECE

The story of Jason and the Golden Fleece is told at length by Apollonius Rhodius in his poem *Argonautica*, which he wrote in the third century before Christ. The story is a collection of many legends: some of them are pure make-believe, others were invented to explain strange customs or occurrences, while others have a grain of actual history in them. So the voyage of Jason to Colchis may be founded upon real merchant journeys from Greece to the Black Sea, while the fall of Helle may be a story invented to explain the name Hellespont. There are often different versions of the same story: we shall give only the general outline of the story of Jason and the Golden Fleece.

Phrixus and Helle, son and daughter of Nephele, flee from Boetia to Colchis on the back of the ram with the golden fleece.

BACKGROUND TO THE STORY

There was a king called Athamas, in Thessaly, which is part of North Greece. He married Nephele, who bore him two children, Phrixus and Helle. His second wife, Ino, hated these two step-children, and decided to kill them. So she persuaded the Thessalian women to commit the crime of roasting some seed-corn, instead of keeping it for sowing. The gods were angry and sent a famine on the land: the people asked the oracle at Delphi how they could stop the famine, and Ino bribed the messengers returning from Delphi to answer that Phrixus and Helle were to be sacrificed. Their

mother, Nephele, rescued them by carrying them off on a golden-fleeced ram to Colchis, on the Black Sea. Helle fell off the ram, and the sea where she fell was thereafter called the Hellespont—Helle's sea. Phrixus was received by Aeetes, king of Colchis, and the ram was sacrificed to the honour of Zeus. Its fleece was hung in a grove guarded by a dragon.

Back in Thessaly, Athamas' brother Cretheus had been king of Iolcos. When he died, his son Aeson became king, but was deposed by his step-brother Pelias. Aeson's son, Jason, had been sent away into safety, and when he grew up, he decided to return and demand his father's kingdom from the usurper Pelias. He set off wearing only one shoe: he could get a better grip in the mud with one foot bare. An oracle had warned Pelias to beware of a man with only one shoe: so when Jason arrived, Pelias decided to send him as far away as possible. He invented the tale that the ghost of Phrixus haunted him, and asked for the golden fleece to be brought back to Iolcos: this was to be Jason's task. Jason agreed, and collected a crew to man his ship, the *Argo*, which was built with the help of the goddess Athena. The crew, called Argonauts, contained among other people Argus the craftsman, Tiphys the pilot, and Nylas, who was captured by water nymphs at a stop on the voyage.

The ship set sail from Pagasae, the nearest port to Iolcos,

Jason in his ship, the Argo, *leaving the shores of Thessaly to search for the Golden Fleece.*

and went north and east to the island of Lemnos. There they lingered, warmly welcomed by the women who had just killed all the men on the island. At last the Argonauts left, and reached Cyzicus: they left this town after being well received, but were driven back by a storm at night, and mistaken for raiders by the people of Cyzicus. A battle was the result, and the king who had recently welcomed the Argonauts, was killed by them.

They sailed onwards to the north, and reached the land of the Bebryces. Here they were refused water from the spring until one of them agreed to box with Amycus the king of the Bebryces. Polydeuces volunteered and defeated Amycus. The Bebryces were so angry that they attacked the Argonauts, but they too were defeated.

Eventually the ship reached the Bosporus straits, at the northern end of the sea of Marmara. There an old man, Phineus, warned them of dangers soon to threaten them. They would soon reach the Symplegades, or Clashing Rocks, at the entrance to the Black Sea; these rocks could move together and crush passing ships. The Argonauts were to let loose a dove; if the dove passed safely between the rocks, the ship would do so too. So the Argonauts set sail, and when they reached the rocks, the dove flew through just in time, losing a few tail-feathers. The sailors strained every muscle and, with the help of the goddess Athena, they just passed through, while the rocks clashed together behind them. These rocks never moved again.

The ship sailed on along the south-eastern coast of the Black Sea, which is now Turkey, and eventually came to the mouth of the River Phasis, on which Colchis stood. The crew rowed some way up the river, hid the *Argo* in a clump of reeds, and arrived at the court of King Aeetes. Aeetes first took the Argonauts for pirates, and was very hostile to them. He then demanded that one of them should try to plough a piece of land using two fire-breathing bulls, sow the ploughed land with the teeth of a dragon, and defeat the armed men who would spring from the seed. Jason agreed to be the Argonaut's champion. Luckily, the king's daughter Medea had fallen in love with Jason, and being skilled in magic, she gave him good advice and some ointment which he was to rub on his body and armour. This ointment protected Jason from fire and weapons for one day. Jason rubbed on the ointment, and managed to plough and sow the field with Medea's help. When the crop of warriors sprang up from the seed, Jason threw a stone into their midst. This started a fight among them, which lasted until they had all killed each other. Jason now asked for the golden fleece, his promised reward, but Aeetes asked him to wait. He was planning to attack Jason and the Argonauts that night and kill them all. But Medea discovered her father's treacherous plan, warned Jason, and escaped with him and the crew to the *Argo*, which lay hidden in the reeds of the River Phasis. They all sailed secretly down the river to the grove where the fleece hung, guarded by the dragon. Medea charmed the dragon to sleep while Jason stole the fleece, and returning to the ship put out to sea.

King Aeetes and his men pursued the *Argo*, and followed close behind the ship. But Medea had taken her brother Absyrtus on board the *Argo*. She now murdered him, cut him in pieces and scattered the pieces in the wake of the *Argo*. While Aeetes stopped to collect the remains of his son, the *Argo* sailed ahead in safety. Many more adventures ensued, and it is not certain what route home the *Argo* took. Some say that she went round the edge of the world in the great stream of Ocean: others say that she went by Africa, or sailed up the Danube. But eventually, Jason and Medea reached Iolcos, carrying home the golden fleece in triumph.

Jason now had to win the kingdom from the usurper Pelias, who had sent him to fetch the golden fleece. Medea falsely persuaded the daughters of Pelias that if they murdered their father, cut him up, and boiled him with special herbs in a cauldron, he would become young again. They were deceived by this trick, murdered their father, and found that Medea's advice was a lie. Medea and Jason were driven out of Iolcos by Acastus, the son of the murdered Pelias, and they took refuge at Corinth. What happened there is uncertain. Either Medea's children were murdered by the Corinthians, or else Medea murdered them herself to spite Jason, who no longer loved her. Jason himself died quietly: he was killed by a stone which fell from the roof of the shrine near Corinth in which he had dedicated the *Argo* to the god of the sea, Poseidon.

With his mission successfully accomplished and the Golden Fleece hanging over the prow of the Argo, *Jason and his Greek heroes returned home in triumph. Legend has it that Orpheus, the divine singer, was one of the Argonauts who accompanied Jason and his music was reputed to be so wonderful that he charmed alike, water nymphs, wild beasts and even the trees and rivers.*

THE POET VIRGIL

Publius Virgilius (or Vergilius) Maro is reckoned by many to be the greatest Roman poet. His reputation rests mainly on his epic poem, the *Aeneid*.

Virgil was born on 15th October, 70 B.C. at Andes, a village near Mantua in North Italy, which at that time was part of the province of Cisalpine Gaul. His father farmed a small estate. He was sent to school at Cremona and Milan, and then went to complete his education at Naples, and probably also at Rome.

It may have been Virgil's weak health which kept him from the usual Roman careers of oratory and military service; he probably went back to his father's farm after finishing his education. In 49 B.C. all the people of Cisalpine Gaul were given Roman citizenship, so Virgil obtained full rights in this year. After the battle of Philippi in 42 B.C., when the defeat of Brutus and Cassius by Mark Antony and Octavian brought one phase of the civil war to an end, many soldiers were discharged and given land. Virgil's farm was taken over and given to a soldier, but Virgil appealed to Octavian and was allowed to take possession of it again. His first *Eclogue* commemorates this restoration: he may have been evicted a second time.

About 40 B.C., Virgil was introduced to Maecenas, who became his patron, and encouraged him to write the *Georgics* four poems which occupied Virgil from 37 to 31 B.C. He

Publius Virgilius Maro, born near Mantua in 70 B.C., became the greatest poet of the Golden Age of Roman literature.

then received patronage from the Emperor Augustus (formerly called Octavian) and became wealthy and famous: but he maintained his farm as well as a town house at Rome. At the Emperor's request, he wrote his most famous poem, the *Aeneid*, which may not have been fully revised when he died at Brundisium on 22nd September, 19 B.C.

GOLDEN AGE OF LATIN LITERATURE

Virgil lived through the twenty years of civil wars which marked the end of the Roman Republic and the beginning of the Empire. References to political events are frequent in his poems, though none of them were written with a political purpose alone. He lived to see peace and order restored under Augustus, and his works together with those of Horace and Ovid, form part of the great flowering of poetry in what is called the Golden Age of Latin literature.

Apart from a few poems which may be early works of Virgil, or may have been written by another poet, Virgil's poems fall into three groups—the *Eclogues* (or the *Bucolics*), the *Georgics*, and the *Aeneid*. The *Eclogues* are ten poems, averaging about eighty lines in length, with which Virgil began his career. They were followed by the *Georgics*, four poems just over five hundred lines long. Virgil's last work, the *Aeneid*, is an epic poem divided into twelve books, each about seven or eight hundred

Virgil in conversation with his patron, Maecenas.

Virgil receives the patronage of the Emperor Augustus.

71

After studying at Cremona and Milan from 55-50 B.C., Virgil attended Elpidio's famous school of Rhetoric, where he had as his companion the future Emperor Augustus.

lines long. All these poems are written in hexameters. This metre, which had been used before by Lucretius in his poem *De Rerum Natura*, is basically the metre of the Homeric poems, with certain different rules applied. The line can be divided into six feet, with a break normally falling in the middle of the third foot. It is a heavier and more sonorous metre than the elegiac metre (alternate hexameters and pentameters), which makes it more suitable for serious epic poetry.

THE *ECLOGUES*

The *Eclogues* are pastoral poems, which closely follow Greek models, especially the Idylls of Theocritus. The poems are artificial and full of conventions. The country life which is shown is not that of real hard work and day-to-day farm labour which is described in the *Georgics*. Shepherds and goatherds sit in the shade of beech-trees singing songs to each other, oblivious of real farm work and country life. Nevertheless, the poems have a refined prettiness which is appealing. *Eclogue* I is a dialogue between two shepherds, and celebrates the restoration by Augustus of Virgil's farm after his dispossession. *Eclogue* II is a lover's lament. *Eclogue* III is a competition between two shepherds singing

of the charms of their lovers. *Eclogue* IV has been called Messianic. It is addressed to the consul Pollio, and deals with the birth of a child who will bring a Golden Age to the earth. It is uncertain what child is referred to, but the idea that this is a prophecy of the birth of Jesus Christ is now abandoned. On this poem rests the exalted honour which the medieval Church gave to Virgil.

Eclogue V is a singing contest over the death of Daphnis. *Eclogue* VI touches lightly on philosophy and the Creation. *Eclogue* VII is another poetic contest. *Eclogue* VIII tells of an enchantress trying to attract her lover's attention by means of spells. *Eclogue* IX is a lament for farmers who have been dispossessed, as was Virgil. *Eclogue* X is a poem of comfort to Gallus, a man who has been deserted by his mistress.

In *Eclogue* VII, lines 53-60, represent the pastoral mood. Corydon: " Junipers and shaggy chestnut-trees rise up, while strewn all under the trees lie the fruits of each. All things now smile: but if fair Alexis left these mountains, you would even see the rivers run dry ". Thyrsis: " Thirsty is the field: the grass is parched to death by the destructive air. Liber grudges the hills their shade of vine tendrils. My Phyllis when she comes, will make all the woodland blossom, and Jupiter's flourishing rain will fall in abundance ".

THE *GEORGICS*

The *Georgics* also owe a great deal to Greek models, but Virgil was more concerned to sing of the natural beauty and greatness of Italy. The *Georgics* are not meant to be a practical guide for managing a farm, but they extol the virtue of simple farming life, and in particular the value of hard work as the way to achieve real dignity as a human being in the sight of other men and of God. These ideas were in harmony with Octavian's policy of settling people as farmers in the country, but there is no reason to suppose that the *Georgics* were merely written as political propaganda.

Georgic I describes ploughing and signs for weather-forecasting. The incomplete treatment of these subjects is typical of all the *Georgics*, and proves that they were never intended as a practical farmer's manual. *Georgic* II deals with the vine, its growth and the wines it produces. *Georgic* III is concerned with farm animals, especially the horse. *Georgic* IV is the most famous of these poems for its account of bee-keeping and for the inserted story of Orpheus and Eurydice

Virgil dictating part of the Aeneid *to a scribe.*

which concludes the book. The whole episode of the life of bees may be a parable referring to Rome. All four poems abound in references to Italian and Greek mythology and religion, and country customs and beliefs.

The instructions for making a threshing floor (*Georgic* I, 177-186) show the *Georgics*' style. " First of all, the threshing floor must be levelled with a heavy roller, dug by hand, and hardened with stiffening marl, to stop grass coming up, or dust and cracks gaining the upper hand. Then various blights mock your work: often the tiny mouse builds her house under ground and constructs her granaries: or the blind moles make their beds. There is the toad found in hollows, and all the creatures which flourish on earth; and the high-piled heap of grain is robbed by the weevil or the ant, fearful of needy old age ".

The story of Eurydice is the most renowned part of *Georgic* IV, and reaches its climax in lines 484-503. " 'Orpheus' she cried, ' what madness, what utter madness is the cause of my ruin and yours ? See, the cruel fates call me back again, my weeping eyes are shrouded in sleep. And now, adieu. Vastness of night encircles me, and bears me away, holding out to you my hands, alas no longer thine '. So she spoke, and vanished suddenly from his sight, as smoke mingles with the thin air: she saw him no longer, clutching in vain at the shadows, with so much still unsaid: and the ferryman of Orsus refused to let him cross again the marsh which lay between them."

THE *AENEID*

The *Aeneid* is often compared to Homer's *Iliad*. It is quite likely that one of Virgil's intentions was to become the Roman Homer. But what was fresh and spontaneous in Homer was deliberate and scholarly in Virgil. The *Aeneid* is a literary epic, which means that it is more artificial and more carefully composed than primitive epic (like the *Iliad*), more meditative and deeper in feeling and meaning.

The purpose of the *Aeneid* is not to glorify the Emperor Augustus in particular, but to express faith in the destiny and greatness of Italy and Rome, her capital. The story describes the wanderings of Aeneas, who typifies the true Roman character, and his eventual winning of a kingdom in Italy. There are frequent references to Roman customs and institutions: Greek religion is cleverly mixed with Italian. The main characters, Aeneas, Turnus, and Dido, all have wider significance, as their characters embody important principles. Over all of them hangs the power of divine Providence, with which the mission and greatness of Rome in the world is identified.

The plot is as follows:

Book 1. Aeneas has fled by sea after the sack of Troy by the Greeks, and is near Sicily. Juno, the goddess of Carthage sends a storm to wreck Aeneas on the Carthaginian coast. Aeneas is welcomed at Dido's court.

Book 2. Aeneas tells Dido of the fall of Troy through the wooden horse, the sack of the city, and his flight.

Book 3. Aeneas continues by telling of his wanderings under divine guidance, in search of a new homeland. The journey occupies seven years, and ends with his shipwreck at Carthage.

Book 4. Dido falls in love with Aeneas, who deserts her to follow the call of destiny. Dido's suicide.

Book 5. Aeneas in Sicily. Funeral games.

Book 6. Aeneas visits the underworld.

Book 7. Aeneas reaches Italy. Landing in Latium and beginning of war with the ' Italian ' natives.

Book 8. Aeneas and his ' Italian ' allies.

Book 9. The attack by Turnus, the ' Italian ' hero, on the camp of Aeneas during his absence.

Book 10. A council of the gods. The battle begins between Aeneas and Turnus.

Book 11. The battle continues, and the defeat of the ' Italian ' forces begins.

Book 12. The fight between Aeneas and Turnus. Death of Turnus.

The subject of the *Aeneid* is so varied that many extracts would be representative of the poem. Aeneas's descent to the underworld is perhaps the most famous episode. There he meets the shades of the dead (Book 6, 426-30) " Next were heard wailing voices, a mighty mourning sound, the souls of children crying on the threshold of life, who had no part in sweet life, but were snatched away from the breast by the black day of death, and plunged into bitter lifelessness. Next to them were people falsely condemned to death."

Virgil was recognised in his own lifetime as a genius, and his poetry immediately became a standard work in the classroom. His influence can be seen in every age: Dante and Milton are two of his most famous followers. Virgil remains the greatest Latin poet of all.

Virgil at Cumae, in the Sybil's cave, which he later described in the Aeneid.

73

THE STORY OF THE PASSION

The last days of Jesus on earth give us the greatest drama that has ever been played out against the back-cloth of time. The events of these last days are usually referred to as Jesus's Passion, because they were the period of His most acute suffering for the world's salvation and they fall naturally into successive scenes.

The drama really begins far back. Jesus's progress to the Cross where He was to be crucified might indeed be said to begin when He was born. Even through the happy days of His boyhood in Nazareth the tragic end was, slowly but surely, drawing nearer.

But the Passion Story may be taken to begin properly when Judas Iscariot, one of Jesus's disciples went secretly to His enemies and offered to betray his Master to them. This was the opening scene of the greatest drama of all.

These enemies of Jesus were the Jewish authorities—the ruling classes, made up of Priests and Scribes and Pharisees. For a long time they had been looking on Jesus with growing suspicion, dismay and anger. And for some time now they had been anxious to put Him out of the way.

Led by Caiaphas, the high priest and president of their Council, or Sanhedrin, along with Annas, father-in-law of Caiaphas and former high priest, they reckoned that Jesus was a nuisance who could not be tolerated.

His teaching annoyed them because it meant that in so many matters if He was right, they must be wrong and they were not prepared ever to admit to being wrong. His actions,

too, had often antagonised them; such as His healing on the Sabbath day and claiming to be able to forgive sins. As a result, they were firmly of the opinion that He must be put to death. But there were difficulties in the way.

For one thing, their land was in the control of the Roman Empire and the Roman Empire liked to keep the power of capital punishment in its own hands. This meant that if they desired to secure the execution of Jesus they would require to have sentence of death passed on Him by the Roman Governor, who was at this time a man called Pontius Pilate.

But this was not their only difficulty. They had first to face the difficulty of getting hold of Jesus. From one point of view this presented no difficulty at all. They were the authority and Jesus was not in hiding. They could arrest Him at any time. The trouble was, that Jesus was very popular with a great many of the common people. To arrest such a popular figure would be to risk riot and trouble and the authorities were afraid of the possible consequences.

Their mounting hatred of Jesus and their increasing determination to be rid of Him meant that, if they had to, they would take the risk of arresting Jesus publicly but they were hoping that they might find some way of effecting the arrest with the minimum of publicity and the least possible danger of stirring up a hostile crowd.

Judas Iscariot came to them as the answer to their need. For some reason which we cannot know with certainty, he came to see them and to offer to betray his Leader into their

Judas Iscariot receiving his thirty pieces of silver as his reward for betraying Christ. In the background, Jesus is led away by the Temple guard to be brought to trial before the Sanhedrin, or Jewish Council.

Jesus and his disciples partake of the feast of "The Last Supper".

hands. Whether it was simply to make some money or because he was piqued about something, or because he was disappointed in Jesus, or because he thought this would be a way to hurry Jesus on and force Him to use His remarkable powers to save Himself and thwart His enemies, we cannot be sure. But, whatever the reason, Judas struck a bargain with the priests, the most infamous bargain in history, and agreed, for the payment of 30 pieces of silver (the market price of a slave), to deliver Jesus into their hands.

That was the first scene in the final act of the drama. The next came on the Thursday evening. Jesus gathered with His disciples in the upstairs room, the guest room, of a friend's house in Jerusalem, and there they had that meal together which we now call The Last Supper. During this meal Judas stepped out into the night to carry out his awful pact. He knew that Jesus intended to spend a quiet time later in the garden of Gethsemane on the Mount of Olives, a favourite haunt of His, and Judas hurried off to see his new associates in order to arrange with them the details of the arrest.

The consequence of this came an hour or two later when Jesus, accompanied by Peter, James and John, was at prayer in the garden of Gethsemane. He had just risen from His knees when the flickering of torches through the trees and the murmur of voices borne on the breeze gave notice that a crowd of people was approaching. In a moment Judas appeared in the company of a squad of the Temple police who, in turn, were accompanied by some members of the public curious to know what was going on. Knowing that the darkness of the night would be intensified by the surrounding trees and that the torches that they carried would not illuminate the scene very clearly, Judas had arranged with the police that in order to ensure that no mistake was made he would identify their quarry by kissing Him.

A kiss was regularly used by a pupil or disciple to greet his teacher. And so when Judas came upon Jesus in the garden of Gethsemane that night he went forward and embraced Him. At once the police took Him under arrest. There was a slight scuffle when Peter drew his sword and looked as if he might defend his Leader to the death until Jesus ordered him to put his sword back into its sheath.

And so Jesus was taken away to be put on trial before the Sanhedrin, the Jewish Council. He would, of course, if they were eventually to have His life, require to go on trial before Pontius Pilate. But first they wanted to try Him before their own court. This was the Sanhedrin, or Council, which consisted of 71 members drawn from the ranks of the Sadducees, the Pharisees, the scribes and the elders, with the high priest as chairman.

But even before Jesus was taken before the Sanhedrin, He was taken to Annas. Annas had been high priest earlier but had been deposed by the Romans and no longer held any official position. Nevertheless, he still commanded a great deal of respect and exercised a large amount of influence. And it was to Annas that Jesus was taken first of all.

After Annas had interviewed Him, Jesus was led to the palace of Caiaphas, the high priest, and to trial before the Sanhedrin. It is a measure of how strongly the authorities desired to get rid of Jesus that this trial was attended by so many illegalities. The Jewish people had long been proud of their system of justice, and with good reason. It was one of the fairest and most merciful in the world, with every care being taken to give the prisoner the fullest possible chance, but in this particular instance the law was ignored at many points.

The Sanhedrin had other functions beside that of conducting judicial trials but, when it was conducting a trial, certain rules were supposed to be rigidly observed and usually were, but in this case many of these were broken. The Sanhedrin was not allowed to meet during the hours of darkness, but it did here. The Sanhedrin was not permitted to meet during any of the great feasts, but it did here. Leading questions were forbidden, but they were asked here. The Sanhedrin could not meet except in its official meeting place, called the Hall of Hewn Stone, but here it met in the palace of Caiaphas, the high priest. The Sanhedrin was not permitted to announce a guilty verdict or to carry out a sentence on a prisoner before at least twenty-four hours had elapsed, but here the verdict was announced immediately and a carrying out of the sentence was sought at once. The Sanhedrin was not supposed to search out adverse witness against a prisoner, but it did here.

The Sanhedrin was clearly, in this instance, determined at all costs to get rid of Jesus. There was, therefore, never any real doubt what their findings would be. And so, in due course, they found Jesus guilty of blasphemy and decided that He ought to be put to death.

But they were unable to carry out such a sentence themselves. Only the Roman Governor had the authority to order such a thing.

That was why, in the early hours of the first Good Friday morning, Jesus was hustled before Pontius Pilate. Caiaphas and the Sanhedrin had not achieved their purpose yet. They would have to get Pilate to see things their way first.

And it was no good coming before Pilate with a charge of blasphemy against Jesus. That was a religious matter and Pilate would simply have told them it had nothing to do with the laws of the Roman Empire and so had nothing to do with him. For the trial of Jesus before Pilate, the Sanhedrin had to find some other ground for complaint against Him, and that was why the accusation made there was not of blasphemy, but a three-fold charge in which blasphemy was not even mentioned. The charges levelled against Jesus in Pilate's hearing were: 1—seditious agitation; 2—attempting to persuade men to withhold their taxes; and 3—claiming to be king.

DILEMMA FOR PILATE

Pilate, it seems clear, saw through all this right from the start. He seems never to have had any doubt about the innocence of this Galilean carpenter brought before him in this summary fashion. More than that, he seems to have been much impressed by the manner and the bearing of his prisoner. It was a most remarkable thing that a carpenter from Nazareth should make such an impact on a Roman soldier in a very high position. Yet this seems to have been the case and all this added up to a sharp dilemma for Pilate.

On the one hand, he was convinced that Jesus was innocent and clearly wanted to see Him go free. On the other hand, the Jewish authorities desperately wanted to see Jesus dead and Pilate was afraid to cross them too much.

It might appear strange that the Roman Governor should have any fear of the Jewish authorities, when his position and power were so much superior to theirs. But the reason lies in the story of Pilate's record of government up to that point.

Pilate had been appointed Procurator, or Governor, of the province of Judea in A.D. 26 and already, on several occasions, he had been involved in quite serious clashes with the populace. The first incident occurred almost as soon as he took office. Previous procurators had been careful to respect the religious feelings of the Jews as much as possible and, in particular, to avoid offence they had instructed their soldiers to remove the images from their standards before entering Jerusalem. These standards, which the Roman soldiers carried were not flags but poles on which either the figure of an eagle or the image of an emperor was affixed. Knowing how strongly the Jews felt about graven images and realising that it would be regarded as a serious offence to carry such things into their Holy City, Pilate's predecessors had always made their men remove the images from their standards before entering the city. But not Pilate. He seems to have had rather more than his share of arrogance and pig-headedness. The images stayed on the standards. The soldiers marched into Jerusalem flaunting them before the people and, of course, offence was caused.

A deputation of the chief men of the Jews came to plead with Pilate about the matter. Obstinately he refused to see them. Just as obstinately they waited on underneath his residence. This battle of wills went on for five days and then Pilate sent his men with drawn swords to tell his unwelcome visitors to depart or die. The Jews bared their throats and said they would die before they went away without their object achieved. Pilate gave in and the images were removed.

But Pilate did not seem to learn much about the art of discretion from this experience. Other troubles followed. Some time later, for instance, he put up on the walls of his Jerusalem residence certain golden shields that bore the name of the emperor. This was regarded by the Jews as a deliberate attempt to introduce the Caesar worship which was already widespread throughout the empire. A delegation went to Rome to complain to the emperor and the emperor himself sent an order to Pilate to stop doing this.

Pilate ran into further trouble when he decided that Jerusalem's water supply must be improved. Accordingly, he set about having a new aqueduct constructed. This was a very good idea and a much-needed improvement. No one was likely to have quarrelled with him over that.

But practically everyone quarrelled with him about the manner in which he met the expense of the aqueduct construction. He simply extracted the money from the Temple treasury. This high-handed action, however worthy the motive, also caused a great deal of offence. Indeed, it sparked off a riot and the riot was not quelled without bloodshed.

The consequence of all this was that Pilate's position as Procurator of Judea had become a rather precarious one. The Roman Empire liked its governors to get on well with the people they ruled and to keep the peace as much as possible. Pilate's succession of troubles, especially when it appeared that with a little bit of tact some of them at least could have been avoided, had earned him some disfavour in Rome. And Pilate was well aware that he could not really afford to have another full scale riot on his hands or to have any more complaints about his administration finding their way to Rome. Any more trouble and Pilate knew that whether he was in the right or in the wrong, it would likely be the end of his career.

His dilemma, therefore, when Jesus was brought before him was very acute. He dare not, at the risk of his career if not his life, offend the Jews. Yet he was sure that Jesus did not deserve any punishment at all, far less death. What was he to do? The story of what he did is one of the most gripping parts of the whole drama.

As a start, after his preliminary examination of the prisoner, Pilate tried to get the Sanhedrin officials to with-

". . . and they crowned Him with a crown of thorns and brought Him before Pilate."

draw the charges against Jesus. " This man has committed no crime," he said. " I propose to set Him free." But the volume of protest that greeted this suggestion let Pilate see just how strongly the officials desired Jesus's death and just how difficult it was going to be for him to release Jesus without running foul of the Sanhedrin.

Pilate made several attempts to release himself from the horns of the dilemma on which he now found himself impaled. On discovering that Jesus belonged to the Province of Galilee he decided to send Him along to Herod, tetrarch of that province, who was in residence in Jerusalem at the time.

This Herod was Herod Antipas, a son of that Herod called the Great, who was King of Palestine under the authority of the Roman Empire at the time of Jesus's birth. When Herod the Great died, his kingdom was split up among his three sons. In particular, Archelaus became king, or tetrarch, of Judea and Antipas of Galilee. Archelaus however, did not rule well and in A.D. 6 he was deposed. From then on, Judea was governed directly by the Roman Empire in the person of its procurators, Pilate being the fifth in the succession. But Antipas managed to stay in office until A.D. 39 and it is this Herod Antipas who appears in the story at this point.

Pilate was on poor terms with Herod because Herod was suspected of being a spy for the Emperor and Pilate had reason to think that Herod had carried stories concerning him to the Imperial Court. But, when Pilate learned that Jesus was a Galilean, he thought this was an opportunity to kill two birds with one stone. He would send Jesus along to Herod with a message saying that, since Jesus was a Galilean and since Herod happened to be in the city at the time, he (Pilate) would like, as a mark of courtesy, to offer to delegate his authority and invite Herod to try Jesus. Pilate hoped that this would accomplish two things. He hoped it would produce a better relationship between himself and Herod, as in fact it did. He hoped, too, that it would solve his present problem concerning Jesus; if Herod accepted the offer and put Jesus on trial then at least Jesus's life would be saved. For even if Herod found Jesus guilty, he could not sentence Him to death since that power belonged in Judea only to the Roman governor. In his own province of Galilee, Herod had the power of life and death over his subjects—he had for example put John the Baptist to death—but not here in Jerusalem. Therefore, if Pilate's stratagem worked, either Jesus would be acquitted altogether by Herod, or, at the worst, he would be sent to prison. In either event, Jesus's life would be spared.

But the stratagem failed. Herod thanked the governor for his courtesy and returned the prisoner to him. Whether this was simply in order to return a courtesy extended to him or because of a prudent desire not to offend the Jews or because of sheer disinterest we do not know, but it left Pilate back where he had started.

Pilate's next attempt to resolve his dilemma was an attempt at compromise. He suggested that Jesus might be punished but not put to death. " Behold ", he said, " this man is completely blameless. This is not only my opinion it is clearly Herod's as well. I propose to have him beaten with the scourge and then to let him go. How say you to that? "

But this suggestion received short shrift. The authorities and the people refused to agree to it. They wanted Jesus to die. Still Pilate would not admit defeat. He was wriggling desperately in an endeavour to struggle free of the hook on which he was caught. And he had another idea.

It was the custom at Passover time for the Roman Governor to make a gesture to the Jewish populace by releasing to them someone who was being held in custody. Pilate thought that he would tell the crowd that he intended to observe this custom now and proclaim that they could have either Jesus or Barabbas. They would be bound to choose Jesus.

Barabbas was a notorious character—a murderer—and Pilate reasoned with himself that the people could not possibly ask for such a man to be set free. But Pilate's reasoning was faulty. He had misjudged the people he was dealing with and underestimated the extent of their hatred for Jesus. When he put the choice to them, egged on by the priests, the people shouted for Barabbas. And so he had to let Barabbas go free.

Once again, Pilate was back where he had started as far as the problem of dealing with Jesus was concerned. He made another attempt to persuade the Jewish people that Jesus ought to go free. He could of course have set Jesus free without asking them, but he was trying not to offend them. He therefore suggested to them once more that Jesus was innocent of any crime and ought to be released.

But the more Pilate argued in this strain the louder and the more vehemently the crowd called for Jesus's blood. "Crucify Him! Crucify Him! " they screamed. Pilate could see that he was making no progress and the matter was settled when a voice from the crowd called out, " If you release this man, you are no friend of Caesar's."

Any thought Pilate might have had of defying the Jews and of releasing Jesus in spite of them was banished now. The threat in those words was obvious. If he refused to co-operate with them in having Jesus put to death, another complaint about his administration would find its way to Rome and Pilate simply could not risk anything like that. It would mean the end of his career. So Pilate gave up the struggle and passed sentence of death on the prisoner.

The sentence was carried out at once. Crucifixion was the method of execution employed and the execution party, a squad of Roman soldiers, took the matter in hand at once. They took Jesus along with two other prisoners also under sentence of death to the place of execution. This was a little hill just off the main road outside the gates of the city. There, with Jesus in the middle, the three prisoners were crucified. It was still quite early in the morning (Friday morning, the first Good Friday) and by 3 o'clock in the afternoon Jesus was dead.

This seemed to be the end of the drama and a very tragic conclusion it was. But to everyone's surprise there was another act to come.

When Jesus was dead, Joseph of Arimathea, who was a member of the Sanhedrin but had secretly sympathised with Jesus's teachings, went to Pilate and asked if he could be allowed to bury Jesus's body. Pilate readily granted permission and Joseph made haste to attend to the burial. He made haste because time was very short. The Jewish day ended at 6 o'clock in the evening. This meant, in this particular case, that at 6 p.m., Friday would come to an end and Saturday would begin, and Saturday is the Jewish Sabbath. The Jews were not permitted to do any work on the Sabbath, so if Joseph did not manage to get Jesus buried before 6 o'clock he would have to leave the task over until the Sabbath was ended.

Since it was already past 3 o'clock in the afternoon time was very short. Joseph was not able, as a result, to make

Mary Magdalene and Mary, the mother of James, and Salome find the stone rolled away from the tomb entrance.

suitable preparations. The usual custom at a burial was to embalm the body with spices, but Joseph was not able to do this in the thorough fashion he would have liked although he did attend to it in a hurried sort of way. However, Joseph did succeed in having Jesus's body buried before the Sabbath came.

With the assistance of his friend Nicodemus, also a member of the Sanhedrin and also a secret sympathiser, Joseph took Jesus's body to a new tomb of his own which was nearby. This tomb, like many of that time, was a sort of cave hollowed out of the rock with ledges inside it on which bodies could be placed. Jesus's body was placed on one of these ledges and the mouth of the grave was closed by rolling across it the great stone provided for that purpose. Placed just outside the entrance to the tomb, this stone, in appearance rather like a large circular grindstone, was pushed along a groove prepared for it.

Some of the women in Jesus's party watched the burial and decided to come back with spices, at the earliest opportunity, in order to complete the embalming which Joseph and Nicodemus had been unable to do properly. This meant they would return on Sunday morning to the grave. They could do nothing while the Sabbath lasted and when the Sabbath ended at 6 p.m. on Saturday, darkness was falling. Therefore, the earliest opportunity they had to carry out their intention was at dawn on Sunday morning. They made their plans accordingly and first light on Sunday morning found them making their way to the grave of Jesus. But a tremendous surprise was in store for them. When they reached their goal they discovered that the tomb was empty.

They had been anxious in case they would not be strong enough to push back the stone and, in fact, had been discussing this very matter on the way. But when they got there it was to discover that the stone was already rolled back and the body of Jesus was gone. Their first reaction was that someone had moved the body to another place.

This distressed them but their distress changed to joy when the true explanation of the facts was made known to them that Jesus had risen from the dead and was alive again.

This seemed so remarkable and so wonderful that they were not inclined to believe it at first. The disciples, when they heard of it, were also very doubtful. But when Jesus actually appeared to them, and spoke to them, they realised that strange and wonderful though it was it was really true. Jesus was risen and alive!

He was clearly different from what He had been. It was not just a case of His body being brought back to life the way it had been. He was different. Although He was plainly the Jesus they had always known, at the same time, He was changed. He was no longer as He had been, subject to the restraints and limitations of the flesh. He could now, for example, appear and disappear at will and closed doors were no barrier to Him.

Jesus was risen! Jesus was alive! This was the glad news of that first Easter day. What a difference it made to his followers. On Friday night they had all been in despair. Their Master was dead and the exciting adventure they had been sharing with Him was at an end.

They had come to think and to hope that Jesus was Messiah, the anointed one of God. But the crucifixion of Jesus had shown them, or so it seemed, how terribly wrong they had been. For God would never have allowed His Messiah to be put to death.

So far as the Jews were concerned there could be no worse way to die than by crucifixion. Their scriptures said that anyone who died on a cross must be accursed by God. Therefore, when Jesus was crucified it would appear quite clear to all concerned, to His friends as well as to His enemies, that no thought of His being the Messiah could possibly survive any longer.

All the fine dreams that His followers had cherished concerning Jesus and His work were now in ruins. His enemies had been right after all. He was a fake. What a bitter blow it was and how broken-hearted they were. Not only broken-hearted but afraid, afraid they might be arrested too and perhaps even share their Leader's fate.

This was how it had been on the Friday night. But here on the Sunday all that was changed. Their fear and their despair were gone and they were full of joy. For Jesus was risen from the dead. God was with Him after all. What had seemed the worst of tragedies had become a victory. Jesus was risen. Jesus was alive again and they need not be afraid of anything any more.

THE SPREAD OF CHRISTIANITY

The Christian Church really began its life on the first Easter day. In a sense, of course, it had begun much earlier. But Easter was its real birthday.

On that day, a Sunday, it was discovered that Jesus of Nazareth, who had been crucified to death on the Friday, was alive again. His grave was empty and He showed Himself to some of His friends and spoke with them. God had raised Him from the dead and what had seemed to His followers to be final, crushing defeat, was now found to be glorious victory.

During the three years that He had spent preaching and teaching and healing up and down Palestine, Jesus had attracted large numbers to His side. But, as time went on and it became increasingly clear that following Him was to be no easy matter but rather something involving danger and sacrifice, many of these followers gave up. Even the apostles, those men who were closest to Him, took fright when He was arrested in the Garden of Gethsemane and they ran away. And when He was put to death on the cross, they were shocked and broken and afraid. It was only their Leader's Resurrection that put new heart into them and made them ready to brave anything and everything for His sake.

Therefore when the Christian Church began, it did so with only a small number of people. But on the day of Pentecost or, as we more often call it, Whit Sunday, the Church began to grow.

After His Resurrection, Jesus appeared a number of times to His followers, sometimes to one of them, sometimes to a group, sometimes to a large body. During these meetings, He tried to explain to them the message of new life through faith in Him which they were now to proclaim to the world. At the same time He was preparing them for the great task of building up His Church.

This went on for nearly six weeks. Then Jesus told His followers that they would not be seeing Him any more. He would still be with them. Indeed, He would always be with His followers in every age, ready to guide and strengthen and help them, but He would no longer be appearing in visible form to them. They must learn now to stand on their own feet without the prop of His visible presence. And so Jesus went out of their sight for the last time. They never saw Him again although they were very much aware that He was always close beside them.

SPREADING THE GOSPEL

One of the last things Jesus told them to do, was to go and wait in Jerusalem until they felt the Holy Spirit of God come upon them and then to go out and start preaching. This was an order which surprised and puzzled them. But they obeyed. And so it came about that ten days later, on the first Whit Sunday, they were gathered together, about 120 of them, in Jerusalem, when they had a strange and wonderful experience. They felt that the Holy Spirit was entering into them and filling them with great power.

That was the start. Peter rose there and then and preached to the crowd which, attracted by the noise and general excitement, had quickly collected. He told them about Jesus and how He had been crucified and raised from the dead. Then Peter invited his hearers to follow Jesus, too, and a large number of them did.

Three thousand, the record states, attached themselves to the new faith on that first day. In the following days their number increased steadily. But it was far from being plain sailing all the way. The Jewish authorities, the chief priests and others, who had plotted Jesus's death, were furiously angry when the report of His Resurrection began to

After His resurrection, Jesus appeared on the road to Emmaus before Cleopas and his companion. At first they did not know Him, but later recognised Him from the way He broke bread, and they reported what they had seen to the other disciples.

After one night's imprisonment for preaching the gospel, Peter and John were brought before Annas, the high priest.

be circulated. And, when Jesus's followers began to win more and more people over to their side, these men became even angrier and they determined to take immediate steps to stamp out the new faith.

As a result, they put every possible obstacle in the path of the apostles. On one occasion, for instance, they arrested Peter and John while they were preaching to the people and before releasing them, gave them a stern warning to discontinue this practice. Peter and John, however, kept on preaching as before and so the same thing happened all over again. Once again they were arrested, and once again they were rebuked and warned before being released.

FIRST CHRISTIAN MARTYR

The opposition and interference from the authorities that they had to contend with did not discourage the apostles and they persisted in their efforts to spread the gospel of Jesus. However, the Jewish authorities were fast losing patience with the apostles' activities and tempers were dangerously short. The climax came with the murder of a young man called Stephen. He was a very devoted convert to the new faith and was the means of converting many others. A charge of blasphemy was made against him and he, too, was arrested and brought before the Sanhedrin for trial.

Stephen made such a spirited defence of himself before the Sanhedrin that they became furiously angry and all restraint was cast aside. Abandoning legal procedure altogether and paying no heed to the fact that, under Roman rule, they had no right to exact a death sentence, they rushed Stephen out of the city, flung him down a cliff and rolled boulders on top of him until he was dead.

Stephen's death acted like the bursting of a dam. All the hatred the authorities had for the Christians, which up till then had been kept under some control, was now released and a great wave of persecution swept down on the followers of Jesus.

To the infant Church in Jerusalem, which had been steadily building up its numbers and its strength, this was a great blow. Although the Jewish authorities had been hostile and had been making things difficult, there had been no general persecution so far and the members of the young Christian Church had been able to meet together regularly and to carry on their work of evangelism.

PERSECUTION

Now all this was changed. The young Jerusalem Church became the target of violent persecution. So violent was it that the followers of Jesus were no longer able to stay on in the city in safety. In a very short time, except for the apostles, scarcely any of them remained. The others had been scattered throughout the land. But what looked like a terrible disaster helped, in the end, to spread the young Church and its gospel farther and quicker. The Christians, who had been expelled from Jerusalem, continued to bear witness to their faith in the new districts to which they had been driven. The result was that fresh outposts of Christianity were created all over the place. It was as if someone had kicked a camp fire apart and the various burning sticks had started up fresh fires wherever they fell.

And so the young Christian Church spread from Jerusalem throughout Palestine. But it was to spread even farther with remarkable rapidity.

SAUL OF TARSUS

The persecution the Christians had to face was not confined to Jerusalem and the fact that they had escaped from

81

Saul fell to the ground and heard a voice saying to him, "Saul, Saul, why persecutest thou me?"

Jerusalem did not necessarily mean that they had escaped their persecutors completely. In some cases, at least, persecution followed them. One such occasion led to the conversion of Saul of Tarsus, an event which was to have far-reaching consequences for the spread of Christianity.

Saul was a young Pharisee who was bitterly opposed to the new Christian faith. Considering it blasphemous, he hated it so much that when the persecution began, he offered his services to the authorities to help crush Christianity completely.

This offer was gladly accepted and soon Saul found himself in the position of chief agent for the task of exterminating the Christians. He took this position very seriously and harried the followers of Jesus without mercy. When Acts 8 : 3 says that Saul "made havoc" of his Church, the word used in the original Greek (*elumaineto*) is the same word that is used of a wild animal savaging a body.

When he learned therefore that there was a fairly strong and active colony of Christians in the Syrian city of Damascus, he asked the authorities for permission to go to Damascus after them. This was granted and he was issued with letters giving him authority to bring back these Christians to Jerusalem for punishment. However near the end of the journey to Damascus, which in those days took a week, something very extraordinary happened.

CONVERSION OF SAUL

Although accompanied by a detachment of the Temple Police from Jerusalem, Saul, because he was a Pharisee, walked alone. Suddenly he had a vision of the Risen Jesus,

Who said that He wanted Saul to stop his persecution and to become His disciple instead.

This dramatic experience changed Saul of Tarsus completely. From being one of the most fanatical opponents of the Christian faith, he now became one of its most ardent supporters and one of its most eloquent ambassadors. As a sign of the change, he was always afterwards called Paul and that is how we know him to-day.

Paul contributed greatly to the spread of Christianity after his conversion, probably more than any other single person. He was, of course, not the only man responsible for the growth of the Church in those early days. Nearly every Christian acted as missionary and evangelist and it was due to the efforts of them all that Christianity moved steadily farther afield. But Paul was especially successful and was the means of taking the gospel, for the first time, into many places.

He had three main missionary journeys in which he covered many miles by sea and by road and carried the good news of Jesus into many different regions, not only to countries lying close to Palestine but also to far-off parts of Asia Minor and even into Europe.

Through the endeavours of Paul and his fellow Christians the gospel of Jesus spread throughout the world of the first century like a forest fire. As a result, in a remarkably short space of time, the new faith which had begun in Palestine in a rather small and obscure corner of the earth, had reached even far-off Rome, capital city of the great Roman Empire and mistress of the world at that time. For when Paul went to Rome about A.D. 60 as a prisoner the Christian Church was there in strength before him.

ARCHITECTURE : II
Early Christian to Gothic

Early Christian architecture grew out of the old Roman style after the Christians were allowed to worship as they wanted in A.D. 313. They did not build their churches like the temples to the pagan gods, but chose to make them like the Roman *basilicas*. Basilicas were the big halls which were used by the judges. The centre was a long nave supported by columns, and on each side were aisles. The altar was at the east end, and very often it was raised up over the tomb of a saint. The east wall of the church, semi-circular in shape and called the *apse* was behind the altar. In front of these early Christian basilicas was an atrium, which was like a courtyard with arches round the sides. St. Paul's Outside the Walls, the most magnificent of these basilicas, is to be found in Rome. It was built in A.D. 380, but was badly damaged by fire in 1823, and had to be rebuilt. Another great early Christian church that looked very like St. Paul's Outside the Walls was St. Peter in the Vatican, which was pulled down when building began in 1506 on the present St. Peter's.

MOSAIC DECORATIONS

Inside many of these churches the walls were covered with pictures called mosaics. These pictures were made up of thousands of tiny pieces of marble or coloured glass, and showed scenes from the Bible and portraits of saints and leaders of the early Christian Church. Some of these churches were built in a circular shape, rather like small copies of the Pantheon. One of the oldest in Rome is St. Constance, built by Constantine the Great for his daughter. Many of these round churches were used as baptistries—places where people were baptised into the church.

BYZANTINE CHURCHES

In the fourth century the Emperor Constantine divided the old Roman Empire into two parts. The east part had *Byzantium* or Constantinople as its capital, and there the type of architecture we call Byzantine grew out of the early Christian style. Byzantine architects loved to build their churches with domes supported by columns and arches, and they covered the whole of the inside with beautiful marbles and mosaics. The largest and most magnificent Byzantine church is Santa Sophia in Constantinople, now called Istanbul. It has a two-feet thick dome measuring more than one hundred feet across, and has been standing since the year A.D. 537.

Outside the city walls of Rome is the Basilica of St. Paul's, which was built for Valentinian II.

This reconstruction of the old temple of St. Peter in Rome is an example of a primitive, cross-shaped basilica.

The interior of the Basilica of Saint Constance in Rome.
Several of the finest Byzantine churches are at Ravenna, a small town which became the capital of Italy after Rome was captured by the barbarians. Above all, these churches are famous for their fifth and sixth century mosaics. The tomb of Galla Placidia (A.D. 420) is built in the shape of a cross. Most of the great cathedrals and churches built in the Middle Ages and later are in the shape of a cross. The arms on either side that make the cross are called the *transepts*. The biggest and most beautiful Byzantine church in Italy is St. Mark's in Venice (1042-1085) which has five domes, one in the centre and one each over the choir, the nave and the two transepts.

SAXON ARCHITECTURE

In the rest of Europe, especially in the north, people did not have the skilled architects and marble deposits needed for such buildings, so they used a simpler style. In England, before the Norman conquest, the buildings were in the Saxon style. All the houses and even royal palaces were of wood; only a few remains of these wooden buildings have been found. But several churches are still standing which were built of stone. You can see fine examples at Escomb in County Durham (seventh century), Deerhurst in Gloucestershire (seventh-eleventh century), and there is even a tiny eleventh century wooden church at Greensted in Essex. Compared with early Christian and Byzantine churches they are very simple. They are without carved capitals and there are no mosaics on the walls.

NORMAN-STYLE BUILDING

The style we call Norman was brought to England about the time of the Conquest in 1066. In the rest of Europe the style is called Romanesque, because it was rather like the architecture of ancient Rome. Many of the great English cathedrals were built by the Normans, though some were altered later on. Norman architecture is easy to tell by its massive walls and pillars, called piers. Also, all the doors and windows have round tops. The Normans liked to cover their walls with *arcading*, or little columns and arches fixed to the walls as decoration. The finest Norman cathedral is at Durham. The nave and choir are separated from the aisles by huge, round pillars, some of which are carved with simple zig-zag patterns.

After the Conquest the Normans built many castles which are in the same style as their churches. In the Middle Ages "church architecture" was no different from that used in castles or private houses. The windows and doorways are smaller, but would look in place in a church. The most famous and largest Norman castle keep is the White Tower in the Tower of London (1078). The keep is the strongest part, usually right in the centre of a castle. The White Tower contains dungeons, large rooms for the soldiers, a beautiful chapel, and at the top the rooms used by the king.

In the early Middle Ages cathedrals, churches and castles were built all over Europe in the Romanesque style. Round arches and thick walls are to be found in all of them, but the details are not the same in different countries. The Leaning Tower of Pisa, which is in fact the bell-tower of the cathedral, is a very good example of Italian Romanesque architecture and quite unlike anything in England. The men who designed these buildings were not architects who worked only in offices. Often they would also take part in the actual manual work. In the twelfth century these builders gave much

The interior of the mausoleum of Galla Placidia in Ravenna.

The interior of the Basilica of St. Mark in Venice.

Canterbury Cathedral, one of the largest and most magnificent Gothic churches in Britain.

thought to making their churches more graceful and less massive. Up to that time the only way to build stone vaulting over the nave and aisles was to make the church rather like a tunnel. But this was extremely heavy and needed very thick walls, with buttresses, to help to support the vaults. Then in France they discovered that by building their vaults with pointed arches instead of round ones, they could make them lighter, taller and more graceful. This new method was first used in the church of St. Denis (1132) just outside Paris. Only one year later the first pointed vault was built over the Norman nave and choir of Durham Cathedral. Then a Frenchman called William of Sens came to Canterbury to build the whole of the new choir of that cathedral in the pointed style. This style is called Gothic, and all the details such as windows, doorways and arcading have pointed arches. The new style did not take over at once from the old, and sometimes you will find pointed and round arches side by side in a church. Most cathedrals and churches were built with the altar at the east end, facing towards Jerusalem, so the main entrances were at the west end. The west front of a

church is usually the most impressive part, with big doorways, called portals, and a large window in the centre. Cathedrals like Canterbury and York have two towers on either side of the west front, and another taller one in the centre where the transepts are built out on each side. Many parish churches have spires on top of their towers. Usually these spires are built of wood and covered with sheets of lead or slates, but sometimes they are of stone. The very beautiful spire of Salisbury Cathedral is stone, and is 404 feet high. The tallest stone spire built in the Middle Ages is on the cathedral at Strasbourg in France. It is 468 feet high, and has a stairway right to the top.

Because Gothic builders made their windows much larger than before, and filled them with painted glass, the walls needed extra support to hold up the vaulting. This was done by building *flying buttresses* on the outside to help take the weight. These flying buttresses are like thin arches built above the aisles, and their job is to help to take some of the weight off the piers, and also to stop the vaulting from pushing the walls outwards. Nearly all the great Gothic cathedrals in

85

France have them because the French preferred to make their churches very tall indeed.

Most Gothic churches are decorated with sculpture, especially on the portals of the west front. Carvings in churches are not always of serious subjects. In Wells Cathedral there is a little figure of a man with toothache! The sculptors also liked to carve the rainwater spouts into fantastic shapes of people or animals. These are called *gargoyles*.

Gothic architecture lasted from about 1130 until the sixteenth century, and is divided into several periods.

In England these periods are Early English, Decorated, Perpendicular and Tudor. Early English (about 1150 to 1300) was the simplest, with long narrow windows and little decoration. Salisbury Cathedral is built in this style. After about 1300 the sculptors added much more decoration both inside and outside their churches, and made the windows larger. Much of Exeter Cathedral is Decorated. But this very elaborate style did not last long and about 1370 Perpendicular became more popular. Perpendicular means upright, and all the lines in a church in this style do seem to carry the eye straight up. It is light and airy, with very big windows, and the stone vaulting is nearly flat and covered with designs such as stars. The most magnificent piece of Perpendicular architecture is Henry VII's Chapel in Westminster Abbey. Most buildings in the Tudor style are not churches, but houses. Usually they are built of small red bricks, and the finest example is Hampton Court.

In a town of the Middle Ages most of the houses were built of timber, with plaster or bricks set between the wooden posts. This gives the black and white striped look you see on old houses in some country towns like Stratford-on-Avon. The main part of a really big house was the Great Hall, which was shared by the family and their servants. Life must have been very uncomfortable there because the fire was lit in the middle of the room, and the smoke escaped as best it could through the roof. We can still see such a Great Hall in Stokesay Castle in Shropshire. There is no glass and the wooden shutters which cover the windows would not have been much use for keeping out the icy winds in winter. Life in a Roman house with its central heating must have been much more pleasant than life in Medieval England.

Banquet scene in the Great Hall, Stokesay Castle, Shropshire.

KING OF THE BRITONS
The story of Arthur

On Arthur's tomb was written " *Rex Quondam, Rexque Futurus* ", which means " The once and future king "; because it was believed Arthur was not really dead and would return to restore peace to a troubled Britain. Arthur's life, like his death, was full of magical happenings, some based on fact and some on fantasy, and the best course is to begin by looking first at the historical facts we have, and then at the stories which grew up around Arthur's romantic person.

THE " HISTORICAL " EVIDENCE

Arthur is first mentioned in the tenth century by early historians, though they never make clear who he was, or tell us much about his life. A hundred years later, in 1100, a historian called Geoffrey of Monmouth gives us the first full picture of Arthur, including many stories which were not historically true, but were used and embroidered by later writers, like Sir Thomas Malory in his *Morte d'Arthur* so that the original historical source was quite hidden by a mass of fascinating legend. King Arthur thus became a myth.

Geoffrey of Monmouth describes an Arthur who was son of a king of Britain called Uther Pendragon, and who came to the throne aged fifteen on Uther's death. The first years of Arthur's reign were occupied with fighting the Saxons whom he eventually defeated in a great battle near Bath. The account states that Arthur always fought with his sword Caliburn, forged in the Isle of Avalon, his lance Ron, and his shield Pridwen. (These names changed in later histories of Arthur.) Arthur married Guinevere, and his court became the most famous in the world. Leaving Britain in charge of Guinevere and Mordred one of his knights, he conquered Norway and Gaul. He was preparing to go into Italy, when he suddenly heard of the treachery of Guinevere and Mordred; Mordred had married Guinevere and become King. Arthur hastened back to Britain and after several battles was slain. Geoffrey writes:

" And the famous Arthur too was wounded to the death, and being borne thence for the healing of his wounds to the island of Avalon resigned the crown of Britain to his kindsman Constantine, son of Cador, Duke of Cornwall, in the five hundred and forty second year from the incarnation of our Lord."

So Arthur died, according to Geoffrey of Monmouth, in A.D. 542, a date which is probably correct. After Geoffrey's time, Arthurian legends were told and retold by both British and French poets; each poet added something, by inventing or elaborating on a character or a happening.

ARTHURIAN LEGEND

By the time Sir Thomas Malory wrote his *Morte d'Arthur* while he was in prison during the years 1460 to 1469, there was a vast number of stories about Arthur to draw upon. He wove them all together into a long and beautiful book. After Malory, no one improved further upon the Arthurian legends, and the stories we know about Arthur are all to be found in Malory.

When Arthur, son of Uther Pendragon, was born, the magician Merlin took charge of him, to keep him safe until he was of an age to rule wisely and well and perform all the wonders prophesied for him. Merlin put Arthur in the care of Sir Ector and his son Kay without explaining that Arthur was a king's son.

KING OF BRITAIN

Then, when Arthur was a tall, strong youth, Merlin commanded the Archbishop of Canterbury to call all the chief men of the land to London at Christmastime. When all the nobles came out of church on Christmas Day, they saw a great stone and on it an anvil, thrust through which was a sword; written on the stone was:

" Whoso can draw forth this sword, is rightful King of Britain born."

Knights of the Round Table. The empty seat next to Arthur is called the Siege Perilous.

Tristan being challenged by an unknown knight. The fight ends in a draw because the challenger is Lancelot, his equal in arms.

Of course all the nobles clamoured to try it, but none succeeded no matter how hard he pulled. It was not till the following Easter that the young Arthur, needing a sword for his friend Kay, and unable to find one, went to the great stone and pulled the sword easily from the anvil. Thus was Arthur revealed as the new King of Britain.

THE KNIGHTS OF THE ROUND TABLE

After he had quelled his unruly nobles, he married Guinevere, the daughter of a king, against the wishes of Merlin who had foreseen trouble and sadness in the future for the young king. On his wedding day, Arthur founded his famous Order of the Round Table. This Round Table had been made originally by Merlin to show plainly to all men that the earth itself was round. One hundred and fifty knights could sit at it, and their seats were called sieges. To fill the places, Arthur created one hundred and twenty-eight knights; the other knights were appointed each year at the high festival of Pentecost. Only one siege, the Siege Perilous, remained empty; no one could sit at it unless he was completely free from sin, and the Siege Perilous remained empty until the coming of Sir Galahad.

Among the most famous Knights of the Round Table were Sir Launcelot, the bravest, most courteous, and gentlest of knights, Sir Tristram, the only peer of Sir Launcelot on the field of arms, Sir Bors, Sir Percival, Sir Pellinore, Sir Gawain and his three brothers, Sir Gareth, Sir Gaheris, and Sir Mordred, the traitor, Sir Palamides, the heathen knight who was baptised by Arthur, Sir Lucan, Sir Bedivere, Sir Geraint and many, many more.

EXCALIBUR

Early in his reign Arthur, with Merlin's help, found his sword Excalibur in a lake deep in the Forest Perilous. There, sticking out of the water the King saw an arm, clothed in white samite (silk), and holding a fair sword which gleamed brightly. There was written on one side of the blade " Keep me ", and on the other side, " Throw me away ". Merlin explained this to Arthur: " Keep it, the time to cast it away is not yet come ". The sword had a beautiful scabbard which would magically prevent Arthur from bleeding to death. But this scabbard was later thrown into a lake by Morgan

Le Fay, a sorceress and Arthur's bitter enemy. When Arthur finally died, he died of blood lost from wounds received in battle.

THE QUEST FOR THE HOLY GRAIL

With the coming of Sir Galahad, an event took place which changed the lives of Arthur and all his Knights of the Round Table. When Sir Galahad came in at the next feast of Pentecost at Camelot, to the astonishment of all the knights, he sat unscathed in the Siege Perilous. Suddenly there was a crash of thunder, and a dazzlingly bright beam of light filled the hall. There, in white samite so that it was hidden, was the Holy Grail. This Grail was said to be the chalice which Jesus Christ had used at the Last Supper, and was visible only to the good and pure in heart. Sir Galahad's presence had brought about its appearance, and now all the Knights vowed they would go on a quest of the Holy Grail in order to have a perfect and unveiled sight of it.

The Knights scattered themselves all over Europe in their search; only Sir Galahad, Sir Bors and Sir Percival achieved a perfect sight of the Holy Grail. Sir Launcelot saw it imperfectly, and returned a saddened man to Arthur's court. There he discovered that Mordred had plotted against him, telling exaggerated stories about the true love which existed between him and Guinevere. They had always loved each other, but Launcelot had continued to serve Arthur faithfully. Now Arthur in anger at his treachery banished Launcelot to France, and then later went over to France to fight against him. He left Mordred in charge of Britain. In his absence Mordred turned traitor, and declared himself king. Arthur had to return to try to regain his crown, and in the vicious civil war which followed, nearly all the Knights were killed, and Arthur, fatally wounded, was left with only Sir Bedivere beside him. He gave Excalibur to Sir Bedivere and told him to throw it in a great lake. After three hesitations Sir Bedivere finally threw the sword, and as it touched water a hand caught it, brandished it three times and drew it into the deep. A barge then appeared; in it were three tall women who took the body of the dead king on board and to the Valley of Avalon, the last resting place of the heroes. So ended mysteriously the life of Arthur, the once and future king.

Sir Galahad has a perfect vision of the Holy Grail and the spear which pierced the side of Christ.

TAPESTRY AND CARPET MAKING

One of man's earliest inventions was that of interlacing at right angles a series of threads. Those running lengthwise are called warp threads, or simply, the warp. Those which run across are called weft threads, or the weft.

The threads can be spun, or twisted into various thicknesses, or dyed. By using one or more of these treatments a great variety of texture can be produced by the weaver. A later development was the use of knotting, as in carpet weaving.

Man's delight in decoration and ornament has led to an infinite number of ideas in the use of threads on the loom.

TAPESTRY WEAVING

Tapestry weaving is a very ancient craft, the origins of which are lost in antiquity, but specimens of the work of the Coptic weavers in Egypt, who flourished in the early centuries of the Christian era, may be seen in many museums.

These early Coptic examples are, like all tapestry, built up by inter-weaving various threads upon warp threads stretched in close parallel lines. By varying the colours of the threads that are thus manipulated upon the warp, patterns of any degree of complexity can be built up by hand.

Throughout the Islamic world, tapestry weaving was widespread. Silk and sometimes very fine spun cotton were used instead of wool.

Fragments found in Central Asia show that tapestry weaving was carried out in China from early times, reaching a particularly high standard during the eighteenth century. The Chinese used silk in both warp and weft, sometimes adding threads of gold and silver to the weft.

ORNAMENTAL TAPESTRIES

One of the best-known tapestries is what is known as the Bayeux Tapestry; in fact, this is not a real tapestry, the work having been embroidered upon the material, not woven into it. First heard of among the treasures of Bayeux Cathedral, it consists of a very long and narrow strip of linen with embroidered figures and inscriptions representing the Norman conquest of England.

The kind of weaving which demands from the weaver highly developed artistic and technical skill is that which produced the great masterpieces of Arras in Flanders. Later named Gobelin Tapestry after the Manufacture de Gobelins in Paris, founded about 400 years ago, the tapestry is produced in Paris to this day.

Such tapestries, used to cover entire walls, were intended to provide protection against cold and damp as well as to convey a sense of luxury. Latterly in the eighteenth century, French tapestries were made solely for ornamental purposes. They became smaller and the imposing subjects, based on sacred and secular history, gave way to pastoral scenes, or mythological subjects, the treatment of which more closely resembled painting. This trend grew when well-known painters of the period began to design tapestry cartoons. The weavers' artistic independence was threatened and they resented the slavish copying which permitted little or no opportunity for personal expression.

At Aubusson, which consisted of a group of independent workshops, unlike the single factories of Gobelin and Beauvais, carpets were made in exactly the same way as tapestries. From their profound knowledge of tapestry weaving, the Aubusson weavers were able to obtain shadowing and highlights, thereby achieving the rich effect of deep pile carpets.

Tapestries are still being woven to-day and whether the subject is traditional or modern the result can be as exciting, as rich, and as beautiful as those of former times.

The pile carpet is a comparatively modern amenity in the Western world. It was little known in the seventeenth century except for rare hand-made carpets from France and Flanders, and a few even more rare from the East. Not until the early nineteenth century, when the power loom became widely used, was the pile carpet regarded as a necessary or, at least, a desirable part of household furnishing.

The making of carpets is however a very ancient craft which has in its long history attained some of the highest levels of art ever produced by mankind.

The remote origin of the art of carpet weaving is suggested by a discovery made in 1949 by Soviet archaeologists in the frozen wastes of Gorny-Altai near the Mongolian border. In a burial mound was discovered a patterned carpet of knotted, sheared pile almost perfectly preserved by perpetual ice for over 2,400 years. It is of fine workmanship and measures 6 feet by 6½ feet. It is woven in what is now called the "Turkish Knot". This carpet may now be seen in the Hermitage Museum in Leningrad and is the oldest carpet in existence.

It is almost certain that carpets were first made by the nomadic tribes of Central Asia. For these wandering shepherds in cold and mountainous regions, where walls and floors had to be covered as a protection against the cold, carpets were a matter of life rather than luxury. Their flocks

Cardinal Scipione Borghese (1576-1633), a great patron of the arts, examines a seventeenth-century Flemish arras.

of sheep provided them with ample supplies of the ideal raw material.

From these nomadic tribes the carpet was introduced into the dwellings of their more settled neighbours, gradually spreading throughout the Middle East, to China, and much later to Europe.

That fine carpets were already regarded in the East, in the tenth century, as familiar symbols of wealth and luxury is evident by the frequent admiring references to them in *The Arabian Nights*.

Of the many ancient and splendid examples of antique carpets still surviving, perhaps the most famous is the Ardebil carpet from Persia, now in the Victoria and Albert Museum in London. Measuring thirty-four and a half feet by seventeen and a half feet, it contains about thirty-three million knots, or three hundred and forty to the square inch. Translated, an inscription woven in the carpet, reads—

"I have no refuge in the world other than thy threshold. There is no protection for my head other than thy door. The work of the slave of the threshold, Maqsud of Kashan in the year 946 ".

The date 946 corresponds to A.D. 1540.

Possibly the largest Oriental carpet ever made by hand, was one formerly in the Hall of the Forty Columns at Ispahan. It is estimated to have measured seventy feet by thirty feet, but now only fragments remain.

CHINESE CARPETS

Marco Polo makes frequent references to the textile industry of China, and although he specifically commends the quality of the carpets of Asia Minor, he says nothing about their manufacture by the Chinese. But, in the fourteenth century, the arts were flourishing in China and carpet designs of that period show a high standard of artistic achievement. Chinese carpets of to-day are of a standard of beauty which claims world-wide admiration. A notable feature of these carpets is the way in which the pile is clipped around the pattern so that it stands out from the body of the carpet as though embossed.

CARPETS IN EUROPE

It is possible that the first carpets may have been brought to Europe by the returning Crusaders, but it was not until the seventeenth century that carpet weaving became established in France.

In 1604, Henry IV founded a small factory at the Louvre in Paris. In 1626 a factory making hand-knotted carpets was founded at Chaillot, now a district of Paris, in an old soap (*savon*) factory. These carpets, known as Savonnerie, have become famous. In 1672, the Louvre works were transferred to the Savonnerie and in 1712 this factory became known as the " Royal Factory for the Manufacture of Carpets in the Persian and Near Eastern Styles ".

Although the Savonnerie carpet with its deep velvet pile had a textural affinity with the Persian carpet, from the first the French took an entirely independent line in regard to colour and design. Carpets made in France at this time were softly coloured, and incorporated in the designs were large acanthus-leaf scrolls, flowers, and heraldic emblems. They were designed to harmonise with the decorative scheme of a room, unlike the Oriental carpet which is conceived as an entirely self-contained work of art.

Another famous type of French carpet was that known as the Aubusson. This was a smooth, pileless carpet, woven on a low-warp loom such as was used for tapestry weaving and was, in fact, a tapestry on which one could walk. The weavers, by adapting their tapestry looms to produce a smooth surfaced carpet, were able to use less wool and weave more quickly. Thus, the Aubusson carpets were produced more cheaply, while retaining by clever designing much of the beautiful appearance of the Savonnerie.

England was some centuries behind France in civilisation and comfortable living. Carpets were almost entirely unknown and the stone or wooden floors were covered with

A tapestry by Gobelins entitled Children Gathering Flowers, *is now to be seen in the Pizzi Palace, Florence.*

The design department of a modern carpet-manufacturer must anticipate the styles and colours that will be fashionable in any given year. Above, designers at work creating and transferring the design to graph paper; in the background a pile-levelling machine.

rushes or straw, which was changed from time to time, the dirt being swept away with the rushes. Even as late as 1598 it is on record that Queen Elizabeth's presence chamber at Greenwich was strewn with hay. The very few carpets then in use were not spread on the floors but used as table-cloths.

By the eighteenth century, carpets were becoming relatively more plentiful due to increased trade with the Eastern Mediterranean. In 1756, the Society of Arts offered a premium for those who would make carpets in England by the Turkish and Persian knot techniques. Several weavers responded, the most celebrated being Thomas Moore of Moorfields in the City of London and Thomas Whitty of Axminster. The great Scottish architect, Robert Adam, designed for Moore, and some of their magnificent and elegant productions can still be seen at Syon House and Osterley Park.

WILTON AND BRUSSELS
About 1720 the first pile carpet to be made on automatic looms in England was woven at Wilton in Wiltshire.

Although the emigration of skilled workers from France was strictly forbidden, two weavers from the Savonnerie factory were smuggled into England and at Wilton they erected Brussels looms at the carpet factory and taught the weavers there. They also introduced the cut pile to give a smooth velvet surface.

Later, in 1749, a Belgian master weaver, who had also been persuaded to come to England by a firm in Kidderminster, erected the first Brussels loom in that town. Within fifty years there were thousands of looms in Kidderminster, which now eclipsed Wilton as a carpet producing centre. These looms were manually operated and produced their patterned effect by means of heddles. These heddles were replaced by Joseph Marie Jacquard's invention for the loom which was exhibited at the Paris Exhibition of 1801. By reading the carpet design, which is painted on squared graph-type paper, cards can be punched with small holes. These cards when loaded on to the carpet loom, would enable the jacquard mechanism on the loom to select for the pile the colours chosen by the designer.

As so often happens, the inventor died in poverty. His jacquard mechanism is in use throughout the textile industry to-day and has only been mechanically improved by such things as ball bearings. The same principle of punched holes was used for the old-fashioned "pianola"—a mechanical piano— and is used to-day in strip paper form for feeding complicated data into electronic computers.

Wilton carpeting, which is made on a jacquard loom, is widely used to-day in homes, hotels, restaurants, ships, offices and public buildings. It is hard wearing and has excellent acoustic properties in reducing noise. It is seldom that a Wilton carpet has more than five colours in the pattern but there is no restriction on the style of design, which may be oriental, traditional or modern in conception.

AXMINSTER CARPETING
The name Axminster was originally given to hand-knotted carpets made in the factory started by Thomas Whitty in 1755, in the town of Axminster in Devon. In 1878, the British rights of a new American power loom were purchased by an English firm in Kidderminster. The pile was woven into the surface of the carpet, giving the impression of a hand-knotted product. Therefore, it was thought appropriate to call the new carpet Axminster, although it had no connection with the town of that name.

The outward appearance of Axminster carpeting differs very little from that of Wilton, but in construction it differs considerably. There are three kinds of Axminster carpet, Spool Axminster, Gripper Axminster, and Chenille Axminster. The Spool Axminster can be woven in an almost unlimited number of colours, a Gripper Axminster seldom has more than twelve colours. As in Wilton there is no limitation in the design style, though, in general, the appearance is not so fine as that of Wilton. This is due to the fact that the number of tufts to the square inch is usually less than in Wilton weaves.

Axminster carpeting is widely used domestically.

In the centuries-old story of carpet making, British carpet manufacturers throughout Scotland and England to-day produce a greater variety of carpets than at any other time in man's history. The choice of weave and of quality, the ingenuity and variety of design and colour has never been equalled.

THE HISTORY OF COSTUME:II
From the Dark Ages to the Victorian era

Early in the fifth century, when troubles nearer home compelled the Romans to move out of England, the Saxons and their allies moved in. These tribes brought from that part of the continent, which was later to become Germany, a very different sort of costume to that worn by the Romans. The Saxons were not elegant. Their cross-gartered hose or shapeless trousers, called *braccae*, were gathered in at the ankles like ski pants and were practical rather than decorative. But they loved bright colours, and worked beautiful bands of embroidery round the necks and hems of their tunics, mantles and gowns. They also wore a lot of massive, barbarically splendid jewellery. Women's undergowns, or *kirtles*, came right to the ground. Over this they wore a three-quarter length *gunna* or gown, and at all times on their heads a head-rail, or covering of linen. But it was not till the Saxons were conquered by the Normans, that the stage was set for the series of dramatic changes in costume from medieval to modern times.

THE NORMANS (A.D. 1066)

From a province in what was later to be called France, the Norman conquerors brought with them a number of new fashions. It is said that Saxon spies, surveying the Norman host before the battle of Hastings, reported that they were opposed by an army of priests. At that time, the Norman knights shaved the backs of their heads and cropped the rest of their hair short so that their conical metal helmets, with nose-guards between the eyes, fitted more closely. Their shields were kite-shaped, with the point downwards, and they wore hauberks, one-piece defensive garments of leather to which metal rings were sewn. These had a sort of divided skirt, or rather long shorts, for riding astride. The horsemen now had saddles and used stirrups and spurs.

Left to right: *an English woman, a sovereign and a warrior of the twelfth century.*

Off the battlefield, the Norman nobles dressed richly. On formal occasions they wore splendid tunics which came down to the ankle. Shorter tunics were worn for more active pursuits. Servants and workmen wore short tunics all the time and long tights called *chausses*, made of cloth cut on the cross, which were drawn in at the waist with a sort of pyjama cord. Both men and women wore mantles and the practical, hooded cloak, which seems to have gone right through history in one form or another.

Norman women wore a head-covering called a *couvre-chef*. This was kept in place by pressing over it a metal circlet so that the couvre-chef surrounded the face and hung down the wearer's back. Gowns were still worn calf-length over kirtles which came down to the feet. Girdles were important, since their length and splendour indicated the lady's wealth and social position. Another important consideration was the length of the two plaits of hair, which she decorated by twisting ribbons in and out, inserting jewels and lengthening with false tresses, if necessary. Inner sleeves were tight; outer sleeves so exaggerated that they had to be tied in knots to prevent them from trailing.

During the twelfth and thirteenth centuries, costume throughout Christendom was influenced by the Crusades. Those who returned from these expeditions to the Holy Land, brought back new and exquisite fabrics, jewel-studded goblets and beakers, and unheard-of things such as carpets. These carpets were first used as table-cloths and not as floor-coverings. Most important, perhaps, was the beautifully light, linked chain-mail, which was so much less clumsy than the metal and leather hauberks. The Crusades gave a new impetus to the international orders of chivalry, so that the ambition of almost every boy of gentle birth was to pass through the apprentice stages of page and esquire and receive the accolade of knighthood from his king.

THE PLANTAGENETS—c. 1154

As time passed, Angevin and Plantagenet kings followed the Normans, and foreign royal marriages brought new fashions. Eleanor of Aquitaine, who married King Henry of England in 1152, brought a new style of head-dress with her. This was the *barbette*—a strip of linen folded under the chin and tied on the top of the head. A veil, held down by a circlet, was sometimes worn on top of this, and sometimes a little white linen stiffened pill-box cap. The *wimple*, a modification of the barbette, came in rather later. Unlike the barbette, the throat covering was softly draped instead of being tightly folded under the chin. The wimple was completed by a veil, with or without a circlet to keep it in place.

Fashionable women of the thirteenth century wore loose and flowing gowns, with long, tight sleeves. Their mantles, if possible, were lined or trimmed with fur. In England, Sumptuary Laws were often passed forbidding men and women below a certain rank to wear specific furs and materials. The average citizen was expected to wear wool, and these regulations were intended to boost the native wool trade.

Pictured above are costumes from Germany. Left to right: *a soldier, knight and arquebusier.*

Left to right: *English costumes of a prince, a woman of high rank and a dignitary in a Turkish-style habit.*

Both the men and women of the Middle Ages loved bright colours and wore them all freely, except yellow, which was worn only by the Jews. When they got tired of their plain tunics and hose they took to slashing or " dagging " the hems. They also slashed, scalloped, or dagged, the lower margins of their hoods and sometimes wore a gay felt hat on top.

Men's mantles grew shorter after King Henry II had taken to wearing his at waist-length and been given the nickname of *curt-manteau* in consequence. In those days, castles and churches were chilly and winter clothes were still lined with fur by all who could afford it. Men were wearing beards again in the thirteenth century and letting their hair grow long. The " pudding basin " bob, cut straight across the forehead and round the back of the neck, was worn in most of the countries of Europe for several hundred years. The footwear of men and women more or less followed the shape of the foot till the Middle Ages. By the end of the thirteenth century, the medieval " winkle-picker " had appeared.

Then, in the fourteenth century, chain-mail, first brought home from the Crusades, was in its turn being supplemented and later replaced by the much heavier plate armour. This gave the knight and, latterly, his barded horse, much more effective protection, although it added greatly to the weight.

HUNDRED YEARS' WAR

Also, during the fourteenth century, war broke out with France, a war which lasted, on and off, for a hundred years. The Hundred Years' War interfered very little with ordinary people's lives, at least in England, which was not being used as a battlefield. Wars, of course, were still fought mainly by the king, his feudal lords, and their retainers. As is usual, one of the results of the war was a craze for new styles and new materials. After such victories as Crécy and Poitiers (1346 and 1356 respectively), the great lords and knights concerned became national heroes, and heraldic devices were adapted and used for decoration of mantles, gowns, tunics and inn signs. From France came the fashion for the skin-tight *côte-hardie*, which was fastened by a long row of tiny buttons down the front, and so short that it scarcely covered men's hips. With it went gay little capes, closely fitting hose to the waist, and belts made of gold or silver plaques clasped round the hips instead of the waist.

Another fancy was for parti-colours or contrasting stripes. Half the côte-hardie and one sleeve, with the opposite leg of the hose, might be red, and the other halves green. The old-fashioned hood was now worn with a peak so long that it trailed on the ground and was called a *liripipe*. Shoes had such long points that the wearers could scarcely walk. Tradition says that the tips were actually chained to their garters.

FRENCH INFLUENCE

Many of the odd garments now appearing came from France and Burgundy. Such was the *houppelande*, which was a complete contrast to the skin-tight côte-hardies and hose. It was like a high-collared dressing-gown with wide, trailing, scalloped-edged sleeves and tight, wrist-length under-sleeves. Often the shoulder belt, or baldric, which was used for carrying a sword, was ornamented with a multitude of tiny bells. Bells were fashionable, not only on jesters' costumes, but on the gowns and houppelandes of the courtiers. Their tiny chimes must have provided a tinkling background for the music played in the minstrels' gallery.

French fashions of the fourteenth century. Left to right: *a knight, a woman of high rank and a nobleman.*

93

As in our own time, women's particular fantasy was for new hair-styles and headgear. Never before had they worn such freakish fabrications as those which came from Burgundy early in the fifteenth century.

Oddest of all, and anything up to three feet high, was the Burgundian *steeple hennin*. It was a type of dunce's cap, made of gorgeous materials, with a gauzy veil floating from it. There were also hats made in the shape of bull's horns, and heart-shaped edifices of padded silks or velvet, which were worn over jewelled *cauls* or hair-nets, and *truncated hennins* with the top of the steeple shorn off. The ladies who wore those styles also shaved their eyebrows and sometimes the front of their heads to obtain the smooth, domed look of a boiled egg.

THE TUDORS

Life settled down in England when Henry VII came to the throne. The first of the Tudors was a thrifty, even a miserly sort of person, and the long-drawn-out civil war had left almost every great English family either impoverished, or deprived of leadership, or both.

So the spectacular houppelandes were replaced by much plainer gowns—this type is still to be seen at our universities. These gowns were made of brocade or velvet, for those who could still afford it, or of good, serviceable wool. The Tudor *doublet*, or *paltock*, which was often worn under it, was still very brief indeed, and the tailored, close-fitting hose had the central pouch or codpiece, which had been introduced earlier in the century. The low square neckline, so typical of the early Tudor period, owes something to the art of the Italian Renaissance. Under the doublet, men wore a finely pleated and embroidered shirt. Sometimes the front of the doublet was left open and laced across to show more of the shirt underneath.

The king set the fashion for clean-shaven faces at court, but men still wore their hair nearly to their shoulders, and cut squarely across the forehead. The most typical headgear for men was the square Tudor bonnet, a flat-topped, shallow cap, usually of black velvet, with a turned-up brim and slit here and there to fit closely to the crown, the whole held in place by jewelled brooches or medallions. Another significant Tudor change was in the shape of shoes, which

Italian fashions, left to right: *a riding-master of the sixteenth century* (*note the slashing of sleeves and trunks*), *a Florentine lady and a soldier.*

were no longer pointed, but rounded. At a later period, shoes were squarely cut across the toes.

Women's gowns were also square-necked, showing a frilled margin of chemise at neck and wrists; tight-fitting inner sleeves emerged from wide outer ones. On their heads they wore the *gable hood* or *kennel*. These hats were, literally, stiffened to look like a kennel or a dormer window, and had a fitting white undercap underneath. Jewellery was very popular with both men and women throughout the Tudor period.

MAGNIFICENCE OF HENRY VIII

With the succession of Henry VIII the wheel of fashion turned again, for the flamboyant young king was very different from his father. Everything was magnificently exaggerated. Shoulders were squared, sleeves were puffed, and short trunks ballooned over the hips. Wherever possible, on shoulders, sleeves, trunks, and even the squared toes of Tudor shoes, the outer fabric was slashed to show a different colour beneath.

Stockings appeared about this time. Trunks, later lengthened to become breeches, were called *upper-stocks*; the hose attached to them were called *nether-stocks*. As King Henry VIII was bearded, most men grew beards again. Caps were jauntily plumed but extremely flat.

Women's gowns still had square-cut necks but even tighter waists. Outer sleeves were wider still, and the fine white inner ones were often trimmed with a narrow band of velvet at the wrists. Now that Christopher Columbus had discovered the New World for Spain, Spanish influence was apparent in the world of fashion, and new ideas came to England at the time of Henry VIII's Spanish marriage. The greatest novelty at this time was the *farthingale*, a stiffened, richly embroidered petticoat, whalebone-hooped to give the bell-like outline required. The front of the gown was cut back to show the central panel of the farthingale, and the gable hoods were gradually replaced by much softer little bonnets surrounding the face like a halo.

However, it was in the reign of Queen Elizabeth I that English fashion reached its greatest height of splendour. Spanish influence was thrown off as hostility mounted be-

A courtier of Henry VIII's time, a high-ranking woman of Elizabeth I's time and a herald.

tween the countries. The queen herself rejoiced in every new and exaggerated style. The modest neck-frilling of Tudor shirts became the stiffly pleated pie-frill ruffs worn by both men and women. Extraordinary, puffed-out doublets were called *pease-cods*, because they gave men's stomachs a pea-pod shape. *Wheel farthingales* came into fashion giving women's dresses a tent-like appearance. These wheel farthingales were wired stiffly outwards at waist level, so that the skirt jutted out all round the wearer. Bombast, or padding, was used to fill out the ballooning trunks, absurdly-curved doublets and wheel farthingales. So, bombastic became a word to describe a pompous, puffed-out person.

Elizabethan women piled their hair elaborately on top of their heads, and netted it with jewels. If a hat was worn at all, it was only a little cap, although the heart-shaped head-dresses Mary Queen of Scots brought from France were also popular. As always in periods of dramatic hair-styling, wigs were in great demand. Stockings were now knitted in all sorts of colours, but silk stockings were still very expensive. For the first time shoes had low, wedge-shaped heels and were worn with big ribbon bows on the front of the instep. Men's hats were no longer flat, but high-crowned and plumed.

THE STUARTS (1603-1714)

This period started rather uninterestingly for England, for King James VI of Scotland who became James I of England was not a very fashion conscious person. In his reign the " great breeches ", which were rather like the bloomers of the Victorian lady cyclists, replaced the short trunk hose. Sometimes these were stuffed out with bombast, and sometimes left to hang loosely. Shoes had heels, and were decorated, both for men and women, with large rosettes instead of bows. Hats had higher crowns than ever, and men took to wearing them indoors and out.

In the next reign, the Civil War split the country, fashion-wise, from top to bottom. Royalist supporters dressed with studied elegance, Roundheads with equally studied austerity. The Royalists introduced normally shaped breeches, fitting jackets, and riding boots with turn-down, or bucket, tops. Hose and buckled shoes were worn indoors.

With both men and women, lace was popular and it was

English costume, from the left: *courtier, noblewoman and dignitary.*

Left to right: *Court official, a woman of fashion wearing a dress over a hooped petticoat, and a richly-dressed knight.*

used for edgings, bands and Van Dyck collars. And both men and women wore graceful, wide-brimmed hats, trimmed with ostrich plumes. Women's gowns were still square-necked and tight-waisted, with full skirts, lace collars and cuffs. They wore hoods in bad weather, and masks to protect their complexions. The expression " bare-faced " suggests that those who went without them were thought immodest.

During the dreary interlude of the Commonwealth, the ruling party dressed in black or grey belted jackets, matching breeches, black stockings, buckled shoes, plain linen collars and cuffs, and witch-high black hats. Puritan women wore a feminine version of this. On the restoration of Charles II in 1660, the reaction against puritan-style dress was an immediate swing-back to earlier Stuart elegance.

To cover the cropped hair favoured by the Puritans, wigs were worn by those who wished to show loyalty to the new king.

Adopted primarily as an emergency measure, the fashion took hold. It dispensed with the necessity of men growing their hair long and enabled them, when necessary, to appear in ringlets as luxuriant as the king's.

Women's gowns were still tight-waisted, and bodices were almost off the shoulders, with puffed, elbow-length sleeves. Both men and women wore ribbon bows everywhere. Full-skirted gowns were caught back with bows on the hips to show exquisite under-gowns, and men's coats were cut short at the front of the waist to show the billowing frilled shirt beneath. Ruffles were worn at throat, wrists and knees. Everything was gay, exaggerated and rather ridiculous, especially the men's fashion known as " petticoat breeches ", so nick-named because of their extreme width. The wide, open knees were edged with a cascade of ruffles.

Fashion steadied under the last sovereigns of the House of Stuart—William and Mary, and Mary's sister, Anne. Men's coats had big cuffs on the sleeves and were worn nipped in above full skirts. Waistcoats appeared for the first time and, like the coats, came to the knee, so that the breeches scarcely showed. Men carried snuff boxes and handkerchiefs and tricorn hats. Wigs were now so full that hats could only perch on the tops of their heads.

Women's gowns were still elaborate. Their tight-fitting

In the seventeenth century, large doublets, short overcoats and less full gowns were fashionable. Right: *a lawyer's gown.*

bodices required a leather or whalebone corset, and the bodices were open in front, lacing across a decorative stomacher below. They wore their hair in ringlets, with high head-dresses of stiffened lace and ribbons—a fashion imported from France.

THE GEORGIANS

Neither of the first two kings from Hanover had much influence on British fashions. In spite of them, new versions of old designs were brought back into favour. From France came the waistless gown known as the *sacque*. This rather tent-like garment was worn over a hooped petticoat and the bodice was open in front to show the embroidered stomacher inside. The skirt was not cut back to show the under-gown, but swept from waist to hem in front, and at the back fell from a box-pleated yoke to the ground. Sleeves came to the elbow and were trimmed with lace ruffles.

For travelling, women had taken to wearing charming, Red-Riding-Hood cloaks. Men, on the contrary, struck a new

Left: *a typical mantle of the early nineteenth century,* Centre: *a citizen's dress of the same period.* Right: *a short-skirted, high waisted walking-out dress.*

note with overcoats. These were belted and had cuffs and ample skirts. Under them they wore coats, waistcoats and breeches. The coats were still almost knee-length, but more pinched in at the waist than before, and their flared, buckram-lined skirts stood out all round. The vast cuffs reached nearly to the elbows, and were trimmed with a row of buttons and imitation buttonholes. Waistcoats were gorgeous affairs of brocade or satin; breeches, which usually matched the coat, were buckled below the knee and worn with white or coloured stockings of silk or wool; black leather shoes with long, squared toes, upstanding tongues, buckles, and, for a time, red heels, completed the outfit.

Swords were still worn, but the real elegants wore cravats, wigs and hats and carried canes, gloves, muffs and snuff-boxes. Wigs were on their way out and women wore their hair high, with ringlets or plumes for formal occasions. By the beginning of George II's reign, men wanted a change, so they powdered their naturally-coloured, full-bottomed wigs. They made such a mess in doing so that powder-closets were partitioned off for them in fashionable people's houses. Fashion then decreed that the curls of wigs should be tied back at the nape of the neck. These styles were called *ramillie*, *tie*, and *bag wig*. Then politics put an end to powder, for Mr. Pitt put a tax on it. People promptly stopped using it, except in the army, where the custom persisted for some years.

During the rest of the eighteenth century, women's fashions were influenced by the French Queen, Marie Antoinette. She set the fashion for towering hair-styles and *panniers* (basket-like hoops on the hips), over which wide skirts were bunched up to show the elegant petticoat below. The hair was trained over pads, and decorated with all sorts of unexpected things such as a model of a coach and horses, or a ship in full sail. Hats, when worn, were frivolous little straw saucers perched on top of everything else.

Men's fashions were now moderating towards the sober elegance of broadcloth and fine tailoring. For the first time, British fashion for men led the world. Coats were high-waisted, double-breasted, high-lapelled, and were worn with white buckskin breeches and boots, or stockings and buckled shoes.

Children, too, were beginning to be liberated from the tradition of being dressed just like their parents, though, during the nineteenth century at least, the clothes prescribed for them were a very doubtful improvement.

THE VICTORIANS (19th Century)

The great Victorian era did not actually come in until the death of King William IV in 1837. However, many changes at the beginning of the nineteenth century foreshadowed Victorian fashion. Men took to that specially Victorian garment, the *frock coat*, which had the front cut away at waist level and skirts to the knees at sides and back. These coats were double-breasted, with velvet-covered collars, wide revers and six buttons. The rest of the fashionable world followed Britain's lead in substituting trousers for breeches. The first trousers were tight-fitting, with a central buttoned panel instead of the modern single line of buttons or zip. They were made of cloth, buckskin, or corduroy, and were strapped under the instep. Outdoors, knee-length boots were worn, and at home, flat, leather pumps.

Like the men, women were now wearing various sorts of overcoats. The *spencer* was short, the *pelisse* full length, trimmed with fur, and belted. At the beginning of the century,

Women of about the 1850s wore crinolines, while men had broad cravats, long jackets and trousers with looped insteps.

Crinolines were replaced in the late nineteenth century by elegantly-flounced and decoratively-trimmed dresses.

women's dresses were simple and charming and made of filmy, pastel-coloured materials. They gathered their hair back to the nape of the neck into a chignon or bun. *Poke bonnets*, looking very much like coal-scuttles, had appeared by 1800.

As the century went on, men's clothes became more sombre. Only the gay brocade waistcoats struck a lighter note, but after about 1850 even they were replaced by plain, light-coloured ones. At first, waistcoats were cut straight across the waist, and had small revers. Then the revers were dispensed with, to be replaced by the peaked waist-line.

Trousers were wider, though still without turn-up or crease. Short-jacketed tweed suits for country became popular. Tobacco was smoked instead of snuffed. With the pipe came the smoking-room, the smoking carriage, the smoking jacket and matching cap. Less formal styles in hats as well as suits were also coming in. Casual *panamas*, and the stiffer *boater* appeared at the seaside. Men began to wear *bowlers* instead of the almost invariable *top hat*.

The most typical Victorian fashion for women was the bell-shaped skirt and the fitted bodice, over which was draped a shawl or cape. Fringes and edgings were everywhere, on the furniture as well as on its owners. Women wore six or seven petticoats under their full skirts, until the *crinoline*, or frame of horsehair, stiffened with whalebone bands, came in at mid-century. Bonnets, which were neater and smaller now, were worn by women of all classes. Sombre colours such as sage green, magenta, navy blue and purple were worn in daytime. In the evening women wore charming, off-the-shoulder gowns in white or pastel colours, with tiny puffed sleeves, and they wore their hair parted centrally, with ringlets. In the second half of the century, for a short time only, the bustle ousted the crinoline. The bustle was a pad placed in the small of the back which gathered the skirts together so as to show the decorative petticoat. In the seventies it was so exaggerated that it looked like a sort of shelf.

When the Victorian era began, men had long been clean-shaven. But, by 1850, and for the first time since the Stuarts, beards and moustaches were back in fashion. Next came side-whiskers, called " Dundrearies " or " Piccadilly Weepers ", worn either with, or without, moustaches. Men's evening dress was nearly the uniform it is to-day, tail coat, trousers

(at first strapped under the instep), white shirt, collar and cravat. The less formal dinner jacket with a plain black tie, came in towards the end of the century. White ties later replaced the cravats with tail coats, and white gloves were essential.

By our standards, children were still miserably muffled up. Little girls wore shorter dresses, but in the early nineteenth century their lace-edged pantalettes showed below the skirt to cover their legs. Later, during the last half of the century, boys wore knickerbocker suits, Eton jackets, or sailor suits, and both boys and girls wore black, or circularly striped, stockings. Little boys wore petticoats till they were about four.

Everybody was becoming more interested in sport and women were demanding to learn to bicycle, to play tennis, hockey and cricket, to swim and run races like their brothers. The Victorian ladies who courageously wore cycling-bloomers and ankle-length bathing gowns can scarcely have guessed how little their great-grandchildren would be wearing in another sixty or seventy years.

Three later Victorian costumes heavily boned and corseted.

For centuries churches have been beautified by the ancient art of staining glass. There is in existence a letter, written in the tenth century by a Bavarian abbot, which makes mention of the monks at work on the coloured glass for the windows of their monastery. Originally, the monks had four main reasons for using coloured glass—to beautify their monasteries, to educate people through pictures at a time when few could read, to let in light, and to act as a filter to the heat of the sun's rays.

There could be no stained glass windows without glass, and the first thing necessary was a supply of window glass, plain and coloured. Glass is made by heating pure sand and soda ash with a small amount of limestone.

Right: *is the exterior of the Gothic cathedral of Chartres (France)*; Left: *the superb thirteenth-century, medallion-shaped, stained-glass window of the same cathedral.*

Nowadays, window glass is made in endless rivers by machine, but for stained glass windows, the old hand-blown method is often used, because the glass so produced is more suitable.

Hand-blowing means that a glassmaker dips a hollow tube into the melted glass and takes up a soft lump on the end. He blows down the tube and makes a big, hollow ball of glass, which he swings until the globe becomes a cylinder. When it has cooled enough to be hard, the ends are cut off and the cylinder of glass is slit up one side. Then it is heated a little until it is soft enough to be opened out flat like a pancake. When cool, there will be a sheet of glass perhaps two feet broad and three feet long.

Not all the glass is made like this. The artist will also need another kind which is made as " Norman slabs ". The glassmaker blows his glass globe as before, but he blows it inside a square mould. The soft glass has to stretch to fill the corners, and the result is a square box of glass, which is cut up to form five slabs—one from each of the four sides and one from the bottom. Each slab is thin at the edges but thick in the centre. We shall see that this will be very useful for the window artist.

The first step in making a stained glass window is to sketch out the picture in full size, marking the various colours upon the drawing and remembering that the colour will always be in blocks, each shade separated sharply from its neighbours. The sketch is called a cartoon.

No window will look the same in bright light as in shadow, so its position must be taken into consideration by the artist when choosing colours. Weather changes, too, must be taken into account. If the window is to show up well against a dull sky, the artist will use lighter shades than for a window illuminated by bright sunshine.

If the background is sky, possibility of clouds will govern the choice of tints. Furthermore, he may have to use different hues at different levels, if, for example, a wall or a line of hills covers half the background. You can easily see that the windows of older churches in large cities often look dull and

The stained-glass workers of early times probably moved from church to church, manufacturing their windows on the site.

In Italy, in the fifteenth century, it became customary for painters to provide designs for stained-glass windows.

dark because the sunlight in which they formerly basked has been blotted out by huge buildings. New churches in built-up areas, may, however, be made to look quite bright by considering their environment and using colour tints judiciously.

Supports for the window are important, too. A stained glass window is soft and liable to bend and a long one could sag under its own weight or be blown right out of the frame by a strong wind. All but the very smallest have to be held rigid by iron bars which run across them and are set in the stonework at either side. These bars must be correctly spaced, so the cartoon must be planned to include the bars. One could not, for example, have the bars running across the faces of the characters in the picture. So the figures are placed in such a way that the bars cross them where it does not really matter—such as at the wrists and ankles. One reason why many windows look rather stiff and lacking in action or excitement is that all the characters are carefully keeping their hands and feet out of the way of the iron stays.

It now remains to cut out all the pieces of coloured glass and fix them together like a jigsaw. This used to be a really tedious job, because the glazier had to heat up an iron tool and scratch away with it until he had made a sort of furrow along which the glass would break—very much as home-made toffee or fudge will crack along a groove. Nowadays a diamond is used, which will scratch the glass deep enough at once; or a cutting wheel rather like a dentist's drill. If you look at a window you will see that squares and long curves can easily be cut, but a V-shape is not possible without breaking the glass. This is why the legs of animals are usually in separate pieces.

Although coloured windows are called stained glass, the glass is not stained. Wood can be stained and so can cloth, because they will soak up colours into their fibres, but glass cannot be stained at all, and the tints have to be there in the make-up of the glass itself, or melted into the surface.

The glass artist colours his picture in several different ways. First he has his " pot " colours, glasses which are made from a whole pot of molten glass to which the colouring has been added so that the glass is coloured right through. The colourings are not the sorts of dyes used for cloth, nor the pigments a painter will use in his pictures, but salts of various metals. These salts may not look the right colour, but when melted with the glass they produce vivid tints. Yellows and greens can be made with iron salts, and the deep royal blues are usually the result of adding cobalt.

Pot-coloured glass can be made into sheets of Norman slabs, and the colour runs right through it. But not every tint can be made in this way. Sometimes, the artist wants a very special shade, and then he may choose two thin sheets of pot-coloured glass, lay them together and soften them in the furnace so that they stick together. A yellow sheet and a red sheet fused together like this would give a bright orange which could never be produced with a single pot colour.

The artist also needs detailed colouring, perhaps for a peacock's feathers, a brindled cow, or for the markings on aircraft in a war memorial window. He will add these by making a paste of powdered glass of the right colour, and painting it on the surface. The piece is then fired in the furnace, and the powdered glass melts into the surface to make a patch of different colour.

This stained-glass window by N. da Varallo can be seen in Milan Cathedral.

A stained-glass window in Milan Cathedral.

single piece of glass which has the correct change in colour and also the streakiness of the cloth.

CEMENTING AND FIXING

When all the pieces have been made, the glass picture has to be fixed together. The pieces are set with an oil cement or sticky mastic into grooved lengths of lead, the lead being fused with a hot iron wherever one piece joins another. The lead can be used to help the colours stand out from each other, and if the picture is well designed you will hardly notice the black lines wriggling all over it. But if you look at the window from outside, you will see that there is a surprising amount of lead. You can also see that the window is not at all smooth. It is a jumble of thick and thin pieces, and there may be chunky wedge-shaped bits cut from the Norman slabs.

The cement should stay firm enough to hold the glass in place for hundreds of years. But eventually it may begin to crumble and the little panes become loose. That is why you can sometimes hear the pieces of glass rattle when a strong wind is blowing round the church.

The last step is the placing of the supporting pieces of iron. The bars are laid across the finished picture and fixed to the leads beneath. Now the whole window is ready to be taken off and raised to its position, where it will delight people for hundreds of years with the brilliance of its colours.

The most obvious local colouring is in the faces of people or animals. For a long time facial features, wrinkles and eyebrows were added as a paste of brown glass. Melted into the surface it gave a pinkish brown effect. This " enamel " of powdered glass was called " grisaille ", and it is very common in the oldest windows. Everybody had to have grisaille hair unless the whole head of curls was added like a wig on a separate piece of yellow glass above the face. But about the beginning of the fourteenth century, a window artist discovered that silver oxide could be painted on glass; when this mixture was fired in the furnace it gave rich colours of yellow, orange or gold. If you see an angel or a king with golden hair, or royal crown on the same piece of glass as his face, you can be sure that the window is less than seven hundred years old.

Nowadays a glass artist has many new chemicals for pot colours and he can produce tints unknown before. But he still uses Norman slabs for parts of his work and this is because the slabs are streaky and vary enormously in thickness from side to centre. The thinner the glass, the lighter the colour will be, and there may be places in the picture where he wants to have the colour strongly graded. For example, a figure may be wearing a rich, red cloak which falls from his arm in a fold. The recess of the fold should be made much darker than the rest of the cloth which is turned out towards the light, but the artist may be able to cut from a slab one

A sixteenth-century window entitled, The Manger.

100

THE HISTORY OF THE MINIATURE

A miniature is a painting of a person, family group or scene which is on such a small scale that it may be held in the hand. Its size may vary from a painting no larger than a thumb-nail to one as large as a photograph of seven to ten inches, or larger.

The name miniature was not, as one might suppose, taken from a word meaning little, but was taken from the Latin word *minium*, which means red lead or vermilion. It was not until later that the French word, *mignature* became connected with it to emphasise the smallness of the work. Red lead was the colour used to paint the initial letters and borders on bibles, prayer books and letters, which before the invention of printing were all hand-drawn by people who were called illuminators.

" PAINTINGS IN LITTLE "

At the present time the term miniature is given to any small object, but in art it describes small paintings, the majority of which are portraits of people. When the art first began in Britain these were called " paintings in little " or limnings. They can be painted in oil, water-colour or enamel and may be on almost any base such as vellum, card, metal, wood, ivory, paper and, in modern times, hardboard.

The shape of the early miniatures was round, but later oval, rectangular and square shapes were used. The majority of them are painted in water-colour, but those painted in oil or enamel are on a metal base. Enamel paintings have to be placed in a kiln at a high temperature to fix the colours. If the enamel paintings are left in the heat too long, or not long enough, the paintings are spoilt and have to be thrown away.

In the seventeenth century some artists drew small portraits in pencil, or " plumbago " as it was then called, while

The monks of medieval days dedicated themselves to the celebrated art of manuscript illumination.

others drew sketches of the sitters before painting the finished miniature. Then in the nineteenth century a few artists who worked in a china factory painted miniatures on porcelain. These, like the enamels, had to be fired in a kiln.

The early miniaturists, or limners, copied the work of illuminators by using the same kind of water-colour paint, which is called *gouache*. Painting by this method retained the brilliance of the colours throughout the years and gouache was used for both miniatures and the illuminated pages of books. Both miniatures and books often had gold leaf laid down on letters and on the design, so that the general effect was a glowing one—rather like sunlight shining through a stained-glass window.

The base on which the artists painted with gouache was vellum, the same material as that used for pages of books and letters. This was prepared from the skin of calf or sheep. For this purpose the vellum used was thin and it was stuck on to a base of card to strengthen it. Playing cards were ideal for this and if some miniatures are opened up the old card may be seen on the back.

The idea of having small portraits painted of members of a family goes back hundreds of years, long before photography. It was the only means people had of carrying a portrait about. Because there was a danger of the miniatures getting spoilt they were usually placed in a box with a lid, or in a piece of jewellery under glass to protect the paint. Those done in water-colour should not be left in sunlight or they will fade; if they get damp the paint will be spoilt.

Besides the jewelled lockets, rings, brooches and boxes of different kinds, miniatures were also preserved in frames of wood, silver and other metals, ivory, pinchbeck (which is an imitation gold), tortoise-shell and enamel. Many of them were decorated on the back with engraving, or were decorated with designs made with a lock of the sitter's hair. Sometimes

Predating the small portraits known as miniatures were the delicate decorations and illustrations carried out in early manuscripts by illuminators.

the sitter's initials were cut in gold, entwined with seed pearls, the whole set over coloured glass.

In fourteenth, fifteenth and sixteenth century Europe, small portraits of living persons were sometimes included on illuminated manuscripts, some of which have survived on notable documents. These portraits were undoubtedly the beginning of portrait miniatures as we know them to-day.

BRITISH SCHOOL OF MINIATURISTS

Britain is justly proud of the artists who, from the reign of Henry VIII up to the present day, painted so many people of historic interest. The British school of miniature painters is considered one of the finest in the world.

Hans Holbein, a Dutch artist, has always been considered to be the first artist to paint accurate likenesses in miniature. He visited England and undertook commissions to paint portraits. By 1536, he had been appointed by Henry VIII to the position of court painter. One of Holbein's most famous miniatures is that of Anne of Cleves, who was the fourth wife of Henry VIII. This portrait was placed for safety in a carved, ivory box, which may still be seen to-day at the Victoria and Albert Museum in London.

Practically all the sixteenth century miniatures were painted on a blue background. The date on which the miniature was painted and the age of the person in the portrait was often written round the edge of the circle, or on either side of the sitter. A few oil miniatures of this early period exist but as with all miniatures painted in this way, they are slightly dark. As they were hardly ever signed, it is impossible to say by whom they were painted.

In Elizabethan times, thirteen-year-old Nicholas Hilliard, the son of an Exeter goldsmith, began to paint miniatures. Eventually, he became very famous and painted all the well-known people of the day, including Queen Elizabeth, King James I and Sir Walter Raleigh.

The Queen thought so much of his work that she granted him the sole right to paint her portrait. His miniatures varied in shape and were circular, oval and rectangular. The

In India, under the influence of the Persian school of painting, the art of the miniature flourished. Indian miniatures are noted for their richness of colouring.

paint he used was gouache, which was the same as that used by Holbein, and he also painted his sitters against a blue background. However, his miniatures were much brighter than Holbein's because the people of Elizabethan England wore clothes which were more colourful. The ruffs, lace collars and the beautiful jewellery made the portraits very attractive. The frames in which these paintings were placed were often studded with precious stones. Hilliard had a son, Laurence, who also became a miniaturist.

SEVENTEENTH CENTURY MINIATURES

Two other artists, Isaac Oliver who died in 1617 and his son Peter, painted in much the same way as Hilliard. However, they succeeded in drawing faces which showed the roundness of the sitter's cheeks, whereas Hilliard's portraits made the features look rather flat because he did not paint shadows on the faces, but copied the style of the illuminators. The Olivers also painted on vellum stuck on to card, but some of the miniatures were larger in size. Both artists worked for the Royal Family and the Court.

Charles I understood a great deal about art and was so fond of large paintings that he had a number of them copied in miniature so that he could take them about with him. Unfortunately, after his death, when Oliver Cromwell ruled the country, many of the king's treasures disappeared. Peter Oliver had painted a number of these miniatures and when Charles II was restored to the throne in 1660 he tried to recover some of them. He heard that Peter Oliver's widow had some duplicates, so he went to see her and bought them.

By this time, miniature painting had been firmly established and the Olivers were followed by yet another father and son, John Hoskins, Senior, and his son, also called John. These men painted portraits which were even more lifelike. They continued the practice of painting on vellum and card, but instead of blue backgrounds they introduced other colours, such as brown and red, with occasionally a curtain or landscape scene behind the sitter.

By the middle of the seventeenth century there were a number of miniaturists working in Britain—David des Granges, and Richard Gibson (whose family were all artists), deserve to be mentioned; but the artist who has gone

Numerous manuscripts are in existence to-day to bear witness to the intense activity displayed by the miniaturists of the Middle Ages. At that time, abbeys and monasteries were the main centres of miniature painting, and of particular interest are the documents illuminated by Benedictine monks.

down in history as one of the greatest miniaturists the world has ever known was Samuel Cooper. He and his elder brother Alexander, also a miniaturist, were brought up by their uncle, John Hoskins, senior, who taught them to paint. Samuel Cooper became so well known that even abroad people knew of his work. He was interested in music, travelled to many countries and could speak several languages.

His miniatures show him to have been an artist of outstanding skill and his sitters included most of the notable persons in Britain, both during the period of history called the Commonwealth and after Charles II was restored to the throne. His best-known miniature is probably that of the Lord Protector, Oliver Cromwell. Another magnificent portrait by Cooper is of James, Duke of York, afterwards James II. This was in a family collection for many years until it was sold in 1955. The Victoria and Albert Museum bought this miniature for £2,300.

Towards the end of the seventeenth century, there were numerous artists working in Britain where good schools of miniature painters were being formed. At the beginning of the eighteenth century the English-born artist called Bernard Lens was responsible for introducing one of the new ideas and methods of painting which were being tried out at that time. This new method was the use of ivory or bone as a base on which to paint. This was first used by Rosalba Carriera, a famous Italian artist. It was found necessary to cut the ivory very thinly which is a difficult task as it splits easily. In spite of this drawback, ivory became the most popular background on which to paint. Vellum was expensive and it ceased to be used.

EIGHTEENTH CENTURY

From 1740 to 1770, miniatures became rather small in size and, although there were numerous artists working in Britain, the portraits which they painted were not as good as those painted earlier. It was not until the second half of the century that the great eighteenth century miniaturists produced their finest works.

Richard Cosway, R.A. has always been given credit for discovering that it was possible to paint in water-colour on ivory. This technique ensured that the colours had a tran-

With the discovery of transparent colours, ivory became the most popular background for the miniaturists.

sparent quality, the ivory showing through in places, particularly on the face and the backgrounds. Cosway's work was so popular that for many years a great number of unsigned miniatures were said to be by him, when in fact they were by other artists.

Andrew Plimer and his brother, Nathaniel, copied Cosway's style but their work was not as good. Another miniaturist of the same period was Engleheart, who painted nearly 4,000 miniatures. He was a very good artist and he painted in clear, strong colours. John Smart, another outstanding artist, painted some of the finest miniatures of the same period. He did not use a sky background but painted against pale grey or brown. He must have had some knowledge of anatomy because the faces and bone structure of his sitters were so accurately portrayed. It is impossible here to mention all the well-known miniaturists of this period, but their works speak for themselves. The eighteenth century will always be remembered as one of the greatest periods in the history of miniature painting.

In Persia, as early as the thirteenth century, small scenes illustrating religious or historical stories were painted. In India, from the end of the sixteenth century onwards, miniature portraits of emperors and their courts were in demand. Turkey had a few miniaturists and France, Germany, the Netherlands, Italy and Scandinavia all had artists of outstanding ability. In Italy, the Netherlands and Spain, oil miniatures were popular.

In the United States of America, miniature painting did not start before the early part of the eighteenth century—E. G. Malbone being one of their most famous artists.

In the middle of the nineteenth century, photography was invented and the demand for miniatures declined. Naturally enough, people chose the cheaper and quicker method of retaining likenesses of those they loved. And, although the miniaturists tried to alter their paintings to the same shapes and sizes of photographs, the results were not satisfactory. By the end of the nineteenth century, miniature painting had lost its appeal and the art practically died out.

Fortunately, through the years, people had formed collections of miniatures, thus leaving a pattern for present-day painters; and there is now a revival of interest in these fascinating small portraits.

An early miniaturist painstakingly working at his art.

Civilisation and Culture
THE AZTECS

On 8th November, 1519, Hernando Cortes led his Spanish companions to the shores of Lake Tezcoco. The great Aztec capital, Tenochtitlan, lay before them. It represented a triumphant ending to the many battles they had had to fight on their way there. It was, they hoped, the end of hunger and of long cold marches across the mountains.

As the 300,000 inhabitants came out to greet them, the Spaniards felt as though they had stumbled on some fairy city. Before them were great temples, like truncated pyramids, shining, white-painted palaces and thousands of houses. All around were green fields and the blue waters of the lake.

One of them, looking back on that morning, wrote, " Gazing on such a wonderful sight, we did not know what to

In 1519, Hernando Cortes set sail from Cuba with eleven ships, bound for Montezuma's kingdom of Mexico.

say, or whether what appeared before us was real. For on one side the land there were great cities, and in the lake ever so many more. And the lake itself was crowded with canoes. In front of us stood the great city of Mexico . . . we did not number even four hundred soldiers! "

As the Spaniards entered the city, they stared at the people, amazed by the wonderful costumes and the rich jewellery they wore. What they saw, they called Aztec art. But, in fact, the Aztec empire had only been in existence for 90 years. The Aztecs were the inheritors of many earlier civilisations and of the work of neighbouring tribes, many of whom belonged to the same Nahuatl-speaking family. But, however much the Aztecs might owe to the past, on nearly everything they created they left the imprint of their own ruthless, pitiless and tormented vision of life.

NOMADIC LIFE

The history of the Aztecs and the other related tribes is one of constant and bitter struggle. For thousands of years they had been agriculturalists although they had not a settled existence. They were continually on the move, either from the pressure of the more powerful tribes, or in search of new and richer land.

They are first mentioned in the twelfth century when, with the weakening of the Toltec empire, they and related tribes began the trek into the Valley of Mexico. In 1325, they appeared on the shores of Lake Tezcoco searching, as always, for land on which to settle. They were still too small a tribe to win the rich lands along the shores. The best they could find was a marshy, mosquito-ridden island that lay two miles out in the lake. Here they founded Tenochtitlan, the city that was one day to be their magnificent capital.

In those early days, their life must have been extremely

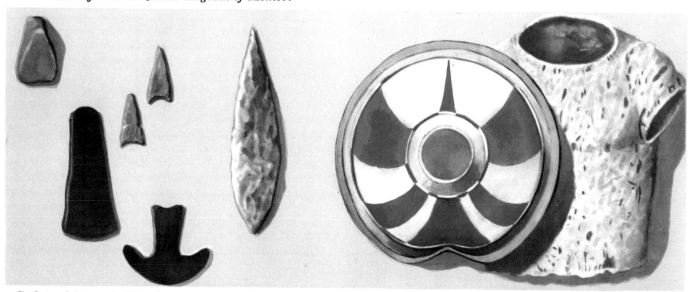

Left to right: *primitive Aztec weapons and armour—axe, arrow- and spear-heads of stone, leather shield and breastplate.*

The first king of the Aztecs was Acampichtli.

The Aztecs were often at war with neighbouring peoples.

hard. But island existence did much to form their character and equip them as future rulers of Mexico. While still a weak tribe, the island offered a secure refuge from which they could send raiding parties. Later on, as other tribes increased in size and had to fight, or migrate, to find new land, the Aztecs found a better solution. They took their canoes out to the shores of the lake and gathered up the rich mud. With this they built " floating gardens " enclosed in wicker work. Gradually these sank and became firm land. By the time the Spaniards arrived, the island had an area of 25,000 acres and a prosperous city.

The inhospitable island helped them in another way. At first the land was so poor that it would not support the whole tribe and many of them had to find other work or become fishermen and merchants. It was the merchants who, by their trade and knowledge of the surrounding tribes, helped to make the Aztecs rich and powerful.

Looking back we can see that Aztec history has four periods. The first lasted nearly 100 years, when they were still very primitive and trying to survive among more advanced peoples. Then for the next 100 years, they were sufficiently

settled to be able to learn from their neighbours and to acquire new skills. For another fifty years, although ruled by others, they were able to build up a strong city-state on their island. Then, for the last ninety years before the Spaniards came, they were strong enough to subdue the tribes for hundreds of miles around them and to grow rich on the tribute and prisoners they exacted.

But, despite this, they were never a happy people. Life in the high plateau lands of Mexico (7,000 feet) is dependent on rain. The Aztecs believed that this was controlled entirely by the gods. The gods did not reward or punish a man because of the life he lived. They were only interested in the respect he paid to them. How, the Aztecs asked themselves, could they show their respect and win the rewards they needed if they were to survive?

HUMAN SACRIFICES

They arrived at the dreadful conclusion that this could only be done by sacrificing the most precious thing they knew—human life. So began the cycle that was to form the basis of their civilisation. When the harvest was gathered in

Some 70,000 victims were supposed to have been sacrificed at the dedication ceremony of Hiutzilopochtli's temple.

The "sun stone" in the National Museum of Mexico.

they had to sacrifice human lives as a token of gratitude. Then, before sowing time, they had to make war to win more prisoners, so as to offer fresh sacrifices to ensure their next year's crops. In this way their life passed from sacrifice to war and back to sacrifice.

PAYMENT TO THE GODS

Their chief god was Tonatiuh, the Sun God. Under him were dozens of other gods and goddesses, of rain, of cloud, of water, of fire, of corn, of childbirth . . . the list could be numberless.

No one knows how many victims were sacrificed at the more important ceremonies, but the Spaniards said that at one there were 12,000 and at another 20,000. Even if the Spaniards exaggerated, we can be certain that the numbers were appallingly large. Added to these must be all the smaller ceremonies that took place. Every important event in life was marked by the offering up of a sacrifice. No merchant would start a journey without buying at least one prisoner and leading him up the steps of the temple to the priests.

There he would be laid across the sacrificial stone. A powder that acted as a pain killer was blown into his nostrils and his heart was cut out and placed on the lap of the implacable god, Chac-Mool.

The Aztecs were not content with sacrificing prisoners only; they, too, had to make offerings. At different times of the year, they would draw their own blood, day after day, as an offering to their gods. Their life was one of work, of penance, of festivity, of war, and then of work again.

EARLY CULTURE

The priests were the possessors of knowledge and it was they who taught the young. They brought them up with the same fears as they possessed themselves. But they also helped the tribe to advance. The more intelligent boys they taught to read the pictographs that recorded past events, or the amount of tribute different cities should pay to the Aztecs.

Nobody was free from the obligation to work and to undergo penance. From the simplest labourer, with his long hair and simple loin cloth, through all the different classes of merchants, doctors, warriors, priests, or emperor, everybody had to play his part in Aztec society.

They were a Stone Age people. Although they had learned to shape gold and silver and to beat out copper, their tools and weapons depended on stone. One can only be amazed as one looks at what they produced with unbelievable patience and skill—the temples and carvings, the pottery and pottery figurines, the woven cloth and featherwork and the works of art.

IMPLEMENTS OF USE

One of their most important materials was obsidian, a volcanic glass that takes a very sharp edge. It was set in wooden handles to make knives, or embedded in heavy clubs to make weapons. With it they cut corn, shaped their cloth, and manufactured bows and arrows and spears.

This still left them without many of the tools that we take for granted to-day. They planted their corn with a simple sowing stick, with which they made a hole in the ground. Nor did they have any kind of plough, only a hoe. The women had a simple loom and the stone-mason chipped away at stone

The richness of the Aztec dress reflects their skill as goldsmiths, leather-and mosaic-workers.

A detail from the pyramid erected to Quetzolcoatl, tribal god of the Toltec race.

The dogs, the warrior in his breast-plate of thick cotton, the whistle shaped like a bird and the bowl are all examples of the art of the Aztecs in terra-cotta form.

with stone, so that his " chisel " had to be constantly reshaped.

WORKS OF ART

Yet the illustrations show some of the marvellous works of art that they produced. It must always be remembered that what remains of the Aztec art is hardly anything compared with what existed when the Spaniards arrived. Nearly all of the works of art were sent back to Spain, where King Charles V melted them down to pay for his wars in Morocco.

The poorest man wore only a loin cloth and when it was cold—a *poncho*—a blanket with a hole cut in the top through which he put his head. But women had fuller clothes, embellished with the most beautiful patterns, which were so beautiful that the masons copied them and used them to decorate their temples.

WAGING WAR

A successful war, one in which many prisoners were taken, was often based on ambush, or treachery, or striking such fear into the hearts of the enemy that they preferred the glory of being sacrificed to the more doubtful honour of being killed in battle.

Therefore, the warriors dressed themselves up for battle to make themselves look bigger and more important. They made head-dresses and coverings of feathers supported on wicker work. A head-dress of the Emperor Montezuma is one of the few Aztec treasures that still exist to-day.

PRECIOUS MATERIALS

Jade, crystal and mosaics were considered more valuable than gold. Many of these have remained, as the Spaniards were more interested in gold than in works of art. They were made with such skill and care that their beauty strikes one first, and their horror only afterwards.

THE NEW WORLD

We have heard America called the New World so often that the phrase has lost its meaning. But to the Spaniards this was literally true. The many things they found, and were amazed by, have now become accepted. European towns were then a mass of untidy streets, but the Aztecs planned their towns carefully. All the streets ran straight into a great central square in which stood the most important temple and the emperor's palace.

The Spaniards were amazed when they saw the markets selling new and, to them, strange plants and foods (including one new domesticated bird—the turkey). Beans, corn, tomatoes (tomatl) and cacao beans (chocatl) had never been seen in Europe and were some of the novelties that were sent back. These new foodstuffs helped to change the whole European economy and to support the rapidly increasing population.

ARRIVAL OF THE HORSE

The Spaniards had stumbled on a civilisation where the horse was unknown. An Aztec chief, who watched Cortes disembark at Vera Cruz, had reported that they had a strange four-legged animal " out of the back of which a man grew."

This was a civilisation where everything had to be carried by man; where there were no pack animals; where the wheel had been used in children's toys, but had never been used to make a cart or become a tool for man; where dogs were rare and were kept as food, but not for companionship.

The stone carvings decorating the Aztec temples were probably representative of the many deities worshipped by the Aztecs.

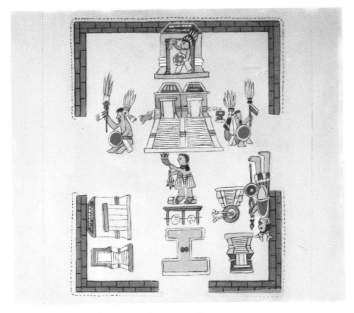

An example of an Aztec mural.

Most of the gold treasure of the Aztec civilisation was sent to Spain for melting down.

The Spaniards have been blamed for destroying the Aztec nation in their greed for gold—there were 9 million Nahuatl-speaking people when they arrived and only 2 million a century later. But it should always be remembered that the Aztecs lived by war and would, one day, have been destroyed by it.

DEFEAT OF A PEOPLE

In 1519, four hundred Spaniards faced 300,000 Aztecs. But the Spaniards brought with them cannons, guns, swords, the horse and, most important of all, superior discipline and technology. This alone would have been enough to defeat the Aztecs. To add to this was the initial confusion caused by legend. The Aztecs had been taught that their gods would come back to live with them, appearing as white men and coming from the East. The Spaniards were white and came from the East. The Aztecs therefore had little choice but to accept them, even if this meant the end of their rule.

The Aztecs were demoralised and when fighting broke out they were eventually defeated. Their city was razed to the ground and most of its people killed.

The Aztecs never recovered from the invasion of the Spaniards. To-day their descendants are among the poorest people of Mexico City. Despite this, much of their greatness still remains and they can be proud to know that many of the churches, as well as the great cathedral of Mexico City, are built from the stones of their temples. The little of their art and architecture that still remains is an unforgettable memory of their greatness . . . just as pitiless, searing and beautiful to look at, as when it was created.

PRONUNCIATION

At first sight, Aztec words seem to be almost impossible to pronounce. But if you have ever learned a code, you will know that what at first seems to be a mere jumble of letters quickly make sense—when you have the key.

Here is the key to most of the words:

	The Consonants					The Vowels
X	usually represents the sound SH					A as in father
Qu	„	„	„	„	K or Kw	E „ „ wet or say
Cu	„	„	„	„	Kw	I „ „ see
Gu	„	„	„	„	G	O „ „ law
Hu	„	„	„	}	W or Hw	U „ „ put
Gu	„	„	„	}		
Oa	„	„	„	}	W	
Ua	„	„	„	}		

Finally, wherever possible a syllable will end on a vowel. The word Teotihuacan is divided into Te-o-ti-hua-can.

Try to work out how the following words are pronounced

—if you have any difficulty look for the answers below.

Aztec	Nahuatl	Tezcoco
Chac-Mool	Olmec	Toltec
Huastec	Popocatepl	Totonac
Maya	Tabasco	Zapotec
Mixtec	Tenochtitlan	
Nahua	Teotihuacan	

As-tek	Paw-paw-cah-toypl
Chahk-maw-awl	Tah-bahs-ko
Wa-stek	Tay-notch-tee-tlan
Ma-yah	Tay-aw-tee-wah-kan
Mish-tek	Tesh-caw-caw
Na-wah	Tawl-tek
Na-wahtl	Taw-taw-nahk
Awl-mek	Za-paw-tek

In the fifteenth century the Italians became very interested in the art, architecture and writings of ancient Greece and Rome. This new interest in the ancient world was strongest in the city of Florence. We call this revival of interest the *Renaissance*, which means rebirth. The Renaissance soon spread all over Europe, and artists and architects were not the only ones to be affected by it. People studied subjects like science, astronomy and medicine, and new universities were opened in many cities. At first Italian architects still made their buildings Gothic, but they had details copied from ancient Rome. In the church of San Spirito in Florence (1436-1482) the arches are round and not pointed like Gothic ones, and they are supported by Corinthian columns. The new style was soon used in the great palaces of the nobles. One of the oldest and finest is the Riccardi Palace (1430). It has a courtyard surrounded by columns like those built in ancient Rome or Pompeii, while the front on to the street is made of big blocks of stone which have been left with a rough surface. It is called *rusticated stonework* and looks very strong.

Soon, architects in other cities like Rome, Venice and Genoa were designing buildings in the new Renaissance style, and by 1500 it had reached France. In Rome the most important Renaissance building is St. Peter's in the Vatican. It is the largest church in the world, and it took one hundred and twenty years to build. The dome is very large. Inside, it measures 137 feet 6 inches across, and it is 452 feet high to the top of the cross on the outside. An architect called Bramante began it in 1506, but it was Michelangelo, the architect, sculptor and painter, who designed most of St. Peter's.

BAROQUE

Most of the early Renaissance buildings in Rome were based on a set of rules made by an ancient Roman architect called Vitruvius. These rules said how thick and how tall columns should be, and left very little room for the architects to think for themselves. After a while the architects in Rome got tired of having to obey these rules, and broke away. Instead of designing buildings that were stiff and formal, they made them with curved fronts and little towers and domes. They decorated the palaces, public buildings and gardens with great flights of steps and with statues of the old Roman gods and goddesses. This style is called Baroque, and it is gay and cheerful. Baroque architects liked to decorate city squares and street corners with fountains, and one of the most famous in Rome is the Trevi Fountain. Some of the best Baroque buildings outside Italy are in Germany and Austria, in small towns like Würzburg and Salzburg.

THE PALACE OF VERSAILLES

By the middle of the sixteenth century, Renaissance archi-

The Palace at Versailles is an outstanding example of Baroque architecture.

tecture had spread all over Europe. In Paris, the Louvre Palace was rebuilt in the new style, and so were many of the beautiful castles, called châteaux, on the banks of the river Loire. The most famous Renaissance palace in France is at Versailles, outside Paris. It was begun in 1661 for Louis XIV. This king lived in such magnificent style that he was called " The Sun King ". The Palace of Versailles is magnificent too. From one end to the other it is a quarter of a mile in length; one room which is 240 feet long has walls that are completely covered with mirrors. Many copies of Versailles were built by kings in other countries such as Austria, Germany and Spain.

INIGO JONES

In England one of the oldest Renaissance buildings is the Banqueting House in Whitehall in London. It was begun in 1619 by the architect Inigo Jones, and was part of Old Whitehall Palace. The rest of the Palace was burnt down many years ago.

SIR CHRISTOPHER WREN

Sir Christopher Wren who lived from 1631 to 1723, was England's greatest architect. Wren studied science, astronomy and mathematics before he became an architect. When he was in France he saw the Renaissance buildings in and around Paris, and they influenced his own designs. In 1666, London was destroyed in the Great Fire and Wren was given the task of designing a new St. Paul's Cathedral and fifty-one new parish churches. All the designs for the parish churches were different, and two of the most famous are St. Mary-le-Bow, which has the Bow Bells, and St. Bride, Fleet Street. St. Paul's Cathedral is Wren's masterpiece. The plan is shaped like a cross with an *apse* at the east end and a huge dome over the *crossing*. The crossing is where the transepts meet the nave and the choir. The two tall towers at the west end were the last part to be built and are Baroque in style. Round the outside Wren used *pilasters* as decoration. Pilasters are like columns, but they are fixed to the walls and do not have to support a heavy weight. Another building

The present St. Paul's Cathedral was designed by Sir Christopher Wren after the Great Fire of London in 1666.

A terrace of houses in Bath, built by John Wood after the style of Nash.

which Sir Christopher Wren designed is the Chelsea Hospital for old soldiers. He also added a new wing to Hampton Court Palace for King William III. Buildings like Hampton Court are of brick; stone was used only for the corners of the walls, the windows and doorways.

SIR JOHN VANBRUGH

Another English architect was Sir John Vanbrugh, who designed Blenheim Palace (1705) for the Duke of Marlborough. It is a huge house with magnificent rooms, but compared with work by Wren the architecture is rather heavy.

Many fine houses were built in towns like Bath and Brighton, as well as in London. These houses were built either in squares or terraces, or in curving crescents. Their beauty lies in the care the architects took to make the doors and windows exactly the right size—not too big and not too small. The most famous architect at this time was John Nash, and we can still see the houses he designed in Carlton House Terrace along the Mall in London.

The most important thing that happened in England be-

tween 1800 and 1850 was the Industrial Revolution. That is the name we give to the time when factories were being built all over the Midlands and the North, and thousands of people were leaving the country to go to live and work in new towns. Instead of inventing a style for new buildings such as railway stations, factories and the like, most of the nineteenth-century architects chose to use the old ones. They built town halls that looked like Italian Gothic palaces, hotels that looked like abbeys, prisons like Norman castles and public baths like Moorish palaces! Some architects still designed beautiful and impressive buildings in the classical style, using the ancient Greek orders. The main front of the British Museum (1828) has Ionic columns, while St. George's Hall in Liverpool is a big building with Corinthian columns. Nearly all the churches built about one hundred years ago were designed in what is called the Gothic Revival. Some were beautiful, but others were dull or ugly. Two good buildings in the Gothic Revival style are the Houses of Parliament (1840-1860), and Liverpool Cathedral (1903), which is still being built.

Civilisation and Culture

THE INCAS

When, nearly 450 years ago, Francisco Pizarro, one of the Spanish conquistadors, or conquerors, set foot in Peru, his aims were three-fold: adventure that would bring him fame and glory, the conversion of the natives to Christianity, and gold. And the last of these was certainly not the least. He found the gold; and he found something else that made his eyes widen with wonder. In that wild and unknown land he stumbled upon a highly organised State with a system of government administration far more efficient than that of his own country.

The story actually begins with Columbus's discovery of America in 1492. One of the sequels to that event was an eager hunt for the fabulous riches of the newly found lands. Cortez marched into Mexico and revealed the elaborate civilisation of the Aztecs and a splendour of gold and silver and precious stones beyond anything the Spaniards had imagined. Pizarro was now embarked on a comparable errand in the Inca Empire of Peru. He had his first real glimpse of the hoped-for treasure when, in 1526, the caravel bearing his little band of soldier-adventurers was sailing southwards down the Pacific coast. A light boat made of bundles of reeds tied together, which the natives called a *balsa*, drew excitedly alongside and the Spaniards, equally excited, marvelled to see that it was laden with finely embroidered fabrics, jewellery, belts studded with diamonds, and other desirable riches. Landing later—after receiving reinforcements—at the port of Tumbez, in the north of modern Peru, they marvelled still more at the sights that there met their eyes. There were stone "palaces" and houses, a triple-walled fortress and great citadel and a temple panelled with gold and silver and stored with articles of the same precious metals encrusted with gems.

By this time Pizarro had seen and heard enough to give him some idea of the power and wealth of the Inca realm. He returned to Spain to report to the king. Five years later he

was back again with a royal commission in his pocket appointing him Governor of Peru—when he had conquered it. Pushing forward at the head of his small army, he doggedly scaled one of the snow-capped, 12,000 foot high cordilleras of the Andes mountains and, in 1532, entered the town of Cajamarca. There, a close-up view of the Inca military power set him thinking. The brown-skinned warriors were a highly disciplined army of perhaps 30,000 men. They were equipped by bronze axes, villainously spiked cudgels, bows and arrows, slings and lances, and their bodies were protected with wadded tunics and helmets and shields. There, too, Pizarro's envoy was presented to Atahualpa, the reigning Inca, who they had already learned was revered by his subjects as a god-king and son of the great Sun-god, Inti. (Here we may note that the ruler was *the* Inca, while the general term " the Incas " comprised the whole concourse of the noble members of the royal clan who were his followers.)

The stately monarch was seated on a gold and jewelled throne. His royal head was crowned with a golden diadem set with diamonds and rubies and decked with two small yellow feathers from a sacred bird. These plumes, the Incas believed, were symbols of their king's divinity, for the Creator made only one pair of the birds for each ruler.

These were impressive revelations; but, presently, when fighting began, neither the Inca's divinity nor his armies could save him from humiliating defeat and capture. And his capture gave the Spaniards a further indication, if they needed one, of the boundless extent of the Inca riches. Atahualpa offered to ransom himself by filling the room in which he and Pizarro stood—it measured about 21 by 18 feet—with gold and the two neighbouring rooms with silver. But even while his emissaries were scouring the country for the requisite treasure the unhappy captive was condemned to death. Later he was strangled.

Next year, Pizarro stood in the capital city of Cuzco, 11,000 feet up in the mountains of southern Peru. Cuzco was the Incas' Holy City. It was dominated by two immense structures: the massive fortress of Sacsahuaman, one of the most impressive and stupendous edifices the world has ever seen, and the magnificent Temple of the Sun. Broad highways connected the capital with the four quarters of the empire. The hanging gardens of the Sun Temple were filled with flowers and trees, birds, animals and reptiles, herdsmen and fountains, all made of solid gold.

After the completion of the conquest much was done to preserve the memory of the vanquished Incas' culture. Spaniards and natives alike wrote books in which many of the ancient customs and ways of life were recorded. One of the most illuminating of these volumes is the copiously illustrated work of Poma de Ayala, a descendant of an Inca nobleman who actually attached himself to the invaders during their career of conquest. In more modern times a succession of enthusiastic explorers and archaeologists have searched and dug the ancient sites and bit by bit reduced at least some of the tantalising gaps in our knowledge.

The people of the Inca empire were skilled metal-workers.

Left: *cross-section showing an underground burial chamber of the Pre-Inca inhabitants of Peru.* Right: *body in sack.*

PRE-INCA CULTURES

One of the first things they have made us realise is that we cannot allow the Incas to walk off with all the honours. Following on the crude settlements of primitive days, quite a number of advanced cultures had arisen along the coast and up in the highlands long before the coming of the Incas. Certain of these cultures dated back to perhaps a thousand or more years B.C. and some of them developed into powerfully organised States.

These pre-Inca cultures, produced some superb weaving as well as beautiful painted pottery, though their operatives never hit on the idea of the potter's wheel. They worked copper, but without learning how to harden it sufficiently to make efficient tools and weapons. Their arms and armour were much the same as those of Atahualpa's Inca troops. They built flat-topped stepped pyramids, on some of which they erected temples to their gods. Their religion embraced a number of Nature gods—deities of the sky, moon, earth and sea—ancestor worship and sacred birds, animals and plants. Their belief in a future life is evident. Like the ancient Egyptians, they preserved the bodies of the dead by mummification or other means, and placed supplies of food and other necessaries in their tombs for use in the after-life. Among the crops they raised were cotton and maize (Indian corn) and—one of America's gifts to the Old World—the potato. The llama and the alpaca were domesticated for their wool and flesh and the former also as a beast of burden. Cows were unknown to the Peruvians. Horses, too, were unknown and the sight of mounted Spaniards terrified the Peruvians.

Roadmaking was among the accomplishments of some of these forerunners of the Incas. Other tribes constructed extensive waterworks and aqueducts for irrigating their land. They were, indeed, masterly builders, both with sun-dried clay bricks (adobe) and with stone, besides being accomplished town-planners. The ruined city of Chanchan, on the coast of northern Peru, covered about eleven square miles and contained palaces and temples and numerous quadrangles of terraced houses. Some of the walls were 50 to 60 feet high and 8 to 12 feet thick at the base. The remains of another city, standing near Lake Titicaca, 1,250 feet up in the highlands, include several huge monoliths and carved stone figures; and there are portions of walls containing gigantic blocks of stone which are shaped into tenons and other joints so as to fit into each other as neatly as a cabinet-maker's woodwork. Plainly the Incas, when they arrived about A.D. 1100 or 1200, could learn a great deal from their predecessors, even though the early cultures had by then fallen into decay.

ORIGINS AND RELIGIONS

We cannot say where the Incas came from, although *they* could. They said that the first Inca, Manco Capac, and his kin issued from the Cave of Creation, wherever that may have been. The Sun-god descended to earth and announced to Manco and his brothers that they were his sons. At the same time he presented them with a golden staff and bade them found a city at the first place they should come to where they were able to make the staff sink into the ground at one blow. After lengthy wanderings their quest ended in the valley of Cuzco. Once firmly established, the Incas embarked on a series of conquests. By 1500, only twenty-odd years before the white men intervened, they had built up an empire larger than any that America had ever before known. It embraced three regions: the almost rainless coastal belt, 2,500 miles long and up to 100 miles wide, stretching from present-day Ecuador to lower Chile; the titanic range of the Andes in Peru and parts of Bolivia and Argentina; and the approaches to the tropical jungles of the Amazon basin.

The Inca religion was distinguished from that of the conquered people by the predominance it gave to Inti, the Sun-god. And it was made a real and visible concern to its followers by the presence in their midst of the very son of the god. The sovereign Inca's power and authority were absolute. All the gold and produce in the empire belonged to him, his word was law and the lives and activities of all his subjects were his to command. There is something Asiatic in such slavish subjection. It is an odious form of flattery which we associate with Mongol or Tartar despots, such as Jenghiz Khan. And this reflection is no exaggeration in the present instance. In the main, the American " Indians ", as we call them (through Columbus's colossal error in mistaking his American landfall for the neighbourhood of India), resemble the Mongolian race in their coppery skin, straight black hair, high cheek-bones and other features; and it is generally accepted that, in early times, their ancestors crossed

The sons of Inca nobles received a rigorous training.

tories ", with stone pillars and sun-dials, they noted the equinoxes and calculated the length of the solar year; but they did not succeed in compiling a complete calendar.

Those sons of the "Big Ears" who were destined for high office were put through a gruelling course of education. Besides receiving tuition similar to that received by Boy Scouts to-day, they were instructed in language, religion, history and astronomy and—what we cannot do to-day—how to read the *quipus*. These were sets of knotted cords, sometimes of various colours, which were the Incas' means of keeping records and accounts. The *quipus* appears to be their nearest approach to writing. The boys' final examinations come as rather a surprise to us. They were more like "games" than class-room work. The fourteen-year-old entrants had to run a two mile race up a steep hill. They also had to show their skill in making sandals and spears and lighting a fire by rubbing two sticks together. Those who passed the tests had their ears pierced by the Inca, who then presented them with the golden discs that made them authentic " Big Ears." Finally, they were equipped with the military arms that marked their initiation into the state of manhood.

over from Asia to North America by the Bering Strait and from there wandered down the whole continent.

THE CASTE SYSTEM

The aristocratic class who thronged the Inca's court consisted of the nobles of the royal family or clan and the favoured ones of the subject tribes. From the former were chosen all the army commanders, civil officials and priests who held office under the Inca's supreme authority. The irreverent Spaniards nicknamed the nobles " Big Ears " from the massive gold discs they wore as one of the outward signs of their rank.

Among, or in addition to, these dignitaries were the Wise Men of the realm. The priests, who formed a very influential class, were also part-time medicine-men. They practised the healing art with fearful herbal and animal remedies, and they even performed the tricky surgical operation of trepanning, that is cutting out part of the skull to relieve the hapless patient's sick brain or evict an evil demon. The astronomers studied the heavens industriously. By means of " observa-

THE WORKERS

When we come to study the position of the common people we find, among other measures, a carefully planned system of official supervision. Every tribe was required to wear its own distinctive dress and hair-style. A census of the population was regularly taken and a graded series of officials kept their eye on the masses. For every ten workers there was an overseer, for every hundred another, and so on in an ascending scale. Each worker was allotted a plot of land. But it was not his to keep. One-third of the produce went to the Inca and another one-third to the priests of the Sun-god. The farm work was hard, the principal instruments used were a hoe and a pointed wooden digging-stick. The worker had to depend on llamas to carry his loads, for he possessed no wheelbarrow, the Incas' powers of invention never rising to discovering the principle of the wheel. He was not allowed to change his occupation. It was his duty to marry and raise children for the service of the State, but he might not marry outside his own group. Neither could he move from his village at will, though he might sometimes

Left: *the* quipus (*record and message cords*); right: *an Inca numbering system.*

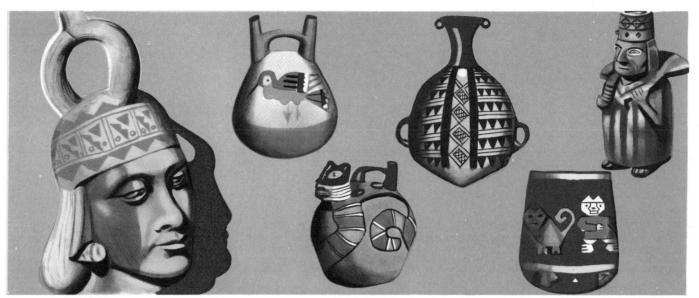

Representational figures of humans, condors and pumas decorated the pottery of ancient Peru. Inca pottery, such as the vase with the long neck and conical base, was usually geometric in design.

find himself doing so under compulsion. If, for political or economic reasons, the Inca so decreed, the overseers would ruthlessly uproot whole bodies of people from their homes and resettle them in another district.

The workers were liable for military service and for labouring on road-making and other State undertakings. Every aspect of their lives was regulated by the State and little scope was left for personal enterprise. The common man was, in fact, a mere serf. In return for his enforced labour, however, the State ensured him from want. As a serf he was valuable property and it was good policy to make him a more or less willing and passively contented subject. His chief relaxations were those he enjoyed on market and feast days. On the latter occasions he revelled in the popular singing and dancing, watched the plays that were acted, indulged himself to the full in strong drink and really made merry.

ROADS AND COMMUNICATIONS

The famous Inca roads—some of which were actually constructed in earlier times—were another of the means by which the ruler kept his finger on the pulse of the empire. One of the main roads was 3,000 miles long and, by connecting these arteries with the lesser thoroughfares, the whole country was covered with a network of communications. Rocks were tunnelled through, steep mountain slopes climbed in steps, and suspension bridges of twisted osiers flung boldly across yawning abysses. Every few miles along the principal routes relay posts were stationed. Between these stations, swift runners, the *chasqui*—blowing their conch shells as they approached—provided a rapid postal service. Military strongholds, too, were erected at strategic points. By these means the Inca was able to maintain contact with the farthest outposts of the empire, to receive early tidings of threatening plots or discontent and to set his armies marching to the centre of trouble.

Unique in character were the terrace works of the Incas and their forerunners. In various parts of the mountainous country they suffered from an insufficiency of level ground fit for cultivation, and the method by which they increased the supply is another remarkable indication of their grandiose planning and industry. They covered the lower slopes of the valleys with rows of earth-filled terraces buttressed with stone walls. Judging from their remains, the terraces must have aggregated hundreds of miles in length.

When we try to form an overall estimate of the Incas it is like examining a pupil who is brilliant in certain subjects and backward in others. The nobly descended native Poma de Ayala, as might be expected, described their rule in highly favourable terms; but a Spanish writer of the times roundly condemned it. Doubtless there is some truth in both estimates. The Incas showed their genius by creating a vast empire, with a population of perhaps 6,000,000, and organising it with the highest degree of efficiency. But they did so as a privileged class. Filled with pride of race and superiority of clan, they imposed a harsh and rigid despotism on the masses of the people. Of their other achievements, the extant remains of their mighty constructions sufficiently demonstrate their mastery in building and civil engineering. They produced superfine work, too, in weaving and pottery and in gold, silver and copper.

Their weak subjects, some of which we have already noticed, make a bold contrast with their strong ones. They had no written language, no wheeled vehicles, no coinage, and they did not learn how to smelt iron for making hard tools and weapons. They have left no great works of art behind them. Their religion, with its god-king and soothsayers and sorcerers, was a mixture of primitive superstitions.

All in all it would seem that their predominating qualities were patience and perseverance in the execution of immense designs rather than artistic or intellectual talent. We need, however, to bear in mind that their career as empire-builders was abruptly cut short by the white men, and that had they been given the time and the opportunity to develop, in all probability they would have progressed.

Those who are lucky enough to make a trip to the modern republic of Peru will find, more especially in the remote highlands, not a few living reminders of its vanished past. The Indians still speak the native language of Inca times. The women do their weaving by hand, while their men-folk cultivate the soil, including some of the early terraces, with the old digging-sticks. The loaded llamas still plod their way along the mountain tracks. The former civilisation has ebbed away, but it has left its wreckage behind in the survival of many of the customs and beliefs of its native descendants.

MICHELANGELO

Of all the world's great artists Michelangelo was undoubtedly one of the very greatest. He was a sculptor, painter, architect, and poet and had he been only one of these things he would still have been accounted great.

Michelangelo Buonarroti was born in 1475 in Tuscany, where his father was a local magistrate. When he was very young he was put in the care of a foster mother, the wife of a marble worker at the quarries of Settignano, not far from the city of Florence. His own mother died when he was six years old.

While still a boy Michelangelo determined to become an artist. His father considered such a career unworthy of a member of the Buonarroti family. They had always been state officials in positions of authority, and for this reason he was distressed at his son's choice of career.

However, Michelangelo got his way and was apprenticed to work under the guidance of two brothers named Ghirlandajo, who were famous painters in Florence. There he learnt the technique of painting on walls in fresco and on panels in tempera. He also made many drawings, a pursuit that he continued to the day of his death, always striving with pen or chalk, to give life and movement to figures.

PATRON OF THE ARTS

At that time the bronze and marble statues of ancient Greece and Rome were being eagerly collected by rich men in Italy, and as eagerly studied by Italian artists. The richest and most powerful man in Florence, Lorenzo de Medici, called " Lorenzo the Magnificent ", had a fine collection of these statues in his palace gardens, where the art students of the city, among them the young Michelangelo, were welcome to come and study.

It was there that Lorenzo saw Michelangelo at work copying the marble head of a faun. Observing how diligent and gifted the lad was, he offered him a place in his own

Michelangelo, aged sixteen, in the gardens of the Medici Palace.

Portrait of Michelangelo in the Uffizi Gallery, Florence.

household to encourage him in his studies. Michelangelo's father was so impressed by the favour shown by the great man that he readily accepted Lorenzo's offer, and no longer opposed his son's choice of a career.

So, at the age of fourteen, Michelangelo took up residence in the Medici Palace, which was then a great centre of learning and art. For the next two years, he was encouraged and befriended by the company of gifted men—writers, artists, and philosophers—whom Lorenzo had gathered into his household. No boy could have had a more stimulating and instructive experience.

Those were the times of great opportunity for artists in Italy, for kings and princes were vying with each other to persuade the most gifted painters and sculptors to work for them; but they were times of great uncertainty also, for Italy was divided into numerous warring states and invading foreign troops were on her soil.

Michelangelo's benefactor died soon after this. The French army threatened the city and the young sculptor left, first to go to Bologna, then on to Venice and back again to Bologna. Everywhere with restless energy he worked and studied.

Soon he was back in Florence. Later he went to Rome, which was then a great centre of opportunity for artists. At the age of 26 he returned to Florence.

THE " DAVID " SCULPTURE

In that city there was a great block of partly-carved marble which had been abandoned by an earlier sculptor. Since then no one had felt capable of undertaking such a very large statue, but Michelangelo was not daunted. From that block of marble he carved a seventeen-foot-high figure of the boy David. He depicted David, his sling over his shoulder, surveying his gigantic adversary, Goliath. In this heroic figure, Michelangelo expressed his own great faith and courage, his confidence and energy and high hopes for the future.

In the " David " sculpture, Michelangelo recaptured the classic nobility of Greek sculpture, which was then so much admired. In marble, Michelangelo expressed the vigour and vitality of the life of his own time; and at once he stepped into the front rank of Italian sculptors.

His fame reached the Pope (Pope Julius II), who summoned Michelangelo to Rome to design for him a splendid tomb to be set up in the new Basilica of St. Peter's. Michelangelo was compelled to change his designs for this tomb again and again, and it was completed only after forty years had elapsed—long after the death of Pope Julius. The great figure of Moses that adorns the tomb ranks with the " David " sculpture as one of Michelangelo's masterpieces.

In the year that Henry VIII was crowned king of England, Michelangelo, then thirty years old, was at work on the first of his great painting commissions, the decoration of the ceiling of the Sistine Chapel, the splendid private chapel of the popes of Rome. On its vaulted ceiling he painted, in fresco, scenes from the Old Testament—the Creation of the World, Adam and Eve, and on to the story of Noah—with many allegorical figures. There are 300 figures in all, some of them twelve feet high. These paintings made a great impression on all who saw them, and established Michelangelo's reputation as a painter.

FRESCO PAINTING

Having, as a young man, depicted the beginning of the world in these great ceiling frescoes, Michelangelo, towards the end of his life, returned to the Sistine Chapel. This time he painted on the end wall, above the altar, a large fresco of the end of the world—" The Last Judgment ". This huge fresco, measuring 48 feet by 44 feet took him seven years and was painted without assistance other than the help of one colour grinder.

The ceiling paintings executed when he was a young man expressed the hope and sure purpose of a young man; but in the later fresco, the figures appear agonised and contorted and the whole design is disquieting and turbulent.

Michelangelo's life had been full of disappointments and

Michelangelo, architect of the dome of St. Peter's in Rome.

Much of the magnificent painting of the Sistine Chapel ceiling, Michelangelo accomplished lying on his back.

frustration. Many of the great projects that he had begun he had never been allowed to complete, or only in a reduced form. He had also seen Rome sacked by the soldiers of the Emperor Charles V, and this had been a great shock to him. The effect of all this showed itself in " The Last Judgment ".

ARCHITECT AND POET

In architecture, Michelangelo's two great masterpieces are the dome, choir and transepts of St. Peter's Basilica in Rome—the largest church ever to be built—and the Medici Chapel in Florence, erected as a monument to members of the Medici family. The Medici Chapel was designed to contain the tombs of Lorenzo and Giuliano de Medici. To fill the central niches of the tombs, Michelangelo carved the seated figures of the two men and the figures reclining beneath them represent Day and Night, Dawn and Dusk.

In his architectural designs, Michelangelo used the classical Roman forms but with a new freedom and originality, just as, in his figures, he combined the classical idealisation of form with a vitality and expression of action that was his own. As a painter he worked with a sculptor's vision, giving his figures the solidity and bold modelling that he achieved in marble. As a poet, too, he seemed to be hammering words to force from them the fullness of his meaning.

THE " DIVINE " MICHELANGELO

Michelangelo never married. He lived for his work, moving from city to city constantly engaged on great projects. At the end of his life he became intensely religious, producing in his old age some of his most beautiful carvings, full of tenderness and pity. Already, during his lifetime, he was called " The Divine Michelangelo ". He had a great influence on artists of his own day and this influence has survived to the present day. Sometimes this same influence led less gifted men, who were without Michelangelo's great vigour and ardent vision, to adopt his " Grand Manner " in works which appear exaggerated, even pompous and ridiculous.

Michelangelo died in 1564 at the age of eighty-nine. The Pope wished to have him buried in Rome, but his body was secretly carried back to Florence so that his native city might have the honour of his grave.

THE BARD OF AVON

William Shakespeare was christened at the parish church of Holy Trinity, Stratford-on-Avon, on 26th April, 1564. At that time children were usually christened about three days after birth so it is generally accepted that Shakespeare was born on St. George's Day, April 23rd, 1564.

His father was John Shakespeare who carried on business as a glover and maker of fine leather goods at the house in Henley Street, Stratford, now preserved as Shakespeare's Birthplace. John Shakespeare had married Mary, the youngest daughter of Robert Arden whose family could trace their descent from before the Norman Conquest. Shortly after his marriage John Shakespeare was made a member of the Common Council which ran the affairs of Stratford as a Corporate Borough. In 1561 he became one of the two Chamberlains responsible for the borough accounts and in 1568 he was made High Bailiff, the mayor of the town, presiding at meetings of the council. Shakespeare's father remained an active member of the Stratford corporation until 1577 when he suddenly ceased to attend council meetings and sold an estate which belonged to his wife. The most likely reason for this is that the Bishop of Worcester was at that time enforcing very strictly the penalties and fines which had to be paid by all who did not attend regularly the services of the Church of England. The greater a man's position the greater fine he had to pay. John Shakespeare actually was fined £40, a very large sum in 1580, and after this he seems to have retired from public business. The council, however, kept his place unfilled until 1585 and excused him many of the taxes which council members had to pay. Obviously his fellow-councillors did not feel that John Shakespeare had disgraced himself in any way.

One of the duties of the Common Council was to maintain the old grammar school of the town. It was a good school for its master would be a graduate of one of the universities and was paid the large salary of £20 a year. The sons of many of the chief citizens naturally attended this school and it is probable that William Shakespeare did so. There he would be taught the elements of Latin grammar and would start the study of the Roman poets and historians. This is very important because his friend and fellow playwright Ben Jonson, in a poem written in Shakespeare's memory, compares him to the great Greek playwrights despite the fact that he had "small Latin, and less Greek." Many people have supposed that this means Shakespeare had not received a proper education since at that time education meant the study of Latin and Greek. But a boy who had been at Stratford grammar school would not be uneducated, although he might not win Jonson's approval since Jonson thought that a playwright should model his own plays on the classical authors.

We do not know when Shakespeare finished his education but in 1582 he married Anne Hathaway, daughter of a family friend. A daughter, Susanna, was born the next year and in 1585 Anne had twins, Hamnet and Judith. For seven years after this we have no definite information about Shakespeare until we hear of him as a dramatist in London. Many extravagant stories have been invented about this but there is only one account that can be relied upon. This is the story which John Aubrey heard from William Beeston in 1681. His father, Christopher Beeston, had at one time acted with Shakespeare. Aubrey says that according to Beeston, Shakespeare must have known Latin and Greek pretty well:

"For he had been in his younger years a Schoolmaster in the country."

A country schoolmaster who was not a graduate of a university would hardly earn enough to support Shakespeare's growing family and so it is probable that about 1584 or 1585 he went to London to seek his fortune.

1584-1594 EARLY PLAYS AND POEMS

What we know of Shakespeare's beginnings as a dramatist fits in well with this account that he had been a country schoolmaster. In a pamphlet published after his death in 1592 the dramatist Robert Greene attacks actors who let playwrights starve and especially one who imagines himself "the only Shake-scene in a country" and is actually writing his own plays. Greene's attack means that Shakespeare was already becoming known by 1592. In his pamphlet he refers to the third part of *Henry VI* so it must have been written before 1592. By this time Shakespeare had probably completed all three parts of this dramatic account of the loss of France and the Wars of the Roses and written *The Comedy of Errors* and *Titus Andronicus*. The comedy is based upon two plots of the Latin dramatist Plautus while the other is a melodramatic "tragedy of blood" developed from the Latin tragedies of Seneca. This Latin dramatic tradition would certainly have been familiar to a country schoolmaster but the way it is used in these plays marks the beginning of a great dramatic career. Plays which may also belong to this period are *Two Gentlemen of Verona*, *The Taming of the Shrew*, *Richard III* and *King John*.

In 1592 the theatres were closed in an attempt to prevent the spread of plague and owing to this disease they were not

William Shakespeare (1564-1616).

properly open again until 1594. During this time the acting companies left their theatres in London and went on tour in the provinces, acting in the yards of inns or anywhere else that was suitable. Shakespeare does not appear to have gone with them. In these years he wrote two narrative poems, *Venus and Adonis* and *The Rape of Lucrece*, based on the poetry of Ovid and designed to appeal to a courtly and educated audience. Both of these poems are dedicated to Henry Wriothesley, Earl of Southampton, and link Shakespeare to the brilliant circle of the Earls of Southampton and Essex. Some scholars think that *Love's Labour's Lost* was written and the *Sonnets* begun at this time.

1594-1599 THE LORD CHAMBERLAIN'S MEN

At this time all theatrical companies had to be under the protection of some nobleman or court official. Actors not so protected were treated as vagrants. Before the closing of the theatres in 1592, Shakespeare had been a member of the company under the protection of the Earl of Pembroke. This company had been forced to break up and in 1594, Shakespeare was with the Lord Chamberlain's Men. He was a sharer in the company, that is an actor who was not paid a salary but was entitled to a proportion of the profits. This company played at the Theatre which was owned by the father of one of their leading actors, Richard Burbage.

In 1598, Francis Meres praised Shakespeare as the great master of tragedy and comedy. At this time the greatest tragedies had not been written but 1594-1599 is the great age of comedy. *The Merchant of Venice*, *A Midsummer Night's Dream*, *The Merry Wives of Windsor*, *Much Ado about Nothing* and *As You Like It* were all written at this time. Perhaps the greatest comic creation, however, is the world of Falstaff in the two parts of *King Henry IV*. But Shakespeare does not neglect the political side of English history. *Henry IV*, *Henry V*, and *Richard II* are all studies of the use and abuse men may make of political power.

In all the plays of this period Shakespeare shows himself a master of dramatic situation. The audience is always carefully told what is going to happen next while the characters on stage are kept in ignorance. This means that Shakespeare can involve his characters in all kinds of extraordinary situations and disguises and test the strength of their love for

At the height of his fame, Shakespeare returned to Stratford, where he spent the last years of his life.

each other—for all the comedies of this period are love stories—without the audience feeling that what it is watching is simply ridiculous.

1599-1608 THE KING'S MEN AND THE GLOBE

The lease of the Theatre ran out in 1597 and the owner of the ground attempted to gain possession of the building as well. After some difficulty Burbage and his company pulled the theatre down and rebuilt it at Bankside in 1599. They also renamed it The Globe. Within a few years the company itself was to have a new name, since after the accession of James VI and I they were appointed The King's Men.

The period at the Globe is the time of the great tragedies. Shakespeare had already written one early tragedy on a Senecan model and in *Romeo and Juliet*, written about 1595, he had produced a tragedy of love to rival the comedies of the same period. At The Globe, Shakespeare wrote one comedy in the old style, *Twelfth Night* (1601), but his main

The ghost of the king of Denmark reveals the truth about his death to his son, Hamlet.

119

The balcony scene from Romeo and Juliet, *one of Shakespeare's greatest tragedy plays.*

interest was tragedy. These follow each other in quick succession, *Julius Caesar* (1599), *Hamlet* (1600), *Othello* (1602), *King Lear* (1605), *Macbeth* (1606), *Antony and Cleopatra* (1607) and *Coriolanus* (1608). *Timon of Athens* probably also belongs to this time but it is not finished in the same way as the other tragedies.

In his tragedies Shakespeare makes full use of the sense of dramatic situation developed in the comedies. But here it is used to create a position in which it seems impossible for men and women to be faithful and honest. Those who attempt it involve themselves and others in terrible destruction. But these plays are not about death and destruction, they are about the courage and devotion which forces men and women to do what they believe to be right, despite all danger. Even Macbeth destroys himself, not only because he was ambitious, but also because he had a conscience. The end of a tragedy does not bring despair but a sense of triumph.

This sense of triumph, of victory in defeat, is much more difficult to achieve in comedy. For this reason two comedies *Measure for Measure* and *All's Well that Ends Well*, have been called "dark comedies" because they do not give the audience the same assurance as the early comedies that all really is well. *Troilus and Cressida*, a play probably written for private performance, is also a problem play.

These problems were solved in the last series of comedies which Shakespeare wrote after his company had taken over the lease of the Blackfriars theatre, a covered hall which could be used in all weathers and gave more opportunity for music and dancing in plays. In these comedies, *Cymbeline*, *The Winter's Tale* and *The Tempest*, the courage of the characters is submitted to the test of tragedy but their choice this time does not involve their own destruction.

On 29th June, 1613, *Henry VIII*, Shakespeare's last play, was presented at The Globe. Unfortunately, one of the cannons being used, set fire to the thatch and the theatre was burned to the ground. It was later rebuilt but by this time Shakespeare had retired from the stage to the house, "New Place", which he had bought for himself at Stratford. He died there on 23rd April, 1616, and was buried in the church of Holy Trinity. In his will he left to his wife, "my second best bed with the furniture." This phrase has caused a great deal of misunderstanding but the "best bed" would have been the one reserved for guests. The second best was the bed he had shared with his wife and was his last gesture of affection to Anne.

Some of the plays had appeared in print during Shakespeare's life-time but the actor companies were not anxious to publish their plays as they were not protected by any law of copyright. Consequently once a play was printed anyone could perform it. Also they thought that if people could read the plays they might not bother to come to the theatre. Occasionally booksellers persuaded poor actors to put together a version of the play made up of what they could remember and published these "bad" versions. The company might then feel compelled to replace these bad versions of the play by a good one. In 1623, however, two of Shakespeare's fellow actors collected his plays and issued them in a book now called the First Folio. To this great service they added the best advice that can be given to the student of Shakespeare: "Read him, therefore; and again, and again."

Macbeth and Banquo returning victorious from the battle are confronted by three witches.

In the seventeenth century, the Symphony Orchestra as we know it to-day came into being. The "infant" orchestra was the one which accompanied the earliest operas. The first of these was Monteverdi's *Orfeo*, written in 1607, and a band including both violins and viols, accompanied the the singers. Louis XIII's famous orchestra, founded in 1626, consisted of the "Vingtquatre Violons du Roi". Later, this was copied by the English King, Charles II. Berlioz (1803-1869) contributed greatly towards the development of the larger orchestra. He was an acknowledged master of orchestration, writing for his instruments with great skill.

To-day, a Symphony Orchestra will have from sixty to more than a hundred players. These are divided into the four families already met: strings, brass, woodwind and percussion.

STRINGED INSTRUMENTS

The violin came into being as a result of many experiments, and descended from various earlier instruments played with bows. At first it accompanied voices or dancing. During the sixteenth, seventeenth and eighteenth centuries, makers in Cremona in Italy brought the violin to a standard of perfection which has not been surpassed. To this day, the violins and 'cellos of such makers as Stradivarius are valued treasures and are played by the world's most gifted soloists.

The violin with its more brilliant tone finally ousted the viol. Public performance demanded more volume of sound from stringed instruments and the family of violin, viola, 'cello and double bass established themselves. To-day's violin is about fourteen inches long and has four strings, tightened for tuning by pegs. The viola is larger, and similar in shape; its four strings are tuned a fifth lower, and the tone is mellower. The violoncello, usually called 'cello, rests on a tail pin, as the player sits down to play. The double bass is over six feet high, and the player stands beside it. In jazz, the sound of its strings plucked by the fingers (*pizzicato*), has been particularly popular.

During the eighteenth century, the perfected violin family inspired the String Quartets, by Mozart (1756-1791), Haydn (1732-1809), then later, Beethoven (1770-1827). In these, two violins, viola and 'cello meet in classical balance and beauty. This small scale music is called chamber music. The string quartet of instruments forms the basis of the orchestra, with the violin as "crown prince" and leader.

The modern harp has a large frame at which the player sits, using his hands to play the strings and his feet to control the seven pedals. The pedals alter the pitch of the notes by shortening the strings' sounding length.

To-day's popular music has given special prominence to the guitar, which has long appealed to amateurs because it is reasonably easy to play. Popular to-day are electric guitars which make use of amplifiers to give greater volume of sound when played with other instruments in small groups. The Spaniard, Segovia, has done a great deal to demonstrate the potentialities of the instrument. Singers who accompany themselves on the guitar may not realise that they are following Schubert (1797-1828) who used to try out his songs with a guitar.

PERCUSSION

Percussion bands, a popular feature of early school life have made most children familiar with these instruments. They include the drum, triangle, tambourine, clappers and cymbals.

Modern Latin American dances such as rumbas and sambas make considerable use of the rhythmic effects of such percussion instruments as maracas (rattles), guiros (scrapers), and claves (percussion sticks). In the Symphony Orchestra, the assortment of instruments, ranging from a big bass drum to tiny castanets making up the percussion section, is nicknamed the "kitchen".

As well as the noise makers already mentioned, there are tuned instruments, which have a definite pitch. You may have seen the kettledrum player tapping his drum, then tuning it by tightening the skin with screws. Usually, three of these rounded, flat-topped drums set on small feet are found in an orchestra. They are descended from the regimental kettledrums, still played to-day by the Queen's Household Cavalry.

Chimes are metal tubes of varying lengths hung within a wooden frame, and tapped with a hammer to produce a bell-like noise. Ordinary hand bells may also be used in an orchestra.

A glockenspiel is a set of steel bars played with small hammers, which produce a ringing sound, as does the xylophone from its hard wooden bars.

WIND INSTRUMENTS: BRASS

In a modern Symphony Orchestra you will find trumpets, trombones, horns and tubas.

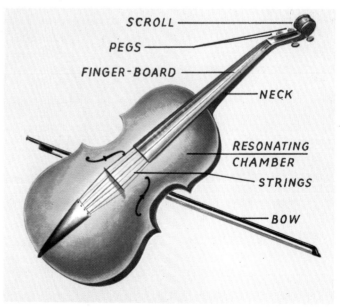

SCROLL
PEGS
FINGER-BOARD
NECK
RESONATING CHAMBER
STRINGS
BOW

An artist's impression of a violin made by Stradivarius.

During the seventeenth and eighteenth centuries, trumpets were called "natural" or simple, and played only in the key which corresponded to the length of their tubes. A typical mid-seventeenth-century one had nearly seven feet of brass or silver tubing, folded in one loop. Additional lengths, or "crooks", were added until, in the nineteenth century, after many experiments, a valve trumpet was perfected. Three pistons pressed down by the fingers could open up extra loops of tube to add to the column of air in the main trumpet.

Orchestras may have two tenor trombones, and one bass one. In these instruments, the loop is made into a slide so that the player "chooses" his pitch by adjusting the telescopic mouthpiece.

About 1705, the modern horn as we know it to-day was developed from the hunting horn. Skilled breath control is needed to play this instrument, which has about eleven feet of tubing, starting at about a quarter of an inch wide at the funnel-shaped mouthpiece, and widening out to a bell from eleven to fourteen inches in diameter.

The tuba was introduced in the nineteenth century, and is a deep-toned instrument with a cupped mouthpiece and valves.

The bugle is a treble instrument of brass or copper, best known for its military use, as in sounding "The Last Post".

WOODWIND

The full woodwind group in a Symphony Orchestra will include in order of pitch: piccolo, flute and alto flute, oboe, cor anglais, clarinet and bass clarinet, bassoon and double bassoon.

The piccolo is a smaller flute, sounding an octave higher than the transverse flute. This name is given to the modern flautist's instrument, because he holds it sideways, blowing across an elliptical mouth-hole placed near the closed end of the tube. He alters the pitch of the note sounded by opening and shutting holes which are covered by finger keys.

The oboe, cor anglais and bassoon are one family, each having a conical tube and double reeds. These reeds are flexible blades of cane set into the mouthpiece, secured at one end, but free to vibrate to the air pressure from the player's lips at the other end. The oboe is highest in pitch; the cor anglais sounds a fifth lower. We do not know how this odd

and confusing name, meaning "English horn", came into being. The bassoon is a bass instrument and has a U-shaped mouthpiece.

The clarinet seems to have a silkier, less woody quality of tone than the other three, and has one reed attached to the mouthpiece. The modern version was invented at the beginning of the eighteenth century.

The saxophone is rather a mongrel, because it is conical and made of brass, and has a mouthpiece like a clarinet, with one reed, six finger plates and other holes controlled by keys. It is most popular in jazz and dance bands, and was invented by Sax, in about 1840.

A globular flute, the ocarina is now found as a musical toy. There also are shrill panpipes in plastic and inexpensive wooden recorders.

The harmonica or mouth-organ is associated with amateur playing, the tiny box being cupped in the player's hand. It has metal reeds which are fitted into slots in a short metal plate and placed in a narrow box. The expert uses his tongue to cover holes which are not required, as he blows and sucks in. The brilliant playing of Larry Adler has inspired Vaughan Williams to write a Concerto for the harmonica. Popular music has used the reedy tones effectively over guitars.

ORGAN

By the seventeenth and eighteenth centuries, it was common practice for larger organs to have "speaking" pedals for the feet to sound notes. In Bach's day (1685-1750), a typical organ would have two keyboards or manuals, and a series of knobs, called stops, at each side. These controlled the particular set of pipes being used. Bach is generally considered to be the greatest composer for the organ. To-day, an organist may play his music on a restored eighteenth-century organ with high piercing tone, or on a modern organ. In this, the wind is obtained from an electrically driven fan, replacing the earlier, hand-pumped bellows. A huge organ may have as many as eight hundred stops, which give it a tremendous range of tones, so that it can imitate many other instruments.

KEYBOARD INSTRUMENTS

The harpsichord, virginal, spinet and clavichord main-

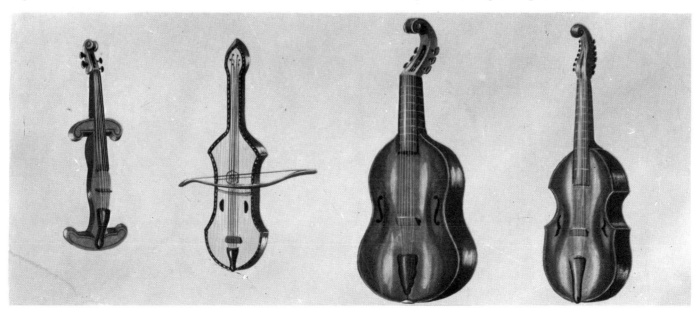

Left to right: *a viola, a sixteenth-century viol, a bass viol and a treble viol.*

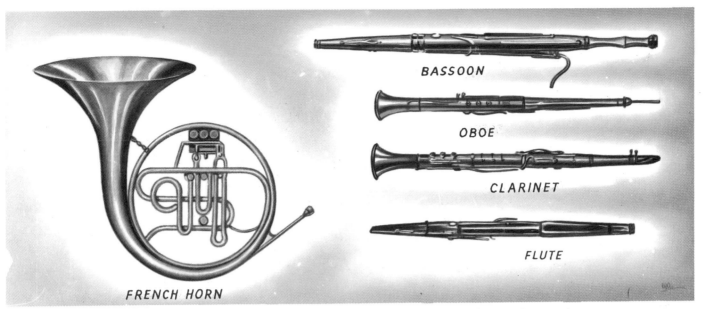

These brass and woodwind instruments form part of the wind section of a symphony orchestra.

tained their popularity until the end of the eighteenth century. During the seventeenth and eighteenth centuries, one of this group would play the *continuo*, a supporting accompaniment to orchestral and sung music. It was frequently played by the composer, who directed the performance from his keyboard.

The first piano as we know it was invented in about 1709, by an Italian, Cristofori. Its full name was pianoforte, meaning " soft and loud ", though in England it was at first called fortepiano. The piano followed the ancient dulcimer and the clavichord in type, for the hammers struck the strings. When the player pressed down the key, the hammer connected to the key struck the string, then returned to its place. The string vibrated until the player let the key up, then pads or dampers fell on to the string and stopped the sound.

The first advantage was that players could now play softly or loudly. By the 1770s, Mozart had begun to write for the piano.

From the 1760s, many square pianos began to be made in England. The name is confusing, because these small pianos were oblong in shape.

From about the middle of the eighteenth century, upright pianos, such as we see to-day, were made. In these the strings are vertical. In time, the piano superseded the harpsichord family, which needed more frequent tuning and maintenance.

Sometimes the celeste, a little keyboard instrument invented in 1886, appears among the percussion. Its keys work hammers which strike steel plates attached to wooden resonators, producing an echoing tinkle.

INSTRUMENTS IN THE TWENTIETH CENTURY

During this century, there have been two distinct developments which affect musical instruments. One is a revival of interest in old music and its instruments; the other development concerns experiments with electronic instruments.

Arnold Dolmetsch, who died in 1940, collected old, forgotten harpsichords and restored them so that he could play old music as the composers had intended, and as they had heard it. Scholars made thorough investigations in order that authentic period performances could be given. Interest

grew, and Dolmetsch and others made copies of old instruments. This literally gave to old instruments a new lease of life, and Stravinsky, for instance, has used the harpsichord in *The Rake's Progress*. Modern mechanisms have made them easier to maintain.

Recording has made it possible for the sound of fragile ancient instruments to be retained permanently for reference. Also it has brought instrumental music into millions of homes where people can see and hear the greatest soloists.

Electronic music is frequently used for sound effects,when it helps to create atmosphere. Sometimes tape-recordings of electrically produced sounds have been combined with the music of traditional instruments. These experiments often include new groupings of instruments.

Looking ahead, it is clear that the use of pre-recorded sounds is in its experimental infancy. But it is safe to guess that there will always be a demand for the live production of beautiful sound, an attempt by musicians to create afresh what a composer first heard in his imagination.

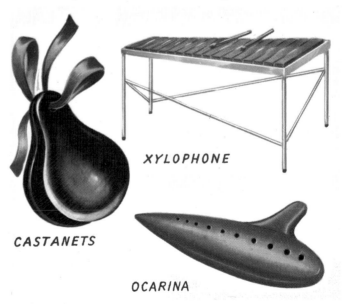

The instruments pictured above are rather specialised. The xylophone has been developed comparatively recently.

REMBRANDT

Rembrandt van Rijn was born of middle-class parents, in Leyden, in 1606. At the age of fourteen, following his parents' wishes, he enrolled as a student in the University of Leyden. After a short time, his parents, realising how unsuitable he was for an academic education, apprenticed him to an artist in Leyden. This apprenticeship lasted three years, during which he reached a standard that encouraged his father to send him to Amsterdam to study under Peter Lastman. According to all existing accounts, Rembrandt stayed only for a short time with this master, before deciding to study on his own.

PORTRAIT PAINTING

During the years 1623-31, little is known of his life, apart from the fact that he returned home and lived with his parents. The paintings that date from this period are mainly compositions of biblical subjects and portraits. It is evident from the number of commissioned portraits as opposed to the self-portraits and portraits of his family, that he soon established himself as a portrait painter. It is also evident that he still had connections in Amsterdam for he painted several portraits of notable merchants of that city. The enormous output of drawings and etchings of this time relate not only to his paintings but also to the visual world around him. The Thirty Years' War coincided with this period of his life, and the large numbers of beggars, cripples, and disbanded mercenaries tramping the roads of Holland were a continual source of inspiration to him.

Rembrandt was soon to realise the limitations of painting in Leyden, and in 1631 he moved to Amsterdam. There was a brisk demand for portrait painting there and Rembrandt could live quite comfortably on the commissions he received from the rich merchants. Trade guilds, each of them with their

In Amsterdam, Rembrandt shared a studio with Jan Lievens.

own Guild hall, commissioned group portraits of their members to hang on the walls of the halls. This type of commission was usually competitive and only the better-known artists obtained them. Also in Amsterdam, Rembrandt came into contact with the works of the greatest artists in Europe, both past and present. The influence of these works and the financial opportunities available, provided the stimuli he needed, and in a comparatively short time he became one of the most popular portrait painters in the city.

The immediate result of this was the important commission he received from the medical faculty of the University of Amsterdam. The result of the commission was " The Anatomy Lesson ", Rembrandt's most important painting to date. It shows a professor of the faculty, Doctor Tulip, demonstrating a particular aspect of surgery to his assistants. Rembrandt's commissioned paintings faithfully portray the sombre character and bearing of each sitter, and are in the direct tradition of Dutch painting. In contrast to this, his self-portraits and non-commissioned works show a preference for bright colours. His sitters wear gay clothes and Rembrandt, himself, adopts fancy dress for his self-portraits. It is these paintings which are an indication of the way Rembrandt's art was destined to go.

MARRIAGE TO SASKIA

One sitter who posed for her portrait was Saskia van Uylenburch, later to become his wife. Saskia, a rich orphan, married Rembrandt in 1634, against the wishes of her guardian. With money at his disposal, other than the income he received from painting and teaching, Rembrandt could now afford to live and paint as he wished. Always interested in the art of the past, he now collected all manner of paintings and sculpture, together with rare Oriental draperies. These he displayed in lavish fashion in a large

Rembrandt was one of the greatest representatives of seventeenth-century Dutch painters. His output was prodigious and there remain to-day about 600 paintings, 2,000 drawings and 300 etchings. These include many landscapes and portraits.

Rembrandt van Rijn, a self-portrait, in the Pitti Gallery in Florence.

house he had purchased in the Jewish quarter of Amsterdam. The gaily-coloured turbans of the Jews and the gleaming fabrics of the Jewesses, provided the colour which his life and art demanded.

For the six years following his marriage, Rembrandt's paintings moved increasingly away from the accepted painting of the time. From this period date his glowing portraits of Saskia and his rich paintings of religious subjects; a typical example being the " Reconciliation of David and Absalom " in the Hermitage collection.

MISFORTUNES ACCUMULATE

In 1641, Saskia, who for several years had suffered from ill health, died, leaving Rembrandt the father of a small son, Titus. Further misfortune was to follow. For several years his portrait commissions had been steadily declining and, finally, in 1642 his painting, " The Night Watch " met with complete disapproval. It had been commissioned for an Amsterdam military company, but instead of being hung on the principal wall of the company's headquarters, it was cut down in size and hung on a side wall where it could hardly be seen. Completely out of popular favour through his indifference to the demands of his time, Rembrandt turned his back on society and withdrew into the refuge of his home.

The effect of Saskia's death and the loneliness and solitude in which he now found himself, resulted in a marked change in his work. His paintings still retained their bright colour, but the gaiety is replaced by a more subdued, tender quality. In his drawings, etchings and paintings of biblical subjects, the splendour and romance of the Old Testament is replaced by the more tender stories of the New Testament. Probably no artist has ever conveyed with so much feeling the life of Christ. At this time he started working on a series of drawings, etchings and landscape paintings. These landscapes are some of the most visually accurate accounts of the beauty of nature ever recorded. It is from these works that the great tradition of Dutch landscape-painting stems.

FINANCIAL DIFFICULTIES

From 1642 onwards, Rembrandt's domestic problems

The devoted and loyal servant of Rembrandt, Hendrickje Stoffels, lived with the painter and cared for him and his children. The beautiful portrait of the "Lady" in the Salon Carré of the Louvre and the "Venus and Child" in the same gallery may represent Hendrickje and her child.

became increasingly more difficult. Under the terms of Saskia's will, Rembrandt benefited only for as long as he remained unmarried. In 1649, the nurse he had engaged to look after Titus left his service, but by the ruling of the Courts he was ordered to pay her an allowance. Prior to her leaving, a new servant had entered his household, Hendrickje Stoffels. The attachment of Rembrandt to this young girl aroused a lot of ill-feeling and criticism. Financially dependent on Saskia's will, he could never afford to marry. So, Hendrickje Stoffels lived with him and, in 1654, after the birth of their second child, she was expelled from the Reform Church. Nevertheless, this country girl of peasant origin showed a loyalty and devotion to Rembrandt which was never to diminish in the difficult years ahead. Hendrickje appears in many of Rembrandt's paintings and drawings, usually as the principal figure in the large compositions of biblical subjects, such as " Susanna and the Elders " and " Bathsheba at her Toilet "; she is also the model for " A Woman Bathing " which is in the National Gallery in London.

Rembrandt's misfortunes continued. His financial position, always precarious, finally collapsed and in 1656 he was declared bankrupt. Always a lavish spender, he had refused to acknowledge the fact that his inheritance was slowly dwindling away. He had continued to spend extravagantly on antiques, rare prints, jewellery, and paintings by the Italian masters. The house and his collection were put up for sale, the proceeds passing to his creditors.

Virtually cast out on to the streets, Rembrandt lived for practically three years in obscure hostelries where he was unknown. Somehow he managed to continue painting. The magnificent portraits of Hendrickje and Titus testify to the fact that now only death could stop him painting. Despite cramped living conditions, he still managed to paint large compositions, and far from diminishing, his stature seems to increase picture by picture.

In the meantime, Hendrickje and Titus were trying to find some sort of means to support themselves and Titus went round, from house to house, trying to sell Rembrandt's etchings. Hendrickje became an art dealer and opened a small business, where she displayed his paintings and drawings. The combined efforts of these devotees enabled Rembrandt to have the money he required for materials. In 1660, they re-established themselves in a house in the Rosengracht, an area conspicuous only for its poverty. Instead of the richly-furnished rooms of his previous abode, he now worked in the cold, bare rooms which characterised this quarter. His daily diet is said to have consisted of bread, pickled herrings and cheese.

BEGINNING OF THE END

In 1661 and 1662, he was given the two most important commissions of his life, solely through the influence of two of the few friends he possessed. These commissions, the " Syndics of the Clothmakers Guild " and " The Conspiracy of the Batavians ", are the crowning achievement of Rembrandt's commissioned works. The completion of these works and the death of Hendrickje in the same year mark the beginning of the final phase of Rembrandt's life.

Once again on his own, Rembrandt continued to produce works of penetrating beauty. It is only in the self-portraits that his physical decline is apparent. This decline, hastened by his addiction to alcohol, resulted in his death in 1664, one year after the death of Titus.

JOHANN SEBASTIAN BACH

The Bachs were the largest and most prolific of all the great German musical families. They lived in the Thuringian province of Germany from the early sixteenth century onwards. For more than a hundred years before the birth of their greatest member, they followed their profession of music in their homeland. Later on, when the great Bach himself moved farther afield in Germany, and his gifted sons ranged all over Europe, the family's exclusive connection with Thuringia was broken. But well into the nineteenth century, various Bachs were in the habit of returning to their original soil for reunions, although the musical fame of the family passed away with the death of J. S. Bach's son, Carl Philipp Emmanuel. The Bachs were a remarkable family, not only in their musical talents, but no less in their moral character, their religious devotion and the unostentatious simplicity of their personal and domestic lives. In every respect Johann Sebastian Bach was typical of them, except that the overwhelming power of his genius was far ahead of anything the musical Bachs had known before, or were to know again.

J. S. Bach was born in March, 1685—the same year in which his great contemporary, Handel, was born less than a month later—at the pleasant town of Eisenach. His father, Johann Ambrosius Bach, his elder brother, and all his many relations were practising musicians; so there was little doubt that the newcomer would adopt the same profession. And indeed, Sebastian Bach showed considerable interest in and talent for music from the beginning. But there was nothing of the infant prodigy about him. He developed slowly but surely, both as man and musician, although it was not long before the real nature of his gifts began to show themselves.

HIS EARLY STRUGGLES

Bach was not quite ten years old when, within a few months of each other, first his mother and then his father died. The double tragedy disrupted the family. Young Sebastian, together with his brother Jakob, three years his senior, went to live in Ohrdruf with their recently-married eldest brother, Johann Christoph. Sebastian had already received instruction from his father on playing the violin and viola, and had attended the Gymnasium at Eisenach for his religious and general education. After the move he went to the Ohrdruf Lyceum, where he showed himself an excellent pupil. Johann Christoph, himself an experienced organist, gave him systematic lessons on the clavier. But the elder brother appears to have been of a jealous and harshly authoritarian disposition; when the young Sebastian began to show unusual talent and strong independence of mind, he tried to apply an unnecessary curb.

In the household library was a collection of manuscripts of the music of the famous composers of the period. These young Sebastian wished to study. He was forbidden to do so. They were kept in a cupboard behind locked, latticed doors and the key was withheld from him. But Bach was never to be frustrated in his ambitions. He had a passion for learning from other people, a passion which stayed alive in him for the rest of his life. So, with infinite care, when the rest of the

household was asleep, he managed to extricate some of these precious documents and copy them out in his small bedroom by moonlight, candles being unavailable to him in that frugal establishment. For six months he worked thus; then his activity was discovered, and his precious copies were confiscated. It was a mean and stupid thing to do; but although Sebastian lost the results of his labours, nothing could take away what he had learnt from them. More serious was the way in which the necessity of working in inadequate light, both in making his copies of other people's compositions and in writing down his own, began that weakening of his eyesight which was to affect him for the rest of his life and which finally ended in the blindness of his last years.

Bach's subsequent life is not remarkable for colourful adventures or dramatic conflicts. It is largely the story of his official appointments, enlivened now and again by disputes with unimaginative employers, of his steadfast devotion to his calling and to the Lutheran Church, and of his contented domestic life. In Bach's day musicians did not usually compose for themselves. They were servants and served their masters loyally. All his life Bach worked in the service of various courts or municipalities. Much of his greatest music was written for a specific purpose, or to advance his claim when seeking some new appointment.

THE INFLUENCE OF BÖHM

When he left his brother's house, Bach was fifteen years old. He secured a place in the St. Michael's Church at Lüneburg, where he stayed for three years. Here he had unrestricted access to a large library of music. Also at Lüneburg, at another church, was the great German organist, Georg Böhm, who was to have a great influence on his subsequent mastery of the organ, a mastery for which he was more than anything else famous during his lifetime.

Working for six months by moonlight only, young Bach copied out a collection of manuscripts by famous composers, which were cruelly taken from him by his brother.

Poor and unknown, Bach walked many miles to hear the great organists of his time.

During these years, probably at Böhm's suggestion, Bach made several journeys to hear the great organists of the day, including trips to Hamburg where Johann Adam Reinken, Böhm's own teacher, lived. Poor and unknown, Bach walked many long miles on these expeditions. Once, on the road to Hamburg, tired and hungry, he stopped outside an inn. The smell of cooking food was tantalising, but he had no money. Suddenly, someone threw two fishheads out of a window. Not much, but something for a hungry lad. Bach stooped to pick them up. Imagine his surprise and delight when he found inside each head a coin. Bach had his meal, and continued his journey much refreshed.

TROUBLES AT ARNSTADT

From Lüneburg, Bach went briefly to join the orchestra of the Grand Duke Johann Ernst of Weimar. But he did not stay long. The post of organist at the town of Arnstadt, where a new organ had been installed, was open and he secured it. It was the first time in his life that he had an independent appointment, and an organ of his own. At Arnstadt, Bach began to show his exceptional powers as an organist and composer of organ music. But his musical mind was too adventurous for his new employers and the congregation of the church. There were complaints that his playing was " extravagant " and " impious ". An immediate crisis was avoided when the famous Swedish organist and composer, Dietrich Buxtehude, appeared at Lübeck, and Bach, after securing the services of his cousin Johann Ernst as his deputy, was given a month's leave to go there. He went —and he stayed for four months instead of one. How he got to Lübeck, which is three hundred miles from Arnstadt, is not known for certain. Probably, it was by his usual combination of walking and hitch-hiking. Anyway, the Lübeck visit was of immense value and importance to Bach. It had a decisive influence on his subsequent work.

MARRIAGE

When he returned to Arnstadt, he naturally found himself in trouble with the authorities. He stood his ground, and was not sacked, as many of the town officials wished. But he soon became tired of all the quarrelling and before long he left Arnstadt to take up a position at Mühlhausen in his native Thuringia. The town had recently been ravaged by a great fire and was a pretty desolate place. But Bach soon settled in and, almost at once, he was married to his second cousin Maria Barbara, whom he had first met at Arnstadt. If he had wished, Bach could have succeeded Buxtehude at Lübeck. But as well as Buxtehude's job, Bach would also have been required to take Buxtehude's daughter in marriage. He did not find the lady sufficiently attractive (probably he was already enamoured of Barbara), so he turned it down. Handel had also rejected the same proposition shortly before.

Bach did not stay at Mühlhausen as long as he expected. In 1708, he returned to Weimar as organist to the court of Duke Wilhelm Ernst, and remained there for nine years. In 1717, having to his great disappointment been passed over for the post of Kapellmeister (or director of music) in favour of someone inferior, he accepted an appointment with Prince Leopold at Cöthen. Bach was on good terms with his young

Johann Sebastian Bach and his family were gifted musicians and his sons carried on the musical tradition. Bach loved his family deeply and delighted in their private musical evenings.

Bach and his second wife, Anna Wulken and their children.

prince. At Weimar he had composed many of his great organ works. At Cöthen there was no call for religious music of any kind as the court adhered to the Reformed Church. Bach was in charge of the orchestra: consequently nearly all his music of this period was orchestral and instrumental. From it come the Brandenburg Concertos, the orchestral Suites, the clavier and violin concertos and the sonatas for various instruments.

BEREAVEMENT

In 1720, three years before he left Cöthen to take up his position at Leipzig, where he was to stay for the rest of his life, Barbara Bach died suddenly while her husband was away on a trip with his employer. Bach's grief was profound, and perhaps some of it is expressed in the six sonatas for violin and clavier which he wrote about this time. There were seven children of the marriage. Two years later, Bach was married again, this time to Anna Magdalena Wulken, whose name is inscribed on the " Little Book " of small pieces which she and her husband played and sang together, and who bore him a further thirteen children.

Refusing a job as organist at Hamburg, Bach was appointed Cantor of St. Thomas's, Leipzig, in 1723. Here he stayed until his death in 1750, working hard and composing among other things, that great series of Cantatas, Passions and various church music which is so important to any final understanding of his genius. Bach had written much church music before this, but the Leipzig works are the products of his highest and most mature genius in this field. His relationship with his employers was, again, not always easy. His reputation was by now great all over Germany, but he suffered all manner of hindrances and annoyances. In 1730, Bach seriously considered leaving Leipzig and finding more congenial employment. However, he changed his mind after he had been given the title of Court Composer of Saxony. This title carried considerable weight of reputation but little else. His life became easier and remained so until he died.

From Leipzig, Bach made several journeys to other parts of Germany. The most memorable was his last when, in 1747, he paid his famous visit to Frederick the Great at Potsdam. His son, Carl Philipp Emmanuel, was already in the employ of the Prussian Court, and Bach went to Berlin in the first place to see his newly born and first grandson. Frederick the Great was a music lover and an accomplished flute player. The king and his orchestra were preparing to make music, when a note was handed in and, at once, Frederick, the most powerful monarch in Europe, exclaimed with obvious pleasure: " Gentlemen, Old Bach is here ".

The visit was an immense success. Bach played on the king's collection of harpsichords and improvised so brilliantly on a theme his royal host gave him that everyone was delighted and " Old Bach " made an honoured guest. After he returned home, Bach used that theme for one of his last and greatest instrumental works, *The Musical Offering*.

In order to understand fully the genius of Bach, it is necessary to recognise two things—his lifelong devotion to and mastery of the organ and his profoundly creative response to the requirements and innermost meaning of the Lutheran liturgy. In his organ music—the great Preludes, the Toccatas, the Fugues and in the meditative Chorale Preludes—and in the Passions and cantatas which he wrote for every occasion in the church calendar, is to be found the true heart, soul and spirit of Sebastian Bach. That is not to say that the Brandenburg Concertos and the other popular orchestral and instrumental works are not great masterpieces. They are. But outside the church and the organ loft only part of Bach lives.

It is difficult for us to imagine how, for a hundred years after his death, the genius of Bach lay more or less unrecognised. When he died he was honoured as a great master of the organ and as a hard working cantor. But the universal nature of his genius and its key position in the history of music had to wait until Mendelssohn and others rediscovered it in the middle of the nineteenth century. The great *St. Matthew Passion* lay unheard until Mendelssohn performed it. A few individual musicians knew Bach's worth, but by the time he died the art of music had taken a new direction and it was his sons, especially Carl Philipp Emmanuel, Wilhelm Friedmann and Johann Christian, all gifted musicians who worked in the new styles, who had the public ear. They, themselves, though honouring their father's memory, tended to regard him as a rather old-fashioned fellow. We know better to-day. Music without Bach would be unthinkable. Schumann's words that music owes as much to Bach as Christianity owes to its founder, are hardly an exaggeration.

GOYA Y LUCIENTES

Goya was one of Spain's greatest painters and one of the world's greatest satirists, holding up to derision all the stupidity and wickedness of his times.

Francisco José de Goya y Lucientes, to give him his full name, was born in 1746 in Fuendetodos in Northern Spain. Little is known about his early days. While he was quite small his father was working as a gilder in nearby Saragossa, and he himself was apprenticed at the age of fourteen to a mediocre painter named Luzan, who seems, however, to have given his pupil a good grounding in his craft. Later Goya studied in Madrid and in Italy, returning to Saragossa when he was 25.

He was employed for a time in Saragossa painting frescoes in some of the churches there, which he did in the then very popular rococo style. Two years later he was back in Madrid once more, where he married Josefa, the sister of Francisco Bayeu, one of the leading artists of the time, who had befriended Goya as a student. Another influential friend was the painter Mengs, who obtained for him a commission to design a series of tapestries for the Prince of Asturias.

TAPESTRY DESIGNER

Goya was then 30. During the next four years, he produced thirty coloured cartoons from which the tapestry weavers were to work. They were mostly gay, light-hearted scenes of everyday life in Spain, quite dissimilar in character and subject to the work he was to produce later, though here and there we see hints of drama and fantasy which give a foretaste of the true Goya to come.

From about this time we can follow Goya's steady progress as a portrait painter to his full development at about the age of fifty. He usually had to paint quickly and some of his portraits were executed without enthusiasm and solely for money; these were often dull pictures. When some quality in

Goya serving his apprenticeship with Luzan.

the sitter intrigued him, Goya could put the sitter's personality on to canvas with uncanny forcefulness.

COURT PAINTER

Goya had the gift of reading character in a face. Every trace of cruelty, meanness or cowardice that most of us would miss was clear to him, and he acquired a skill in painting that enabled him to convey these qualities to us with equal clarity. He was fearless and independent himself, and disdained to flatter even his most influential sitters. When, in time, he became an official court painter, he portrayed his royal patrons with equal candour. He showed us King Charles IV of Spain as the kindly, complaisant, rather stupid man he was, and Queen Maria Louisa as the gaunt, overbearing dictator of her own family, and the country.

No one escaped the penetrating eye of the painter. When you consider his famous " Family of Charles IV ", in which he portrayed the whole royal family on one large canvas, his skill in portrait painting seems well-nigh miraculous.

Goya certainly had a poor opinion of humanity in general, an opinion which he did not disguise in many of his portraits. But, sometimes, the sincerity or the pathos of the sitter's face moved him. On these occasions he gave us portraits seldom equalled in tenderness or dignity. We see this in the wistful face believed to be that of his own wife, " Josefa Bayeu de Goya ", and the " Dr. Peron " in the National Gallery.

When Goya was 46 he had a very serious illness and for a time he was near to death. Eventually he regained his strength but was left completely deaf. For one with his aggressive vitality, the loneliness of utter silence was, at first, unbearable. However, from the time of this affliction, his true character unfolded and his work gained a richness hitherto only hinted at.

NEW TECHNIQUES

While he was still too weak to paint he took up etching,

Francisco Goya y Lucientes (1746-1828), Director of the Spanish Academy of Art and court painter.

and finally discovered a method of combining the techniques of etching and aquatint to produce an effect similar to wash drawings. From that time on he produced many prints which have gained him as much renown as have his paintings.

Bullfights provided subjects for one series of these prints. Danger, courage and death fascinated him. The small figures of man and bull, so different, yet equal, confronting each other in the great arena, gave endless scope for vivid, dramatic aquatints.

Another series of prints, 80 in all, is called "Los Caprichos" (Caprices or Caricatures). These prints portray Spanish life in its most dramatic and bizarre aspects. All the evils and follies of the times are depicted vividly and candidly. In these prints, every cruelty and depravity is derided and condemned unsparingly. Witchcraft, corruption and superstition are repeated themes, and often a haunting, nightmare quality is achieved.

The same mood is echoed also in some of the paintings. In the "Madhouse", he depicts vividly the horrors of a lunatic asylum of those days. In the "Colossus" a vast, nude giant, as big as a cloud, strides across the land, striking panic into men and animals alike. In such canvases Goya gives a foretaste of the Surrealist paintings of recent times.

In 1808, the French army invaded Spain, and war at once stimulated Goya to comment. Two pictures—" The Charge of the Mamelukes; the 2nd of May " and " The Execution of the Defenders of Madrid; the 3rd of May "—show the Spanish patriots, in the first withstanding the invaders, and in the second being executed by the firing squad at night.

The invasion also inspired Goya to produce a series of prints called " The Disasters of War ", which show scenes of heroic courage and loathsome brutality with a vividness never surpassed.

These scenes of war and slaughter were clearly prompted by intense sympathy for suffering humanity, but not by patriotism on Goya's part; for when the invasion was successful, he readily collaborated with the enemy, accepting a post under Joseph Bonaparte, Napoleon's brother, to assist in the pillaging of Spanish art treasures.

Later, when Ferdinand, son of Charles IV, returned to the Spanish throne, it is reported that he said to Goya, " You deserve banishment, nay, worse, the garotte (Spanish form of

Goya was commissioned to paint the portraits of the Spanish Royal family, which he did with complete candour.

execution), but you are a great artist, and we will forget." So Goya, like the Vicar of Bray, changed sides once more.

A few years after this Goya's wife died and he retired to a house in the country, near Madrid. His neighbours called it *Quinta del Sordo* (" The House of the Deaf One "). There he determined to paint, not for money, but simply to satisfy himself. He produced a series of pictures, known as " The Black Paintings", in which he really expressed himself without restraint. Each of these strange, dreamlike murals is like a cry of protest, an exclamation of horror, expressed not in words but in paint. Gone are the charming, trivial tapestry themes of his youth. Goya is now compelled to voice his distress at all the corruption and folly in the Spain he knew, at the disasters and the judgments that he foresaw were to come.

In the end, Goya's independent outlook aroused the suspicion of the corrupt government of Spain, and he was compelled to go abroad. His last years were spent in Bordeaux, in France, where he was virtually a political exile. He died there in 1828 at the age of 82.

Goya painted four successive Spanish monarchs, their wives and their families, including famous men and women of his country and the Spanish court. These portraits were lifelike and without restraint, and no attempt was made to flatter the sitter.

From time immemorial men have hunted wild animals in forests, tilled the soil, caught fish in the sea and rivers—all with the object of obtaining food, that basic commodity essential to existence. Agriculture is part and parcel of life, and is as old as mankind. Yet even in the most primitive times man always had certain tools, hunting implements, knives, spears, and flints, to help him conquer nature and support himself. As knowledge progressed over the centuries, so man developed more and more devices to aid and adorn his life; the corn from the soil was ground into flour and baked into bread; textiles and clothing were made, and buildings such as medieval castles and churches were created, some of which still stand to-day. The art of printing was discovered, and this led to the production of more and more books. Metal goods were turned out at forges and workshops throughout the country; great sailing vessels were constructed and a whole host of goods, ever increasing in variety as time went by, were manufactured by men.

Industry, which is the name given to those occupations in which something is manufactured, has thus for a very long time been an important part of man's existence. Tinkers, tailors, candlestick makers, ironmongers, blacksmiths, tanners, weavers, spinners, and many others were all an essential part of life in olden days. For these were the people who manufactured the goods and articles that society wanted and needed.

Man's life in industry was very different then from what it is now, or what it was just one or two hundred years ago.

Unlike to-day, very few people in medieval England lived in towns, or worked in industry, the majority lived and worked on the land as farmers and farm labourers. Agriculture was by far the most important source of employment. Whereas nowadays only one person in every twenty-five works in agriculture, in the Middle Ages three out of every four were employed on the land.

The manufacturing industry too was very closely associated with agricultural life. Many of the spinners, weavers, and others, did not work in the cities or towns, but in their own cottages in the rural villages. During sowing, ploughing, and harvest time all activity was concentrated on the fields and meadows, but in the long winter months, with little or nothing to be done on the land, industrial work took the place of agricultural. Spinning wheels spun wool into yarn, and weaving looms wove yarn into cloth. In many parts of the country agricultural labourers in summer became industrial workers in winter.

DOMESTIC INDUSTRY

Such was the traditional pattern of industry, with manufacturing essentially a part-time employment with agriculture. This type of industrial organisation was known as the "domestic system" because the work was done at home. And although the domestic system was not typical throughout all England or all industries (some industries, such as mining could not be done at home), it was very widespread, especially in woollen textiles, then the greatest of all industries.

Industry that was not based on the domestic system was usually undertaken in small workshops in towns and villages. Here a master craftsman might employ two or three workers. This handicraft industry unlike domestic work, was generally skilled.

The workers who produced goods in their own homes did not buy or own the raw materials, or often even the simple machinery. Instead, a merchant, or some other businessman, would lend the equipment and materials and then call to collect the finished products. Payment was made according to how much was ready. In the textile industry, for example, the spinner would receive wool from the clothier. The clothier would call again when the yarn was ready, and put it out to a weaver. When the cloth was made, the expensive operations of bleaching, dyeing, and finishing were usually carried out by skilled craftsmen working in towns.

A feature of industry under the domestic system was the irregularity of employment. Not only was cottage industry seasonal to fit in with agricultural labour, but the lack of supervision at home encouraged periods of idleness. The times of idleness alternated with intense activity when the time drew near for the clothier to call for his yarn or cloth. When the work was due for completion, long hours would be worked, and all the family would take part. Defoe, touring through England at the opening of the eighteenth century, noted with satisfaction that in places even three-year-old children were earning their living.

Town industry in the workshops was more regular, but even here periods of unemployment could leave workers destitute. And such depressions were frequent as business activity was dominated by the uncertain harvest; a failure of crops would mean high food prices and precious little money would be available to buy manufactured goods. Many skilled workers formed unions and fraternities to help one another in such times of difficulty, and a special feature of this help was that of "tramping". An artisan, armed with a union card showing him to be of good standing in the society, would set off on a long journey in search of work. His route, sometimes covering 2,000 miles, would be carefully planned, and at each resting place he would be provided with a meal, a bed, and work if there was any. The resting places were frequently inns and taverns, and reminders of this practice can still be seen in public houses with such names as Bricklayers' Arms, and Carpenters' Arms.

This industrial scene of two hundred years ago and more is totally different from that of to-day with our vast cities, huge industrial plants, and high standards of living. The big break with the past occurred at the time of what is known as the Industrial Revolution.

THE INDUSTRIAL REVOLUTION

The period was called an industrial revolution because of the important change that took place, from about the mid-eighteenth to the mid-nineteenth centuries, when Britain became an industrial instead of an agricultural country. These years saw many changes, above all, the great expansion of industry and commerce. Particularly rapid was the growth of the cotton textile industry, which soon replaced wool as the nation's greatest manufacture. Associated with this growth were the use of steam power by James Watt, the development of iron and coal mining and the metal trades, the introduction of all kinds of new machinery, and the subsequent growth of factory towns.

During the Industrial Revolution, instead of most manufacturing being done by men labouring in their homes or small workshops, large factories began to make their appearance, employing many scores and sometimes hundreds of workers.

These factories brought with them a new way of living and many new problems. Now, new workers were wholly dependent on industrial earnings for their livelihood. When a depression hit trade and unemployment followed, there were no side earnings in agriculture to fall back on. As factories spread, economic fluctuations affected a greater and greater proportion of the population.

The factory also introduced a new phenomenon—discipline. The essence of the new system of industrial organisation based on power-driven machinery was continuity of production. Work was regular, hours were long, and holidays limited. The workers had to arrive at and leave their workplaces at fixed times, their work was supervised, and absenteeism and drunkenness were punished. Slowly men had to change their working habits to fit in with those of the new machines.

STEAM-ENGINE

Towns grew as workers flocked to live near their places of work and merchants and manufacturers no longer had to rely solely on villagers working in their country cottages. The old sources of power—human muscles, the pull of a horse, the thrust of a water-wheel, the force of a windmill—gradually gave way to or were supplemented by the steam engine. Steam-driven machines encouraged the growth of urban areas. They ensured the regularity of employment which enabled men to leave agricultural areas where industry was a part-time occupation. Moreover the steam engine was not limited, like the water-wheel, to regions of fast-flowing streams; industry could be concentrated in a single locality which would eventually become a factory town.

The factory was not new in the England of 1760. Long before that time some wealthy manufacturers had crowded workers together in a single establishment, provided raw materials, tools, equipment, and machinery, and set the men to work. But what was impressive after 1760 was the scale and extent of the factory system, for never before had factories made their appearance in such large numbers, or come to dominate whole industries and whole areas.

The transition from domestic to factory production was not sudden and was never complete throughout industry. Instead, a very few industries became rapidly dominated by the factories, while others retained their simple forms of organisation. Nor were factories seen in equal numbers throughout the country. There was a factory concentration in the northern parts of England and in Lanarkshire in Scotland. Above all it was seen in the cotton spinning industries of South Lancashire, centred on Manchester, and of the Glasgow area. Parts of the woollen textile trades of the West Riding of Yorkshire also adopted the factory system, as did the manufacturers of silk goods in Spitalfields, near London.

But the coming of the factory was just one part of the change that took place in industry during the Industrial

A weaver working at home in his cottage.

Revolution. Many trades expanded, whether in the factory or not, and it is important to remember that, at first, the factories only employed a very small proportion of the total British labour force. Even as late as 1850 the typical industrial worker was not a factory hand. As their predecessors had done one hundred years earlier, skilled craftsmen were still setting off on their hopeful "tramps" in the 1840s.

The domestic system and small craft workshop existed side by side with factories throughout the nineteenth century, and always employed a greater body of workers. The domestic system remained predominant in the clothing, nail-making, and woollen-weaving trades, long after cottons were a factory industry. Metal manufacturing was still based on workshops in the mid-nineteenth century. In Birmingham and the surrounding Black Country there were hundreds of small engineering establishments, employing only a handful of men and using little or no machinery. These engineers were highly skilled and turned out all kinds of metal goods, tools, and machinery, which were sold all over the world. Yet these men were not factory workers.

Similarly, in London, the skilled furniture manufacturers produced tables, chairs, and desks in much the same way in 1850 as had been done a century earlier. Sheffield had been famous for its cutlery in the fourteenth century, and well after the Industrial Revolution these products were still being made in small workshops by skilled craftsmen.

MINING INDUSTRY

The main mining areas were also untouched by the factory system and little affected by machinery. The tin and copper of Cornwall, lead of Derbyshire, coal of the Scottish Lowlands, Northumberland, Durham and the Midlands, the iron in Staffordshire and South Wales—all were worked as they had been long before the Industrial Revolution.

Although carried on in the traditional way, mining expanded its output rapidly. The demand for coal and iron was especially large. The steam engine used coal as fuel and coal was also used for the manufacture of iron. The output

133

of both iron and coal was stepped up due to greater demand from industry.

The old methods of production thus not only survived the Industrial Revolution but were often stimulated. The mining industry expanded, as did that of engineering, clothing manufacture, and some branches of textiles. But, well into the reign of Queen Victoria, the factory was not supreme even in textiles. Cotton weaving had only become a completely factory-based industry after 1830, in contrast to cotton spinning which was the first to adopt factory organisation. Although wool spinning, cording, bleaching, and dyeing were done in the Yorkshire mills and factories in the mid-nineteenth century, the spun wool was still mostly woven on the hand looms of independent cottage weavers.

The coming of the factory therefore had only a limited impact on the working classes in Britain, the direct effect was felt strongly only in parts of Scotland, Lancashire, and Yorkshire, and then mainly among those workers who spun yarn. The factories were just one part of the Industrial Revolution. Another contributory factor in the revolution was the introduction of machinery in workshops, cottages and factories; and the whole period was characterised by a wave of inventions, changes and new devices flooding into industry and agriculture. This surge of technical discoveries swept large areas of the economy, and those discoveries that affected industry can be thought of as falling into two categories: those that could be applied only to a particular trade and branch of manufacture, and those that had a more general application.

Of those changes which were applied to specific industries the most important were in the textile and iron industries. The discovery of how to smelt iron ore with coke instead of with the increasingly scarce wood charcoal revolutionised pig iron production. Then, in 1783, an inventor named Henry Cort introduced a new way of making wrought iron by a process known as "puddling". A whole series of improvements helped the expansion of the cotton spinning industry. In the 1760s James Hargreaves invented the spinning jenny, and Richard Arkwright developed what was known as a water frame because it was powered by water. In 1775, Samuel Crompton invented another spinning

One of the earliest rotative steam engines of the type perfected by Boulton and Watt.

machine and as it was a cross between the spinning jenny and the water frame, it was known as a mule.

One man could now, with the aid of a machine, do the work of six or more men. But the innovations, although raising the output of the industry, did not mean the further development of factory towns, for the spinning jenny and the mule could be used by the cottager at home, while the water-frame, driven by a water-wheel, was better suited to the mills built along such river banks as the Orwell and the Derwent.

It was the steam-engine that created the new factory towns. The factories were based on steam-driven machinery, and steam-engines were soon applied to many branches of manufacture, mining, agriculture, and transport. At first, steam-engines had been developed as pumps to drain the Cornish tin and copper mines, and later the coal mines of Durham and Northumberland. James Watt's steam-engine, invented in 1769, could not be adapted to textile machinery until 1781, when a rotary movement, instead of a pumping action, was developed. From 1785, when a Nottinghamshire mill first used steam-power, the new invention was soon adopted in the spinning factories of Lancashire and Glasgow. The inventions of Hargreaves, Arkwright, and Crompton were now steam-driven, and the cotton spinning industry could be more and more concentrated in factories in the towns.

Men from rural areas flocked to the first growing town in search of work, and Britain became the first industrial country in the world. Towns like Manchester, Glasgow, Preston, Bury, Oldham, and many others grew far more rapidly than did the general growth of population, though that too was increasing at a fast rate.

The new order of society that was developing in the few scattered regions of Britain began to arouse increased attention as the appalling living conditions of many factory workers pricked the conscience of the nation. This might seem surprising as so few industrial workers in Britain actually worked in the factories and mines. Moreover the government of the day was still drawn preponderantly from the landed aristocracy, and might have ignored developments in industry.

However, almost from the inception of factories, the conditions of their workers aroused widespread interest and emotion. Whereas isolated cases of overcrowding, overwork, or malnutrition could be overlooked and ignored, the new factory towns presented evils on too large a scale to be passed over.

One of the worst evils was the employment and exploitation of child and female labour. Conditions were especially bad for the orphans and pauper children from parish workhouses. These children were apprenticed in the mills, had no protection, and were often cruelly treated. With the introduction of new machinery greatly simplifying many of the manufacturing processes, much of the work now could be done by a boy or girl instead of by a skilled craftsman. And by the opening of the nineteenth century, many cotton mills had about one half of their total workers under the age of twelve, a large proportion of that number under nine years old. Of the adult workers there were, on average, twice as many women as men.

Conditions were appalling in some of these early factories where the workers were often herded together in badly lit, unventilated factories. The atmosphere was kept damp to moisten the cotton thread, with the result that the clothes of the operatives clung to their bodies, and froze when they

Children worked under indescribably bad conditions for seventeen hours a day in unventilated mines and were in constant danger from gas and collapsing walls. The exploitation of child labour led Lord Shaftesbury to campaign for drastic reform.

left the factories in winter weather. Young children of ten, or even six or seven, worked fifteen, sometimes sixteen hours a day. These youngsters often had to work with unsafe, unguarded machinery, and cases of their falling asleep and being maimed or killed by the machines were frequent.

THE FACTORY ACTS

If working conditions were bad, living conditions were no better. The rapid growth of towns raised immense problems of overcrowding and sanitation. The sufferings brought by the factories were too great to pass unnoticed, and the first half of the nineteenth century saw determined efforts made by many social reformers to obtain improved conditions. One of the first great steps was taken in 1802 when an Act of Parliament was passed regulating the employment of parish apprentices in cotton mills. This Act, introduced by Sir Robert Peel, himself a cotton manufacturer and father of a future British Prime Minister, laid down that no pauper child was to work for more than twelve hours a day, and night-work was forbidden. The Act also provided for elementary education for the children, and the factory walls were to be whitewashed at least twice a year.

The struggle against the horrors of the factory was long and uphill. No matter how good the intent of an Act of Parliament, or how zealous the reformers, to enforce the law was a different matter. For example, a Factory Act, passed in 1819, forbade the employing of children under nine years of age in textile factories. It also fixed a limit of twelve working hours a day for all children under the age of twelve. Yet how could such laws be put into effect when there were no inspectors to keep a check on the activities of mill-owners? How, at a time when births were not officially registered, could the exact age of a child be discovered? Moreover, often parents themselves were anxious for their children to contribute to the family earnings as soon as possible.

It was no simple matter to improve working conditions in factories. It was still more difficult in the case of mines where the dangerous and heavy work was carried on away from the public gaze, and often in the remote parts of Cornwall or Northumberland. A Government inquiry into working conditions in 1842 revealed a terrible story of brutality and exploitation in the coal mines. Men, women, and children worked up to seventeen hours a day in damp, unventilated mines, with constant danger from explosives and collapsing walls. The report told of workers misshapen since childhood with twisted limbs, deformities caused by "hurrying" the coal from the seams and crawling on all fours along narrow passages with their load. It spoke also of pregnant women working underground until the moment of childbirth.

The hardships and sufferings endured by the working classes were immeasurable, but conditions improved as the efforts of reformers and parliamentary legislation gradually took effect. Slowly, society became more conscious of the problems created by the growth of industry, and more anxious to improve working conditions. A great step forward was taken in 1833 when Lord Ashley (afterwards to become Lord Shaftesbury) pioneered a Factory Act which not only introduced better working conditions but allowed for the setting up of a body of independent inspectors to enforce the Act. The law could no longer be ignored, and further Bills in 1842, 1847, and 1849 improved the lot of workers, above all that of women and children, in the mines and factories.

The industrial scene in early nineteenth-century Britain was one of contrasts. A new class of factory workers was developing, while elsewhere men clung to the old methods of work and way of living. Hardships were suffered as society struggled to come to terms with the dramatic changes in the economic life. Perhaps the hardest hit were those skilled craftsmen who fought a long but vain battle with the more efficiently machine-produced goods. The handloom weavers especially were injured by this competition, and they took cut after cut in wages as power-looms came into general use. Riots by workers against the introduction of machinery were frequent before 1820.

But machine and factory production did raise living standards in the long run, even though they caused much misery and squalor. By the mid-nineteenth century wages were rising, and the Factory Acts had helped to improve working conditions. Britain was becoming conditioned to the position of "Workshop of the World", and the Briton was becoming conditioned to life as an industrial worker.

MOZART

Wolfgang Amadeus Mozart was born in Salzburg on 27th January, 1756. His father and young sister, Nannerl, were both musicians, and by the time Mozart was three he was already working out tunes and chords on the piano. At four he had made such progress he could learn a whole minuet and trio in half an hour. So rapid was the development of his musical talent that at the age of five Mozart had composed his first concerto.

Mozart's father decided he would show his two brilliant children to the world, so he took Mozart, just six, and Nannerl, now eleven, to Munich, where they gave their first public concert; it was a resounding success.

From then on, Leopold took his children all over Europe; to Vienna first and then farther afield to Paris and to London. Wolfgang and Nannerl were attractive children; Wolfgang was particularly lively and won the hearts of all who heard him, and was never spoilt by the applause and admiration he received everywhere. Every aspect of music came naturally to him; he could play several instruments, sing, and above all compose music on the spot whenever anyone asked him to. He loved travelling to all these great cities, where every day he learnt something new about music; and his genius awed already great musicians into silence.

But the strain of this exciting life was intense and it is not surprising, since he gave sometimes three and four concerts a day, that the boy was frequently ill. He had little stamina and on two occasions before the age of ten nearly died.

When Mozart was thirteen his father, after giving him a much needed quiet year in Salzburg, took him to Italy, the home of opera. Opera had become the real passion in Mozart's life and his great aim was to compose one. He had proved that his genius was not just a flash in the pan; he was no longer a boy prodigy, but a promising young composer with eighty works already written.

Now Italy gave him a great welcome and also his first real chance to fulfil his dream: Milan asked him to write an opera for their new season. Delighted, he and his father toured the rest of Italy—Florence, Rome, Naples—and in each new place Mozart was acclaimed.

He returned to Milan to write his opera *Mithridates, King of Pontus*, and on Boxing Day, 1770, it was performed, Mozart himself conducting. It was a sensational triumph, and for the next two years Italy opened all its doors to the brilliant young composer. Then for Milan he composed an opera, *Lucio Silla*, with some strange and gloomy music. The Italians did not like it, and never asked him to compose another opera. Italy was lost to him for ever.

Mozart was now seventeen—still gay, nonsensical and warm-hearted as ever, never downcast for long by the great disappointments he suffered, or by his poverty.

SEEKING A POSITION

He needed money badly, and in those days the only way a musician could earn a living was by getting a post with a court orchestra—the private orchestra of some great nobleman, prince, or king. Mozart tried all his life to get such a post, but not until the last years or his life, when it was too late, did one come his way. Mozart was poor all his life; when a little money came his way, he spent it gaily and then the bitter struggle began again.

During his early twenties Mozart went from town to town in Germany and Austria—Munich, Mannheim, Vienna—trying to find a permanent post. All the while he was composing at a furious rate—symphonies, masses, concertos. Music poured out of him. People were astonished by his genius, loved his music, loved him, but no one came forward to offer him the job he so much needed for his financial security. To add to his difficulties, he fell deeply in love with a girl singer called Aloysia Weber who, after encouraging him for a while, turned him down suddenly when she became rich and successful.

Then the tide of his luck seemed to turn in 1781, when he was 25. Munich commissioned him to write an opera, *Idomeneo*, and it was a wild success. He went on to Vienna with this behind him; and Vienna for once received him well

Mozart and his sister at the harpsichord.

Mozart was a most prolific composer. Even on arduous concert tours, new works poured from his pen.

In Mozart's time, Vienna was a gay and lively place, with endless rounds of fetes and balls at which the composer was often a guest. However, Mozart, and other musicians of his standing were unhappy at the treatment meted out to them by Archbishop Hieronymus and, eventually, he resigned from his appointment as "concertmeister".

and asked him to write a new opera *Il Seraglio*. While he was doing this he fell in love again: this time with Aloysia Weber's younger sister, Constanze, whom, against his father's wishes, he married in 1782. He loved Constanze deeply, but their marriage was not a calm, happy one; Constanze was moody, unreliable, a bad housekeeper; not the solid support Mozart needed. Their home in Vienna was always chaotic: in nine years of marriage they moved house eleven times; they had six children, four of whom died. Both Mozart and Constanze were frequently ill, and always poor.

A NEW OPERA

Mozart's days were packed with lessons and concerts to give, and composing to do. In 1786 he composed a new opera, *The Marriage of Figaro*, which was the first of his four great mature operas. It is enchanting; full of fun and humour, amusing and very human characters, and passages of exquisitely beautiful music. Mozart himself instructed rehearsals, and a singer who was in it has left us a description of him.

" I never shall forget his little animated countenance, when lighted up with the glowing rays of genius—it is as impossible to describe it as it would be to paint sunbeams."

The Viennese gave *Figaro* an enthusiastic ovation, but forgot the opera after a few months. It was the city of Prague, not Vienna, which fully recognised Mozart's genius; they saw clearly he was the greatest composer in Europe, and gave him admiration and applause to an extent which moved him deeply. They commissioned him to write another opera, *Don Giovanni*, and it, too, was an overwhelming success when it was performed in Prague in October, 1787.

COURT APPOINTMENT

That same year also Mozart was appointed, at long last, composer to the Imperial Court at Vienna. This would ensure him a small salary to the end of his life; but by this time Mozart was so heavily in debt and had so many commit-

ments, it made very little difference to his position. He was overworked, and ill. Constanze was ill too. Yet he continued composing. During a particularly difficult and gloomy six weeks he produced his last three symphonies, all major works. The speed with which he wrote was staggering.

During 1791, tired and ill, he started work on his last opera, *The Magic Flute*. He was also composing, among other things, a Requiem Mass. He was convinced, as his weakness and sickness increased, that this would be his own Requiem; and he was right. He died, in December, 1791, aged 35, making the sound of the drums in the Requiem he had not yet finished. He died poor and was buried in a pauper's grave; but he left behind him over 620 works of music, full of the deep richness of genius.

In 1786, Mozart wrote his first major opera, which confirmed his status as Europe's leading composer.

137

BEETHOVEN

Bonn is now the capital of West Germany: there, just under two hundred years ago one of the supreme musical geniuses of all time was born—Ludwig van Beethoven. The house in which the Beethovens lived, and where Ludwig was born, still stands. It is known as the Beethovenhaus and in it is preserved a collection of pictures, manuscripts and musical instruments connected with the great composer. In an otherwise empty attic, where the boy first saw the light of the world, stands a bust of him on which the slanting light falls through a dormer window.

"THE SPANIARD"

The Beethovens, though German by residence and adoption, were of Flemish origin. They came to Germany from Louvain and Liège where they lived during the seventeenth and the first part of the eighteenth centuries. There may also have been a Spanish strain in the family blood. The Spanish occupation of the Netherlands in the sixteenth century left a strong influence, especially on those Catholic districts from which the Beethovens came. If there was some Spanish blood in the family, it would explain much in Beethoven's own character and his physical appearance that otherwise seems difficult to account for. In his youth he was dark and swarthy. He was actually given the nickname "The Spaniard", and all his life he had the fierce pride, the quick anger and sense of individual human dignity which are so typical of Spaniards.

MUSICAL BACKGROUND

The Rhineland city of Bonn was, at the time of Beethoven's birth, the ecclesiastical centre of the local principality. It was also a centre of music; and music was the profession of Beethoven's family. Ludwig's grandfather, Louis, was a gifted and experienced musician who came to Bonn as court musician to the Elector. He lived to become Kapellmeister, or director of music. His son, Johann, was also a musician— a singer—though not a very talented one. Johann married the daughter of the Elector's cook, Anna Magdalena Laym, who was the widow of the late valet to the Elector of Treves. Ludwig was the second of their seven children.

UNHAPPY CHILDHOOD

Beethoven's childhood was not happy. His father was weak and unscrupulous. He drank too much, and as soon as he saw his son's great talent for music began to exploit it mercilessly. The boy was only eight when he was forced to play the piano in public for the first time; he was not very much older when he was obliged to undertake heavier responsibilities. The father's laziness and wayward habits meant that the Beethoven family was always short of money; and by the time Ludwig was fourteen he was given the post of assistant organist at the Court, and became the sole reliable breadwinner. His general education had been sadly neglected in the interest of forcing his musical talent. Johann van Beethoven soon realised that he had taught his son all that he could, so he gave the lad into the charge of one of his drinking companions, Tobias Pfeiffer, a fine musician but a cruel man. Pfeiffer treated his young charge abominably. Fortunately, Pfeiffer soon had to leave Bonn altogether, and Ludwig began to study with Christian Gottlob Neefe, the court organist, another fine musician and a good man, whose understanding of Ludwig's gifts enabled him to do much to encourage them. Neefe gave the young Beethoven a thorough grounding in technique, based upon Bach's "48" Preludes and Fugues; and some ten years later Beethoven acknowledged Neefe's influence on him by writing: "If ever

The house at Bonn, Germany, where Beethoven was born. It is now a museum and contains many mementos of the great musician.

Beethoven's father drove his son mercilessly and would often force young Ludwig to get up out of bed to play over pieces he had learned earlier in the day.

Thanks to the tuition and understanding he had received as a pupil of Christian Gottlieb Neefe, the fifteen-year-old Beethoven was appointed musician in the court service.

I become a great man, yours shall be a share of the credit ".

But if Beethoven's father was a weakling and a waster, his mother, to whom he was devoted, was a very different person. If it had not been for her quiet courage and determination, the family would almost certainly have broken up. She did all she could to ease the burden of hardship and poverty (Johann was soon unable to hold his job and was dismissed from court service). But the struggle was too great. Frau Beethoven's health failed, and she died at the age of forty, an old woman in everything but years. To Beethoven himself, who had already tasted bitterness in his short life, the death of his mother was the hardest blow of all. It deprived him of the one person with whom he could feel true sympathy and in whom he felt able to confide.

The hardness of his youth left a permanent impression on Beethoven. Much of the overbearing aggressiveness and impatient anger of his later life must be attributed to the feelings of resentment he acquired in his earliest years.

VIENNA AND MOZART

When he was sixteen, Beethoven paid his first visit to Vienna. And there he met Mozart. He had already begun to compose and was a brilliant pianist. He knew that music was to be his life. His meeting with Mozart was a famous one in musical history. Mozart was used to having young men come to show off their talents to him and did not as a rule pay much attention. He did not at first take much notice of his new visitor. But Beethoven was already a man of unshakable determination. After the initial cool reception, he asked Mozart to give him a theme to improvise on. Mozart did so; and Beethoven played so brilliantly that Mozart turned to a companion and said: " Mark that boy. One day he will make the world talk about him ". It was probably through Mozart that Joseph Haydn, the other leading composer of the day in Vienna, first heard of Beethoven.

HIS MOTHER'S DEATH

While Beethoven was in Vienna, he learned of his mother's grave illness. He hurried home, and arrived just in time to be with her in her last days. After her death, and probably as the result of a death-bed promise, Beethoven assumed full responsibility for the moral and physical welfare of the

Beethoven with the young Lorchen Breuning.

The youthful Beethoven meets Mozart.

In 1814, at the Congress of Vienna, Beethoven performed his Seventh Symphony before the crowned heads of Europe. In the same year he received the freedom of the city.

family. He was still only seventeen. Apart from his father, two other sons and a baby daughter survived Frau Beethoven. Three other children had died in infancy.

Slowly Beethoven got over the shock of his mother's death, although it undermined his health. He found some consolation in his friends, especially the Breuning family and the young doctor, Franz Wegeler. In the Breuning's family circle, Beethoven entered a new and better social circle than that into which he was born; and the experience did him a lot of good. It helped to draw the sting out of his resentment against life, and to give him the social polish and confidence he so far lacked. In later years he had good cause to be grateful to the Breunings for their " civilising " effect on him.

Late in 1792, Beethoven went again to Vienna, this time primarily to study with Haydn. He was never to return. For the rest of his life he lived and worked in the Austrian capital.

THE DISASTER OF HIS DEAFNESS

Beethoven's life in Vienna was often stormy and full of

Beethoven had a passion for the outdoor life and his favourite pastime was to walk in the Kahlenberg hills.

personal difficulties. At first things went well for him. Although he composed all the time, he won his first reputation and earned his living as a pianist. His outstanding talents enabled him to gain access to the houses of the Viennese aristocracy who ruled the city's culture. His rough manners and short temper were forgiven because of his genius. But before long a terrible disaster began to overtake him. He had trouble with his hearing and began to go deaf. We can imagine the effect upon a man like Beethoven, still insecure and still dependent upon piano-playing for his living. His compositions were beginning to be accepted; and he probably knew already that it was as a composer that he would win that fame upon which he had set his heart. But deafness! No greater blow could befall a musician.

THE " EROICA " SYMPHONY

He relapsed temporarily into despair. In this passing mood he wrote the famous document known as the " Heiligenstadt Testament " in which he pours out all his grief and desperation, and even mentions suicide. Beethoven, however, could not be destroyed by anything. He recovered his spirits and his strength, and at once composed one of his supreme masterpieces—the " Eroica " Symphony—in 1803. This great work was originally dedicated to Napoleon, whom he, like most young men of the period, admired and saw as a liberator of mankind. But when Napoleon proclaimed himself Emperor, Beethoven angrily tore out the dedication from the title page of the score, saying: " Ah! He is only an ordinary man after all! Now he will turn tyrant and trample the rights of man under foot ". Beethoven was right, of course; that is just what happened.

All his life, Beethoven was a great apostle of liberty. Many of his great works are openly dedicated to the cause of freedom; many others state it implicitly. Beethoven not only freed the art of music from the conventions of the eighteenth century, he also freed the musician from the position of servitude he had previously occupied. To Beethoven we largely owe the idea of the composer as an independent person, earning a living by composition only, and working according to the dictates of his own genius rather than to the requirements of some private or public employer. Beethoven was a staunch republican in politics. He saw at first hand the working of royal courts; and he did not like what he saw. Whether he would have liked any better the ways of popular governments is something we may well doubt.

HIS FINEST CREATIONS

After the " Eroica " Symphony in 1803, and until the year 1812, Beethoven wrote a long series of masterpieces, including nearly all his most famous symphonies, concertos and sonatas. Then there came a strange break of several years during which he wrote very little. We do not quite know the reason for this near silence. Ill health and personal troubles do not fully explain it. It seems that he became dissatisfied with his own work, strange as it may seem to us, and waited until he had come to terms with himself. When he did resume regular composition, with the great *Hammerklavier* Piano Sonata (1818-19), it is as though he had emerged from a great spiritual crisis. From this point on he composed a number of works that remain unique in all European art for their spiritual depth and extraordinary power of creative imagination. They include the Ninth Symphony with its choral Finale, the Mass in D, the last four piano sonatas and the last five string quartets.

Beethoven's health was never good. Apart from his deafness he suffered several bad illnesses. He never married, although he was usually in love with one woman or other. Why he remained single is a mystery. He seems to have had such an idealised picture of marriage in his own mind that when it came to the point of decision he shrank from risking it in practice. We do not know to whom his famous letters to the " Immortal Beloved " were addressed. They are infinitely touching but infinitely mysterious.

KARL

Beethoven's promise to take care of his family at his mother's death remained a point of honour with him. When one of his brothers died, he undertook guardianship of his son, Karl. Beethoven loved his nephew deeply; but the relationship caused him no end of trouble. Karl has often been blamed for this. It is more likely that to live with Beethoven was enough to make any young man despair.

A scene from Beethoven's only opera, Fidelio, *where Pizzarro is about to kill Don Florestano but is foiled by Florestano's wife, Donna Eleanor.*

For long an admirer of Beethoven's music, Franz Schubert attended the composer's funeral in 1827, much saddened by the musical world's great loss.

Beethoven loved to excess, but not at all wisely. Also, he carried on continuous legal battles with Karl's mother, whom he hated. Karl only wanted to live an ordinary young man's life: Beethoven overwhelmed him with a load of possessive love that almost destroyed him. Karl was driven at one point to attempt suicide. It is a sad story, but probably not one for blame or praise, on either side.

HIS FRIENDSHIP WITH GOETHE

As a famous man, Beethoven knew many of the other famous men of his day. One was the poet Goethe. Goethe greatly admired Beethoven, and Beethoven loved Goethe's work and set some of his poems to music. But there was a big difference between the two men. In 1812, Goethe and Beethoven met at the resort of Teplitz, where the Imperial family were also staying. One day the two great men met the royal family on a walk. Goethe immediately took off his hat and stood aside; Beethoven deliberately kept his hat on and walked through the cortege offering a friendly greeting to those he knew personally. Perhaps he was rude; but he wrote some words about the incident that tell us a lot about him—" Kings and princes can create professors, privy councillors, and bestow decorations, but they cannot create great men, master-minds which tower above the rabble ". That is the truth about Beethoven: he believed passionately in great men, and was never in any doubt that he was one. That knowledge sustained him through all the difficulties and disasters of his own life. Early on, when his deafness began, he said to a friend: " I will take Fate by the throat. It shall not overwhelm me ". He kept his word. At the end, he was totally deaf; but it did not matter any more. His spirit had travelled far from the passing trials of this world. He heard in his own imagination the music he had to compose, and he was able to write it down for posterity. He died of a combination of diseases in 1827, aged fifty-seven.

Beethoven's best known works comprise—thirty-two piano sonatas, seventeen string quartets, seven piano trios, nine symphonies, seven concertos (five for piano, one for violin, and the Triple Concerto), the opera *Fidelio*, ten violin sonatas, five cello sonatas, several overtures, many songs, two Masses, one ballet.

SCHUBERT

Many great composers have been associated with the city of Vienna; Mozart, Haydn, Beethoven, Brahms and Mahler are some of them. But there is none whose story is more closely bound up with the city than Franz Schubert, who was born there in 1797, only six years after the death of Mozart.

SCHOOLDAYS

Schubert's father was a schoolmaster in one of the suburbs. Franz himself, partly through his sweet singing voice and partly because of his ability to read music at sight, won a choral scholarship at the age of eleven to the Seminary attached to the Imperial chapel. The Seminary was open to children of all classes, and here Schubert met boys who became his lifelong friends, some of them from wealthy families. He always inspired great affection and devotion in his friends. At school he became friendly with Joseph von Spaun who, on learning that Schubert composed music but could not afford to buy the paper on which to write it, gave him a large quantity of music paper.

He left school when he was sixteen, but continued to take lessons in composition with the court musical director, the opera composer Salieri, who fully recognised the boy's genius. For several years after he had left school, Schubert continued to play the violin in the school orchestra and the first symphony he composed was played by this orchestra in 1813.

TEACHING CAREER

Franz's father did not want him to become a musician, but rather to be a schoolmaster like himself and earn a regular salary. Schubert, therefore, went to a training college for a year, and after that taught at the parish school where his father was headmaster. He did not like teaching and was not a very good schoolmaster, but at least he had long holidays and a certain amount of spare time, all of which he used for composing; he wrote cantatas and masses for church use, string quartets, two more symphonies, and more than a hundred and fifty songs during this time.

After two years of teaching, he persuaded his father to allow him to go and live in Vienna with a young law student, newly arrived in the city to study, who had been so impressed by the beauty of some of Schubert's early songs that he had immediately sought out their composer. This young man, Franz von Schober, became one of Schubert's greatest friends.

INDEPENDENCE

From then on, except for two short periods as music tutor at the country castle of Count Esterhazy in Hungary, Schubert was free to live and compose as he liked. He never again took a permanent salaried post, and though he was often short of money, he was independent, and he always worked hard at his music. His father would have liked him to go back to teaching, but Schubert was determined to concentrate all his efforts on the wonderful gift with which he had been endowed.

He was always poor, but, except when depressed by illness or by lack of appreciation of his music, he had a happy nature and led a carefree existence with his friends in the wonderful old city, with its inns and coffee-houses, its gardens and theatres and its hospitable houses.

FRIENDSHIPS

Schubert's friends are very important, not only because they were important to *him* as companions, but also because they gave him encouragement and appreciation and helped him by making his music known to a wide circle of people. Some of these friends, like Spaun who had given him the music paper, he knew from school; some, like Schober, were attracted to him by his musical talent and by his charm as a person. They were people from many different walks of life; there were poets, writers, painters, actors and musicians— his school friend Spaun became a respected lawyer and civil servant. There were also older, richer people who were always delighted to have Schubert and his friends in their houses. Parties were often arranged at which Schubert was the most important person present, so much so that a special name

Schubert at the age of five playing the clavichord under the tutelage of his father.

At school, young Franz neglected his work for the sake of music. For this he was reprimanded by his father.

142

When he was eleven, Schubert successfully applied for a place in the Convict, the chief school of music in Vienna.

was invented for these parties: they were called " Schubertiads ". The young people, and some of the middle-aged ones too, danced, played games, recited poetry or read plays, sang, and listened to music. Schubert never danced himself (he was less than five feet tall and probably self-conscious about his small stature), but he was always happy to play for the others to dance. When more serious music was wanted, he would play his own piano works, accompany his own songs, and sometimes sing them too, though the singer was more usually a professional such as Michael Vogl, the famous baritone from the Court Opera, another great friend and admirer of Schubert's.

The Schubertiads took place not only in Vienna, but in other towns and country places too. Schubert took several holiday journeys through the glorious Austrian countryside. In 1819, he visited the towns of Steyr and Linz during a summer tour of Upper Austria with Vogl, who was a native of Steyr, and again in 1825 with the same companion, this time going as far as Salzburg. Schubert and Vogl, wrote a friend, travelled like wandering minstrels, welcomed wherever they went. For although Schubert himself was a rather shy and modest man, throughout the country his friends spread his fame as a creator of heavenly music, and in hospitable houses and castles everywhere there would be Schubertiads. His last country tour was in 1828, when, with two companions, he visited the lovely old town of Graz.

DEATH OF BEETHOVEN

In 1827, Beethoven, lying seriously ill in Vienna, was given some of Schubert's songs to study, among them the song-cycle, Die Schone Mullerin, (The Maid of the Mill). He was astonished at their beauty and the skill with which they were constructed. He had only known of some half-dozen of Schubert's songs before, and was amazed to learn that there were already more than five hundred of them. He asked to see some of the young man's piano and opera music too, but when it was brought to him he was too ill to study it, and he died shortly afterwards.

Although they lived in the same city, Schubert had met Beethoven only once or twice. But he was among the great composer's last visitors, and at his funeral was one of the chief mourners. In November of the following year Schubert at the early age of thirty-one, died, it is thought of typhoid.

HIS COMPOSITIONS

If Schubert had written only his songs, he would still have been an important composer. His six hundred songs are unique; no other musician has composed so many exquisite examples of the art-song, or so perfectly interpreted the words he chose to set to music. But in his short life, Schubert had also composed nine symphonies, several string quartets and other chamber music, some piano works, and the music for more than a dozen operas or operettas, of which we hear hardly anything to-day except some excerpts from *Rosamunde*.

Among the best-known of his songs are the settings of words from Shakespeare—*Who is Sylvia?* and *Hark, Hark, the Lark*; while *Gretchen at the Spinning-Wheel* and *Erlkonig* are two of his seventy-one settings of words by the great German poet, Goethe.

Of Schubert's symphonies, the most frequently played are the Unfinished and the Symphony No. 9 in C major, usually called the Great C major symphony, both because of its length and because it is a superb work.

Schubert and his friend, Vogl, a prominent tenor.

143

HANS CHRISTIAN ANDERSEN

Hans Christian Andersen was born on 2nd April, 1805, in the small village of Odense in Denmark. His parents were very poor; his father was a not very successful shoemaker and his mother worked as a washerwoman. The three of them lived in a one-roomed cottage. This tiny, but clean and much loved home was probably very similar to the cottages which Hans so often described later in his fairy tales. He was a nervous, sensitive child, frightened of the dark, observant, but not very strong. Like his parents he was extremely superstitious. His father was a rather weak, discontented man, who always felt that he should have had a better chance in life.

In 1816, the shoemaker died. Eleven-year-old Hans was a long, lanky, awkward boy, who was always getting into trouble with his teacher for being clumsy. One day he just walked out and told his mother that he was never going back to school. He loved reading and was surprisingly deft with his fingers for all his clumsiness. He built himself a toy theatre for which he cut out the most delicate scenery, and made some puppets which he dressed himself. He put on several plays in his toy theatre and wrote his first fairy story, " Abor and Elvira ", which he read to friends.

When he was fourteen, Hans felt that he had better take up a career. Tailoring seemed the obvious choice, but he was stage-struck and he had set his heart on becoming an opera singer. He took matters into his own hands and set off for Copenhagen in September, 1819. With his tall, awkward figure and stumbling, erratic manner, no manager would consider taking him on. Some of them even thought he was a little mad. With no work Hans was soon starving, but he was befriended by two musicians, Weyse and Siboni, and later by a poet called Frederick Guldberg, who helped him to become a dancing pupil at the Royal Theatre.

Unfortunately, Hans did not work very hard and Guldberg refused him further help. But Hans soon found a new friend and staunch ally in Jonas Collin, the director of the Royal Theatre. An even more powerful friend was the king himself, Frederick VI, who realised that underneath his odd, uncouth manner, Hans Andersen had great talent and intelligence. The king arranged for the boy to go, free of charge, to a famous grammar school at Slagelse. Before going to school his first book, *The Ghost at Palnatoke's Grave* had been published.

Hans Andersen did no better at the grammar school than he had at the Dame school in his own village. He appeared to be backward and stupid and the other boys were always making fun of him and he left school in 1827. Many years later, Hans wrote that this was the bitterest and the darkest period of his life. In 1829, he had his second book published, an extraordinary fantasy called *A Journey on Foot from Holman's Canal to the East Point of Amager* which was quite successful. The new book with the long title was followed by a farce and a book of poems. Some of Andersen's old friends, who had snubbed him and been unkind to him because of his odd and eccentric manners, renewed their friendship now that he was becoming well-known.

TRAVELS ABROAD

In 1833, King Frederick allowed Hans a small amount of money for travelling and Hans made the first of his long journeys across Europe. He wrote *Agnate and the Merman* and, in 1835, a novel called *The Improvisatore* which was his first big success. In the same year he produced the first instalment of what was to become his most famous work, *Fairy Tales*. He wrote further parts to the tales in 1836 and 1837. Strangely enough these were not very popular or

With the help of his friends, Siboni and Weyse, Andersen was received at the Danish court where he won the interest and friend-ship of Frederick VI, but it was not until 1835 that real success came his way.

144

widely read to begin with and his new novel *O.T.* sold much better. He followed this with a romance called *Only a Fiddler*.

Hans Andersen now turned his attention back to his first love, the theatre. Again he was not very successful so he wrote more collections of stories, *Picture-Book without Pictures* and *A Poet's Bazaar*. All this time, however, his *Fairy Tales* was growing in popularity and his fame was spreading all over Europe, although many of his own country-people still considered him an oddity rather than a genius. In June, 1847, Andersen came to England to stay with Charles Dickens, the novelist. He got on well with Mrs. Dickens and the younger children, for whom he made beautiful cut-out pictures of trees, flowers and elves. However, during this visit, he went driving through the streets of London in a horse-drawn cab and he thought an attempt was being made to kidnap him. He undid his boots and stuffed all his valuables into them and when Charles Dickens met him at the end of the journey, Andersen was so frightened he could not speak.

In spite of his fame, he still wanted to be known as a serious writer and a dramatist, but the *Fairy Tales* remained by far the most popular of all his work. Drawing on the old tales and superstitions that his mother had passed on to him, Hans Andersen wrote more of these stories and in 1847 and 1848 two new volumes came out. The *Fairy Tales* went on being published in instalments until Christmas, 1872. Before that Hans wrote another romance *To be or not to be* in 1857 and, in 1863, one of his best travel books, *In Spain*.

In the spring of 1872, he had an accident. He fell awkwardly getting out of bed and injured himself quite badly. He never fully recovered from this, although he lived until 4th August, 1875, when he died very peacefully.

Probably one of the best known of Andersen's fairy tales is that of " The Ugly Duckling ". Many people seem to think that Hans was really describing himself and his own feelings. He was always a very awkward man, all knees and elbows and with irregular features. He was abnormally sensitive and so lost in the colourful world of his own imagination that reality was only a dream to him. " The Little Mermaid " is another of his most famous stories and the people of Denmark erected a small, rather wistful statue of the Mermaid on the waterfront in Copenhagen as a tribute and memorial to their famous countryman.

Charles Dickens was a friend of Andersen's.

The Little Mermaid of the Fairy Tales.

Hans Christian Andersen (1805-1875).

Thumbelina is one of Andersen's most delightful fairy tales.

CHOPIN

Almost everyone who learns to play the piano sooner or later comes across pieces by Frederick Chopin. His waltzes, nocturnes, preludes, studies, mazurkas have never gone out of favour during the whole period since his death more than a hundred years ago. They are in the repertoires of all serious pianists, both professional and amateur. Chopin's music is very beautiful, with a wealth of lovely melodies; and, most important of all, it is perfect for his instrument, which he himself played wonderfully well.

Frederick Chopin spent most of his short adult life in France, but he was born and educated in Poland, and it is to Poland that his music owes much of its essential character. His father, who was French, left his native land at the age of sixteen, made his home in Poland, and married a Polish woman. Frederick was born in 1810 in a little house in the country near Warsaw, the capital. His father was at this time tutor to the owner of the estate in which the house stood. Shortly afterwards he became Professor of French in the High School in Warsaw, and the family moved to the city.

Like his three sisters, Frederick was clever, and he showed signs of his great musical gifts at a very early age. His parents were anxious that his talents should be developed to the full, and provided him with excellent piano and composition teachers until he was old enough to become a pupil at the Warsaw Conservatoire. He was a particularly bright, intelligent child, physically small but quick and agile; he played games of all kinds with his school-fellows, and there are stories of his going skating and having tumbles on the ice. Also he was a brilliant mimic; he could do anything he liked with his face, imitating other people and sometimes making such grimaces that he frightened his friends.

Music was always Chopin's chief passion, but he worked hard at all his school subjects and passed all the examinations his father insisted on his taking. During holidays in the country he heard the real folk music of Poland, and it made a deep and lasting impression on him. He began to note down the tunes of folk songs and dances, and suggestions of many of these can be recognised in his piano works, although he seldom used complete tunes.

REVOLUTION AND EXILE

By the time he was nineteen he had finished the course at the Conservatoire and had given several concerts, playing mainly his own works. In 1830 he set out on a journey through Germany and Austria, intending to visit France. While he was in Vienna he heard about the revolution that had broken out in Poland, and later, in Stuttgart, came the news that Warsaw had been captured by the Russians. Bitterly unhappy at the thought of these terrible events in his native country, Chopin travelled on in September, 1831, to Paris, which he was to make his home for the rest of his life.

PARIS

Paris then as now was a wonderful city for the arts. Here Chopin met Liszt, who was already a famous pianist, the composers Berlioz and Mendelssohn and many other musicians, as well as countless poets, writers and painters. His quiet, courteous manner won him many friends, and his genius was recognised and acknowledged almost from his first appearance in the city.

A number of refugees from Poland were also in Paris at this time, and Frederick was at once made welcome among them. They included rich, titled people who introduced him to the leaders of Parisian society. As a result he was asked to give piano lessons to the daughters of many wealthy families, among them the Rothschilds, the famous bankers, and soon he was making a comfortable income from teaching and was a favourite wherever he went.

His success as a concert pianist was not so great. The Paris audiences liked the flamboyant style of Liszt better than Chopin's poetic, sensitive playing, which was in any case less well suited to large concert halls. After a few years he no longer played in public in Paris, though he gave many private recitals.

As his fame grew, publishers became eager to bring out his compositions. They found that, in spite of his quiet manner, Chopin was a clever business man who knew how to get the best price for his works.

Frédéric Francois Chopin (1810-49) Polish composer.

In Paris, Chopin became a favourite of musical society.

Previous to his Paris visit, Chopin was acclaimed in Germany and Austria.

HE FALLS IN LOVE

In 1835 Frederick's father and mother travelled to Karlsbad in Austria for a holiday, and he joined them there for a happy four weeks. When they returned home he went on to Dresden to meet a wealthy Polish family whom he had known in Warsaw, and fell deeply in love with the daughter, Maria.

That winter, in Paris, he was seriously ill with influenza.

The next summer he was allowed to become engaged to Maria, but when he was again ill in the winter of 1836, her parents decided that his health was too delicate for him to make a good husband. His letters were ignored, and three years later Maria married another man.

The effect of the broken engagement on Chopin's sensitive, romantic nature was profound, and it was while he was in this mood of despair that he became fascinated by the famous woman novelist, George Sand.

HIS FRIENDSHIP WITH GEORGE SAND

His health was worsening, and in October, 1838, with George Sand and her young son and daughter, he left Paris for the Mediterranean island of Majorca, where the climate was said to be ideal for lung-sufferers like himself. By now he had developed tuberculosis, the disease from which his youngest sister had died some years before.

Unfortunately the Majorca sun shone on the little party for only a short time. They had scarcely been there a fortnight when the weather broke and violent winds and heavy rain swept over the island. There were no hotels, and they were living in primitive, uncomfortable conditions. Inevitably Chopin became desperately ill. Madame Sand was a good and devoted nurse, and under her care he recovered sufficiently to do some composing, in spite of the miserable little piano which was all he had, and to appreciate the beauty of the scenery once the weather began to improve.

But by February, when they returned to France, his health was worse than it had ever been. George Sand took him to her country house, Nohant, in the province of Berry, south of Paris, and here for the next eight years Chopin spent every summer, except that of 1840 when his hostess had a play produced in Paris. He was waited on hand and foot, given the best room in the house with a fine piano, and everything was done for the good of his health and his work. During this period Chopin composed some of his best music. In winter he lived in Paris, teaching and leading a gay social existence as before.

QUARREL WITH GEORGE SAND

But a misunderstanding caused a bitter quarrel between Chopin and George Sand and after 1846 he never visited Nohant again. In February, 1848, revolution broke out in Paris; many people left the city, including most of Chopin's pupils, and he decided to accept an invitation from one of these pupils, Jane Stirling, to visit her home in Scotland.

For seven months he travelled about England and Scotland, staying with friends, and giving concerts in London, Manchester, Edinburgh and Glasgow. But he was weak and wretched, and in the cold northern weather his illness increased its hold on him. He returned to Paris and there, a year later at his home, he died. Among the few friends with him at the last was his sister Louise, who had travelled from Warsaw to see him. A small boxful of Polish soil was sprinkled on his grave in the Paris cemetery of Père-Lachaise.

In Majorca, Chopin composed the Raindrop Prelude.

147

CHARLES DICKENS

Charles Dickens was born in 1812 in Landport, a division of Portsea. His father, John Dickens, was a clerk in the Navy Pay Office and earned quite a good salary. But he and his wife were a happy-go-lucky, thriftless couple who were continually in debt. Dickens later drew portraits of his father first as Mr. Micawber in *David Copperfield*, then as Dorrit in *Little Dorrit*; while his mother is pictured as Mrs. Micawber and as Mrs. Nickleby in *Nicholas Nickleby*.

EARLY DAYS OF DICKENS

For a short time the family went to live in London before moving to Chatham in Kent. It was in the house in Chatham that Charles Dickens discovered an old parcel of books containing *Robinson Crusoe*, *Tom Jones* and *Gulliver's Travels*. These caught his imagination and opened up a whole new world to him. He went to a school run by William Giles, son of a Baptist minister, who realised that the boy had a remarkable imagination. It was Mr. Giles who gave Dickens the nickname which was to follow him all his life " The Inimitable ". Meanwhile, Mr. Dickens was getting further and further into debt and finally they had to sell up their furniture and move back to London. Just before his eleventh birthday Dickens travelled up by coach to join his family.

They settled in Cheapside, a very poor neighbourhood but one which in those days was still near open country. Charles Dickens was desperately unhappy for he had loved Chatham and had made many friends there. Also, he was now made to work in the house and he missed being at school. Later in life he wrote about this period: " What would I have given— if I had had anything to give—to have been sent back to any other school, to have been taught something anywhere ". To try and forget his unhappiness he began to explore the back streets of London in his spare time. His quick eye and retentive memory provided much of the material for his later

Charles John Huffman Dickens (1812-70), English novelist.

novels. He saw and felt great compassion for the terrible miseries of the poor.

Mr. Dickens's debts rose all the time and when Charles was offered a job in a blacking factory at a wage of between six and seven shillings a week, his father made him accept it. For twelve hours a day, six days a week, he worked in a basement sticking labels on to jars of blacking. He was miserable and frightened and for years afterwards he suffered from a nightmare in which he found himself back in the factory. His father was now arrested for debt and sent to Marshalsea Prison, where he was joined by his wife and younger children. Charles Dickens lived in a home for children run by a Mrs. Pipchin, whom he later described in *Dombey and Son*.

Matters improved when Mr. Dickens inherited some money

In David Copperfield, *David marries Dora who dies not long after, leaving him alone and disconsolate.*

and was set free. Charles was sent back to school for a while, until he too came into a small legacy and went to work as a very junior clerk in a solicitor's office. He taught himself shorthand and studied hard in his spare time as he was very ambitious and was constantly worried about his lack of education. He became a political reporter on a newspaper called *The True Sun*. At this time he had also been secretly writing short stories and he sent one called " Dinner at Poplar Walk " to *The New Monthly Magazine*. It was published anonymously. Fired by this success, and under the pen name Boz, he wrote more stories and a series of articles for his next newspaper, *The Morning Chronicle*.

MARRIAGE

On his twenty-fourth birthday, *Sketches by Boz* was published. It was well reviewed and highly praised. Chapman and Hall, the publishers, asked him to write a short text to accompany a series of pictures by an artist called Robert Seymour—and so *Pickwick Papers* was born. To begin with, the series was not a success.

On the 2nd of April, 1836, Charles Dickens married Catherine Hogarth, whose father, George Hogarth, was editor of *The Evening Chronicle*. She was a pretty, rather moody girl, who probably never fully understood or appreciated the genius of her husband.

Robert Seymour died suddenly and his place was filled by a young artist, Hablot Browne, who worked under the name of Phiz. He was the perfect collaborator for Dickens and later illustrated many of his most famous works. Drawing on his wonderful memory and his experiences as a reporter, Charles began writing *Oliver Twist*, which first appeared as a serial.

He was now becoming a very popular writer and although he had enormous vitality, the strain of so much work was intense. He was also badly shaken by the death of his young sister-in-law, Mary, to whom he had been devoted.

He had a brief holiday and then began work on *Barnaby Rudge*, when, suddenly, he was seized with the idea of writing a book about " cheap " boarding schools. Shelving *Barnaby Rudge*, he began *Nicholas Nickleby* and the first instalment was published in March, 1838. He continued to write *Oliver Twist* and *Nicholas Nickleby* as serials, both of which caught the public's imagination.

Charles Dickens was now extremely popular, not only because he was a celebrity, but also because he was excellent company, a good talker and wanted passionately to improve the conditions of the poor people. He began publishing a weekly magazine called *Master Humphrey's Clock* which did not do very well until the first instalment of *The Old Curiosity Shop* was printed in it. At last he managed to finish *Barnaby Rudge* and, badly in need of a holiday, he took the reluctant Catherine with him on a tour of America. They were mobbed by admirers and later he wrote a book about their experiences called *American Notes*.

The serial story of *Martin Chuzzlewit* followed. Then, while visiting Manchester, he was appalled yet again by the terrible conditions of the poor people and fired by this he wrote *A Christmas Carol*. This was followed by *The Chimes* and *The Cricket on the Hearth*. He was still obsessed by the miseries of his own poverty-haunted childhood and he started to describe them yet again in *David Copperfield*.

In 1850, Charles Dickens began another magazine, *Household Words*, and in 1851 he was inspired to start *Bleak House*. During the next five years he went all over the country giving readings of his work, the proceeds of these

Oliver Twist—*a tale of realism and pathos.*

readings going to charity. Next he wrote *Little Dorrit*. In spite of his fame and all his achievements, Charles Dickens was not happy in his home life and after twenty years and nine children, he and Catherine parted.

His next book was *A Tale of Two Cities*, which was followed by *Great Expectations* and *Our Mutual Friend*. In 1865 he was involved in a railway accident, which upset him very much and gave him a great fear of travelling. But, in spite of his fears, he accepted an invitation to return to America to give readings from his books. The tour was a great success, but he had overworked for years and his health began to fail. He started a new book, *The Mystery of Edwin Drood* but was too worn out to finish it and, in 1870, he died.

Charles Dickens was buried in Westminster Abbey in the Poets' Corner. The poor people, whose suffering he had described so vividly and with such compassion in his books, felt the death of their friend and champion so deeply that for two days they filed past his coffin—a constant stream of mourners.

Oliver Twist with his beloved Rose.

GIUSEPPE VERDI

Just as many people think of Mozart and Schubert always as young men, because they died young, so we tend to think of Giuseppe Verdi as a rather severe-looking old man, because he lived to a great age, and portraits and photographs usually represent him as elderly. His life spanned most of the last century, for he was born in 1813 and died when the twentieth century was already a year old, in 1901.

Verdi's father was an innkeeper and Verdi was born in an inn in a tiny village near the town of Busseto in northern Italy. At the time of his birth, the country was under French rule. In 1814, Napoleon was defeated by the Austrians and Russians, who entered Italy and drove out the French. The story is told that as the foreign troops passed through Busseto they murdered many people who were taking refuge in the church, but Verdi's mother hid with her baby in the belfry, and so escaped.

Giuseppe (or " Joseph ") was a shy child. His father was very poor, but when his son showed a passion for music he managed to get for him an old spinet. This old instrument, Verdi kept all his life. He took music lessons with the village organist but by the age of twelve he knew as much as his master and succeeded to the post when the organist retired.

HIS BENEFACTOR

Verdi's father was too poor to give him a proper musical training. In Busseto, however, there lived a well-to-do merchant named Antonio Barezzi, who was passionately fond of music and it was he who became a second father to the boy. When Giuseppe went to school in Busseto, Barezzi saw to it that he had the best musical instruction that could be obtained in the little town. Eventually, Verdi went to live with the Barezzi family.

When he was eighteen he went to the city of Milan, where he was refused admission to the Conservatoire because he was four years over the age limit. So, he studied privately and made rapid progress. He also made the most of his opportunities, while in Milan, to attend the operas performed at the famous theatre of La Scala. Already he was composing music—piano pieces, cantatas, and marches for the town band of Busseto.

HAPPINESS AND SADNESS

On his return to Barezzi's house, Verdi fell in love with Margherita, the daughter of his benefactor. They had known each other since childhood and had often played piano duets together. They were married in 1836, the year Verdi composed his first opera. After three years he went back to Milan with his wife and baby son. His opera was produced there at La Scala in 1839 and was so successful that Verdi was asked to compose three more operas.

In the meantime his infant daughter had died and shortly after the production of his opera his little son died too. In 1840 he was busy composing a comic opera for the director of La Scala when his wife, Margherita. died. Prostrated with grief at these successive losses, Verdi finished the comic opera, but when it was produced, it was a complete failure. Verdi resolved to compose no more operas, and asked the director of La Scala to release him from his contract. The director, however, had just been sent a libretto which he insisted on Verdi taking home with him to read. In spite of himself, Verdi was so impressed that he began composing music for it. The opera, *Nabucco*, was finished by the end of 1841 and was produced at La Scala in March, 1842, with immense success.

SUCCESS

The following year Verdi composed another successful

Giuseppe Fortunino Francesco Verdi was born at Le Roncole, near Busseto in Northern Italy, on 10th October, 1813.

In 1832, Verdi applied for admission to the Milan Conservatorio, but the governing body rejected him.

In 1846, after the successful performance of Attila *at the Fenice theatre in Venice, Verdi was carried home shoulder-high through the streets. At that time, he was the most popular composer in Europe.*

opera for La Scala and later, in 1844, he wrote *Ernani*, which was produced at Venice. He composed yet another for production in Rome. He was now a famous man and his operas were in demand, not only in Italy but in Paris and London too.

Although several of Verdi's very early works have been revived in recent years, the first of his operas, *Rigoletto*, produced in Venice in 1851, and *Il Trovatore*, composed the following year, are still popular favourites. For more than ten years Verdi knew only success, but *La Traviata*, produced in Venice in 1853 and now one of his best-loved works, was a complete failure. The public later received *La Traviata* enthusiastically.

In 1859, Verdi married again, his second wife being the singer Giuseppina Strepponi. She had appeared in three of his earliest operas, and before her voice was spoiled by over-work and illness, had been one of the most popular sopranos in Italy.

PATRIOTISM

Verdi had never shown any interest, or taken any active part in politics but, in 1860, when the various Italian states

Requested by Radetzky to write a marching song for the emperor's troops, Verdi curtly refused.

Written in answer to a request by the Khedive of Egypt and first performed in Cairo in December, 1871, Aida *has remained one of the most popular and successful operas ever since. Verdi gave his opera an Egyptian setting.*

151

became united as a single nation, he was persuaded to become a member of the Chamber of Deputies. In another way, too, he was forced to concern himself indirectly with political matters; several times his operas got into trouble with the censor on account of their supposed revolutionary ideas. The most famous example is *The Masked Ball*, the story of which is the assassination of King Gustav III of Sweden. The authorities were afraid that this might be a bad example to the Italian people and Verdi was compelled to alter the scene and to change the names of all the characters so that it was no longer a king who was assassinated. The opera was nearly ruined in the process but the magnificent music saved it and to-day it is often produced with its original characters and setting.

The very name of Verdi became associated with patriotic feeling because the letters spelled the initials of " Vittorio Emanuele Re D'Italia " (Victor Emmanuel King of Italy) and, when northern Italy was still under Austrian domination, to cry " Long live Verdi! " was equivalent to calling for the expulsion of the foreign rulers.

In 1848, Verdi bought the farmhouse and estate of Sant' Agata, near Busseto, and here he began to spend as much time as he possibly could. With his second wife he lived there in happy seclusion, planning the gardens, planting trees, and managing the farm lands.

When he was fifty-five he was requested by the Khedive (ruler) of Egypt to compose an opera for the new theatre to be built in Cairo. The opera, *Aida*, with an Egyptian setting, was the result. It was produced in Cairo in 1871 and is one of his greatest works.

For fifteen years after *Aida*, Verdi composed no new operas. The only major work to come from his pen during this period was the Requiem Mass written in honour of the famous Italian writer, Alessandro Manzoni. Then, in 1885, he began to plan an opera on the story of Shakespeare's *Othello*. Shakespeare had always fascinated him, and many years before he had composed an opera based on *Macbeth*. In the creation of *Otello* he had the assistance of Arrigo Boito, a very gifted writer. Verdi and Boito worked together on the opera for more than a year and, when the work was produced at La Scala in 1887, the seventy-four-year-old composer was given the greatest reception of his life.

In 1890 he began work on another Shakespearean play, this time *The Merry Wives of Windsor*. Again Boito was responsible for the brilliant libretto, which was called *Falstaff*. Verdi took two years to compose this, his last and probably his greatest masterpiece. It was produced in Milan in February, 1893, in the presence of the veteran composer, now eighty years old. At the end of the performance there was a tremendous demonstration of enthusiasm, admiration and love for Verdi. There is not the slightest sign in *Falstaff* that it is the work of an old man; Verdi was still at the height of his creative powers.

But he was tired and his health was failing. He died in Milan at the age of eighty-eight.

Altogether Verdi composed twenty-six operas, of which ten are still performed regularly in opera houses all over the world, while several of the lesser-known works are beginning to be revived more often. His Requiem Mass is also one of the great masterpieces of choral music.

Nabucco *was written by Verdi in what is called his early →
period. A middle period is represented by* Aida, *and the third
period by* Otello *and* Falstaff.

JULES VERNE

Ever since men began telling tales, they have imagined lands and times which never existed. For instance, in early days, writers could set such stories in the undiscovered heart of Africa. However, as the world became more thoroughly explored and tamed, writers looked farther afield. Centuries ago, indeed, they were imagining trips to the moon.

Then, at the beginning of the last century, there came real wonders to stir the imagination, such as steam engines, iron ships and electricity. The world was ready for a new kind of adventure story, one in which science and engineering would feature prominently. This is the kind of story especially associated with the name of Jules Verne.

Jules Verne was born on the 8th of February, 1828, on the island of Feydeau at the mouth of the Loire river—a place of old mansions built by planters who had become rich in the West Indies. His parents came of people who had adventurous, stirring histories. Jules Verne grew up with tales of the Seven Seas in his ears and the sight of masts and furled sails at the end of his street.

He was not scholastically inclined and his only outstanding gift—apart from a love of music—was a very good memory. But he was popular, for he had a talent for making up new games. He invented imaginary machines—machines inspired by the horse buses, paddle steamships and the trains which were at that time new inventions.

Jules had three sisters and a brother, Paul, who later became a sea-captain and a writer. At the age of 11, Jules tried to run away to sea—not because he was unhappy, but for the sake of adventure. He offered to change places with a cabin-boy sailing for the Antilles. Luckily his parents managed to catch up with the young stowaway, and made him promise that his future journeys should be, for a while, in the imagination only.

The career for which Jules was intended was the law. As he grew older he became less enthusiastic about this, and

Jules Verne (1828-1905), French author.

preferred to write not-very-good plays. However, at the age of 20, he found himself a law student in Paris. He lived on the Left Bank and wrote letters home saying how hungry he was (yet he lived on stewed prunes for three days in order to buy a volume of Shakespeare). On special occasions he went to the theatre, for he loved plays almost more than books.

Then, in 1850, when he was 22, Jules Verne had a one-act play accepted. The producer was Alexander Dumas, author of *The Three Musketeers*, and leader of the " romantic " movement which favoured adventurous plots and colourful settings. On the strength of this play Jules refused, after passing his final examinations, to have anything more to do with the law other than a little teaching to make ends meet. Even so, there were hard times before he got a job as secretary to the theatre management.

Jules Verne was born and raised within the sight of ships berthed in the busy river port of Nantes.

First published in 1862, The Mysterious Island *was the first of Verne's many adventure stories.*

A dramatic scene from Michael Strogoff *in which the Tsar's courier saves his mother from the executioner.*

He went on writing and had plays and then stories accepted. These were not very original, though some of them showed his love of distant places and others his fascination with imaginary machines. These plays and stories were good enough to win him new friends, who were enchanted by his mixture of knowledge and his boyish love of fun and practical jokes.

Jules was now 30, and anxious to marry a young widow with two children. He could not do this on his uncertain earnings as a writer, so he combined writing with a job on the Paris stock exchange. Several of his friends were also members of the stock exchange, and between buying and selling shares they discussed plots for stories.

He was now able, for the first time, to travel. In particular, he made a pilgrimage to the English Lake District where the founders of the romantic movement had written their poems, and to the Border country of another great romantic, Sir Walter Scott. But he was nearly 35 before he found a literary style of his own.

It came about one day because he was driven out of his house by the noise of his new-born son crying. At his club he met a friend who was building a balloon, or airship, in which he hoped to drift across Africa. (In fact, it crashed at Hamburg.) Jules saw the idea for a short story here, wrote it, and sent it to a publisher.

FIRST NOVEL

He was told that it was too short and too technical, and was recommended to rewrite it as a novel, with more human interest. In fact, Jules Verne was as interested in people as in machines: it was simply that he had never thought of combining the two kinds of story before. Now he did so, and the publisher was so delighted with this first novel that he commissioned Verne to write forty more in a similar vein.

When the book came out its readers were just as delighted —and not only the 15-year-old boys whom its author had had in mind when he wrote his novel, but their sisters, fathers and perhaps mothers too. For this blend of scientific marvels, strange settings and heroic or amusing characters of several nationalities was *Five Weeks In A Balloon* the first of the typical Jules Verne books.

The writer was not to disappoint his hopeful publisher

In Twenty Thousand Leagues Under the Sea, *Captain Nemo patrols the depths in his submarine*, Nautilus.

either, for in the next few decades he was to write over a hundred books, including encyclopedias and his famous romances. Some of these books relied for their excitement simply on being set in strange places, such as the Arctic. The Arctic had always fascinated Jules Verne, more so than the tropics, or the round-the-world trip of *Around the World in Eighty Days*, which was inspired by a Cooks' travel advertisement. Other novels were more fanciful, such as the one which described a journey to the centre of the earth. But many of his stories depended on inventions which, nearly a century ago, seemed to be not possible. There was, for instance, the cannon which could shoot men to the moon, and the submarine of *Twenty Thousand Leagues Under The Sea*.

And all the time Jules Verne travelled the world in search of new ideas. Even when he was hardest at work he had to take an hour or a day off now and then to sail his fishing-boat off the French coast. Later he had a yacht in which he cruised the Mediterranean, and on one trip he was nearly shipwrecked. But his real disaster came one dark night on dry land, when a madman shot at him for no reason and wounded him in the foot. . . .

That was in 1886, when Jules Verne was 58. The wound itself could have been worse; but, somehow, the months in bed which followed it changed the author's whole outlook on life. Once so active and party-loving, he now sold his yacht, gave up his travels, and settled down to a quiet, shy, almost retired life in the provincial town of Amiens. He went on writing—he could not live without that, rich and world-renowned though he now was. But only one famous book, *The Floating Island*, in which he relived a boyhood dream, came from this period.

As the new century dawned Jules Verne, whose health had never been good, began to suffer a series of painful illnesses. And, on the 24th of March, 1905—still planning new books—he died. In one sense such a man never dies and, in fact, Jules Verne has three different kinds of immortality.

One reason for Verne's immortality is that he founded a new kind of story-telling—the " science fiction " type, which the English novelist H. G. Wells took a stage farther in inventiveness and which is still popular to-day. Another is that Verne, like Wells, was a prophet whose visions sometimes came true. He not only predicted things like television,

In Master of the World, *Verne anticipated the invention of the airship.*

submarines, polar exploration, and ideas on which scientists are still working, but inspired boys to become the scientists who would make them possible. Lastly, the most important kind of immortality is that the best of his stories—the adventure stories as well as the science fiction ones—remain as popular as ever.

Because of scientific discoveries, we of the twentieth century can now see the faults in Verne's books. The characterisation is not quite " deep " enough for them to be considered serious literature; the scientific details are often impossible; and some of the things which seemed wonderful when he wrote of them now seem funny. But Verne's simple, direct style and universal appeal makes him easy to read in the original French and easy to translate. His books have been translated into many languages, making his name a household word throughout the world. From time to time, a film is made of one of his books (an idea which would have delighted Verne). We are then transported to a world even more wonderful than that which delighted the Paris of nearly a century ago when an adaptation of *Around the World in Eighty Days* was staged.

An episode from Five Weeks in a Balloon, *where the ropes of the balloon and an elephant's tusk become entwined.*

The adventures of Phineas Fogg and his manservant, Passe-partout, are described in Around the World in Eighty Days.

GEORGES BIZET

On the night of 3rd March, 1875, two men left the theatre of the Opera-Comique in Paris and walked slowly away arm-in-arm. There were few people about, for most of the audience at the evening's performance in the theatre had left before the end. The two men wandered sadly through the quiet streets until dawn. They were the composer, Georges Bizet, and a friend of his, and they had been present at the first performance of Bizet's opera, *Carmen*. It had been an utter failure.

CARMEN—A FAILURE

To speak of the failure of *Carmen* now seems absurd, for to-day it is one of the most popular of all operas. It is performed all over the world, and its rousing tunes, like the Toreador's Song, are known everywhere. Yet on that March night in 1875, only a handful of people in the audience recognised its greatness. One of them was the Russian composer Tchaikovsky, who said: "Within ten years *Carmen* will be the most popular opera in the world". Events proved him very nearly right; but Bizet knew nothing of this.

Although friends tried to comfort and reassure him, he remained in a state of depression and melancholy. A few weeks later he became seriously ill, and in May, 1875, he died.

WORLD-WIDE ACCLAIM

Five months later, a few days before what would have been Bizet's thirty-seventh birthday, *Carmen* was produced in Vienna and given an enthusiastic reception. Brahms went to hear it twenty times, and said he "would have gone to the ends of the earth to embrace Bizet". It was produced in Germany, Italy, England; in cities all over Europe; in America, and eventually, eight years after its first perform-

First encouraged by his father who was a singing master, Bizet showed early promise of his musical gifts. At the Paris Conservatoire he studied under several outstanding teachers such as Gounod, whose music was an inspiration to him.

ance, it was produced again in Paris. This time Bizet's countrymen began to appreciate the opera's true value.

CHILDHOOD DAYS

Georges Bizet was born in Paris in 1838. His father was a teacher of singing, and Bizet as a child often used to listen outside the door of the room where lessons were taking place. One day his father called him in and gave him the music of a song. "See if you can sing that," he said, and to his astonishment the boy sang the song correctly, but without looking at the music. He had learned it all by listening at the door.

By the time Bizet was nine his father thought him ready to go to the famous Paris Conservatoire, or Academy of Music. According to the rules the earliest age of entry was ten, but Georges so impressed the professors at the Conservatoire that they allowed him to enter a few months early. He studied there for eight years. Then when he was seventeen he won the Rome Prize, which entitled him to spend several years in Rome studying and composing music.

EARLY WORKS

He had already composed a symphony before going to Italy, but he never mentioned this early work, which remained hidden in the Library at the Conservatoire until 1933. It was played for the first time in 1935 and since then has become a popular item in concert programmes.

After his return to Paris, Bizet found it difficult to earn enough to live on by composing alone. He earned money by giving piano lessons and by helping other composers with the rehearsals and production of their operas. One of the musicians he worked for was Gounod, a great friend of his, whose opera *Faust* is almost as famous as *Carmen*.

But Bizet was always occupied with his own music too,

Georges Bizet, properly Alexander César Léopold Bizet, died in 1875 at the age of thirty-seven. His early struggles for recognition were unsuccessful and it was not until the last four years of his life that he produced his masterpieces.

devoting as much time to it as he possibly could. He wrote a number of songs and piano works (he was an excellent pianist himself) including the delightful suite of pieces called " Children's Games ". Five of these pieces he later arranged for full orchestra under the title " Little Suite ". His first full-length opera was *The Pearl Fishers*, composed in 1862. The next was based on Sir Walter Scott's novel *The Fair Maid of Perth*. Neither of these was successful, though there is some good music in both.

FRANCO-PRUSSIAN WAR

In 1869, Bizet married the daughter of the man who had been one of his professors at the Conservatoire. For a time he and his wife were very happy. Then in July, 1870, war broke out between France and Prussia, and a terrible year began for the people of France, and in particular of Paris.

The French were heavily defeated at the battle of Sedan, and by September the city of Paris was surrounded by German troops and besieged. Through most of the winter the inhabitants were cut off from all communication with the outside world. No food or fuel could be brought in. German guns bombarded the city, and soon the people were suffering from both hunger and cold. Madame Bizet, wrote the composer to her mother, dreamed every night of chicken and lobster. He was desperately worried about his wife's health and about his own affairs, for with war raging there was no time for music and he was earning no money.

He had enlisted in the National Guard at the outbreak of the war, although he had never been strong. He worked hard training to be a soldier, carrying a gun which was very heavy for him, and spending long hours mounting guard on the fortifications of the city. He was on guard duty when the Prussians entered Paris on 1st March, 1871.

Civil war followed; revolutionaries destroyed the Town Hall and the famous Palace of the Tuileries, and many people were killed. It was so dangerous in the city that Bizet took his wife on the first train he could find into the country. After a short time they were able to return, but now began a period of great difficulty for Bizet. He worked very hard, composing new music, re-writing some of his earlier works,

At the Conservatoire Bizet won many prizes and in 1857, with his cantata, Clovis et Clotilde, *he was awarded the* Prix de Rome. *This prize allowed him to spend three years of study in Rome.*

A theatrical impressario, who thought highly of Bizet's talent, commissioned the young composer to write the music for Les Pecheurs de Perles (The Pearl Fishers). *Unfortunately this, his first full-length opera, was badly received by the press.*

giving piano lessons. He was asked to provide the incidental music for the production of Alphonse Daudet's play *The Woman Of Arles* (usually known by its French title, *L'Arlesienne*). The play was a failure, but Bizet made his music for it into an orchestral suite which contains some of his best work. And while *L'Arlesienne* was being rehearsed, he was already thinking of *Carmen*.

DISPUTES AND QUARRELS

In spite of the interruptions caused by all the other work he had to do, the music of *Carmen* came easily to him, but the opera caused endless disputes with the management of the Opera-Comique, where it was to be performed. One of the directors resigned because he disliked the story so much; Carmen, the heroine, is stabbed on the stage, and the idea of this horrified him. Also, the characters—girls from a cigarette factory, gypsies, smugglers, and common soldiers—shocked many people who were accustomed to operas being about princes and princesses and pleasant, well-bred men and women.

During the rehearsal period there were discussions and even quarrels, involving the authors of the text, the singers, and the remaining theatre director. The orchestral musicians said the music was too difficult to play; the chorus were upset to find that instead of standing quite still while they sang, their eyes fixed on the conductor, in *Carmen* they were expected to enter in twos and threes, to move about and to behave as if they really were soldiers and gypsies and cigarette-girls. They had never been asked to *act* before.

BIZET IS HONOURED

On the morning of 3rd March it was announced that Bizet had been awarded the Cross of the Legion of Honour by the government. This was a great honour, but the decoration was little comfort to him that night as he sensed the coldness and lack of understanding in the audience listening to his opera.

If he had lived only a few years longer he would, of course, have composed more music to delight us to-day, and he would also have known that *Carmen* was, after all, a success.

PAUL GAUGUIN

No one to-day would deny that Gauguin was a great painter. People may argue about his behaviour as a man but all are agreed about his pictures, though during his lifetime his work aroused much hostility and derision.

Paul Gauguin was born in Paris in 1848. His father was French and his mother, half-French and half-Peruvian. From his mother, Paul inherited the heavy-lidded eyes and narrow forehead of the Indians of the Andes.

CHILDHOOD

When he was three years old his parents set out for Peru, where his mother had influential relatives. His father died on the voyage while the ship was passing through the Straits of Magellan, and his mother went on to Peru with Paul and his sister. There they stayed with his mother's relatives for nearly four years, afterwards returning to Orleans, in France.

When he was seventeen Paul went off to sea and visited many tropical ports. He got to know and love the sun-drenched landscapes and the simple native people who were completely unaffected by the complexities of civilisation.

BUSINESS LIFE

This roving life ended when Gauguin was 23. He obtained employment with a firm of stockbrokers in Paris, and settled down to the life of a conventional business man. He was successful in his work and, two years later, married a matter-of-fact Danish girl. At this time he seemed destined to live his whole life in a very ordinary, commonplace way. But this was not to be.

One of his business colleagues was an amateur painter and Gauguin, always restless, was soon spending some of his abundant energy as a " Sunday painter ", becoming more and more engrossed in his hobby. He sometimes attended life

In 1875, Gaugin started painting in his free time. Eventually, he became so interested in art that he decided to give up his post at a broker's office and devote all his time to painting.

classes and drew under tuition. This was the only formal training that he ever received.

THE IMPRESSIONISTS

From the beginning Gauguin showed promise. At first he worked in the realistic style approved in the Salon, where he exhibited in 1876. But he soon became aware of a new movement in painting, called Impressionism, and he had the good fortune to be introduced to Camille Pissarro, the leader and chief driving-force of this movement. At times he painted with Pissarro and, under his guidance, turned his back on the photographic style of painting—concerning himself, instead, more with the light that fell upon the objects that he painted than with the objects themselves. This was the interest of the Impressionists, who were often content to paint the most commonplace scenes, for they took delight in the effects of light.

To most people at that time the Impressionist painters were a laughing-stock, and their pictures found few admirers and still fewer purchasers. Among the purchasers was Gauguin, who not only collected paintings by Manet, Pissarro, Monet and even the revolutionary Cézanne, but also imitated them with his brush. For ten years he was a keen Impressionist.

Gauguin made slow but steady progress in painting, spending more and more time at his easel, and less time at his business. But he continued to make money to provide for his family, for he now had five children.

Then, one day, Gauguin shocked everyone and dismayed his wife by announcing that he had given up his employment on the stock exchange in order to devote all his time to painting. He convinced himself, but no one else, that purchasers would soon come forward to buy his pictures. No purchasers came though many painters, among them Pissarro

At the age of 17 Gauguin went to sea as an apprentice in the French merchant marine, sailing back and forth between South America and France. At the age of 23 he left the sea and entered the employment of a broker's office in Paris.

and the great Degas, admired his work. Gauguin, having failed to find buyers for his pictures in Paris, tried Rouen, but with no more success. Soon he was living with his wife's relatives in Copenhagen, Denmark.

He found them narrow-minded and unsympathetic, and they regarded him as a crazy, ne'er-do-well. After six months he could stand it no longer, preferring to risk poverty in Paris. His wife would not take that risk and he returned to Paris with his oldest son, Clovis, who was six years old.

Then a bitter time began for Gauguin. An incurable optimist, he always believed that good fortune was just round the corner. He believed in himself and in his work; the trouble was that very few other people did so—not even his wife.

NEAR STARVATION

That winter, he and Clovis nearly starved. Clovis became ill and Gauguin got work as a bill-sticker for five francs a day. In the end he sent his small son to a cheap boarding-school and dared not visit him there because money was soon owing for the school fees. Gauguin could not even make a living for himself, though he always dreamed of the day when he could afford to have his family with him. But he refused to return to Copenhagen and face the scorn and censure of his wife's self-righteous relatives. He also refused to give up his painting.

DOGGED BY ILL-FORTUNE

That summer he went to Brittany where living was cheap. But ill-fortune followed him there and, half-starved, he became ill and quarrelled with most of his friends. Then, with a young painter named Laval, he set sail for Panama, in Central America, where he believed he could get work. In this, too, he was disappointed, for the only work available was navvying on the site of the Panama Canal, which was then under construction. Both artists were forced to take this work, toiling with pick and shovel under the blazing sun for over twelve hours each day. It was Laval who rescued him; by painting portraits he earned enough to pay their fare to the Island of Martinique, in the West Indies.

There, at first, they thought they had found their earthly paradise, but they were soon laid low with malaria and dysentery. Laval, who was delicate, was carried off to hospital, and Gauguin worked his passage home on a sailing ship, returning to two years of poverty, now in Paris, now in Brittany, but always painting.

INFLUENCE OF FRIENDS

It was during this time Gauguin met two men who were to influence his work profoundly, Emile Bernard and his friend Vincent Van Gogh.

Bernard, inspired by medieval stained glass and Japanese

Women of Tahiti *by Gauguin is on exhibition at the Louvre in Paris.*

159

At Van Gogh's invitation, Gauguin went to Arles to found a community of artists. The two painters later quarrelled and, in remorse, Van Gogh cut off his ear.

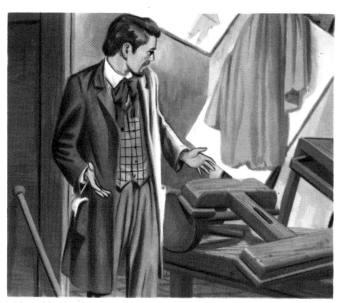

After his return to Paris in 1893, Gauguin's studio was ransacked and his paintings stolen. Now a sick man and greatly affected by his loss, he went back to Tahiti.

wood-cuts, maintained that artists should forget the literal representation of scenes, and concentrate on their feelings about the scenes. Bernard held the view that the important things are those that we remember when we no longer have the scene before us. Then our emotions have selected what is important and rejected what is unimportant. Gauguin at once saw the possibilities that these ideas opened up and began to put them into practice.

POST-IMPRESSIONIST PAINTINGS

Now freed completely from Impressionism, Gauguin painted a number of pictures which at last revealed his true greatness. Among them were the " Vision after the Sermon " with its brilliant red ground, and " Christ Jaune " (The Yellow Christ), in which he used almost flat areas of clear, strong colour and firm, bold outlines. They are rather like children's paintings, but very powerful and moving.

Inspired by the people and conditions prevailing in the lush, tropical paradise of Tahiti, Gauguin produced paintings of superior design and vibrant colourings. His works of art were to have an influence on almost every school of twentieth-century art.

Gauguin, now aged forty, had at last found himself as a painter. Although many artists admired his work, very few people would buy his pictures. Eventually, he was persuaded to go to Arles in the South of France, to live and work with the painter Van Gogh. But neither of them was easy to live with and after two months they parted company. Then Van Gogh had his first bout of madness, doubtless hastened by the strain of sharing a home and studio with the overbearing Gauguin.

SOUTH SEAS PARADISE

Back in Paris, Gauguin had his first taste of success. An exhibition and, later, the sale of his pictures brought him a modest sum of money. Though he still dreamt of the time when he could support his family, he spent the proceeds from the sale of his pictures, not on the family, but on a ticket to Tahiti in the Pacific Ocean. There, in the tropical island of his dreams, he felt certain that he could paint as he had never painted before.

In this he was right, and we can be grateful to him for his decision to turn his back on civilisation.

Gauguin sought out a remote village and in a native hut, there he lived as the natives lived, all the time drawing, painting pictures, and carving figures in wood. While in Tahiti he produced many of his greatest works, giving them titles in native Samoan such as " Te Rerioa " (The Dream), " Hina Marouru " (Fete at Hina), or " Manao Tupapau ". Many have a strange, dream-like quality and all have magnificent, glowing colours.

After two years in Tahiti, Gauguin returned to Paris where his latest paintings were a great success. He visited his family in Denmark and went again to Brittany, but always he hankered for his tropical islands. Within two years he was again on his way to Tahiti, but he was now a sick man.

Gauguin lived in the South Seas for another eight years and painted many more wonderful pictures; but the disease that he had contracted in Europe got a stronger and stronger hold. He was often ill, and being ill, he grew more quarrelsome than ever. In time he moved to an island in the remote Marquesas group, farther than ever from civilisation. He was found dead in his hut one morning in May, 1903.

ARCHITECTURE : IV
Modern Times

The new styles of modern architecture have been made possible by the use of new building materials. The most important of these is reinforced concrete. The Romans used concrete, which is made of cement mixed with gravel, but they could not build upwards to any great height. In the nineteenth century, architects discovered they could build with pillars and girders of cast iron. Girders are beams made of metal. Amongst the oldest buildings made of iron and glass are several of the big railway stations in London—stations like King's Cross, Paddington and Euston, which were built about one hundred years ago. In Britain, the largest building of iron and glass was the Crystal Palace, which was built in Hyde Park for the Great Exhibition of 1851. It was like an enormous greenhouse, and in fact it was designed by a gardener, Sir Joseph Paxton. Later the Crystal Palace was moved to Sydenham, and rebuilt, but it was burnt down before the Second World War when the wooden floor-boards caught fire. The most famous iron building is the Eiffel Tower in Paris, which was erected in 1879 as part of a big exhibition. With the television aerial on the top it is now over one thousand feet high.

A very impressive modern brick-built building is the Town Hall in Stockholm (1911-1923). The architect used ideas from the past, but did not actually copy any of the older styles.

Modern architecture as we know it to-day sprang to life with the use of reinforced concrete, strengthened with steel girders. Since these girders can be riveted together for extra strength, there is almost no limit to the height that a building may be: the result is a skyscraper. Sometimes thin steel rods are fixed together and used between the girders to make the floors of a tall building.

The skyscrapers of New York are built on solid rock, the ideal foundation for the tremendous weight of a tall building. Older skyscrapers on Manhattan Island were made with a steel framework covered with stone or brick, and examples of such buildings are the Woolworth Building and the Empire State Building. The Woolworth Building was built in 1913 and is 800 feet high; the Empire State Building, still the tallest in New York, was built in 1941 and is 1,250 feet high to the top of the observation platform.

It has been said that the electric elevator, or lift, is the mother of the skyscraper and, certainly without some means of rapid vertical transport it would be almost impossible to live and work in a multi-storeyed building. Imagine walking up and down eighty-two flights of stairs every day! Of course New York is not the only city in the United States with skyscrapers, these tall buildings can now be seen all over the world—in Europe, the Near and Far East, Australia and Canada. Due to the high cost of land, New York was forced

The town hall in Stockholm is a magnificent building which combines Italian influence with traditional Swedish design.

The Pirelli Tower in Milan is an imaginative structure of glass and reinforced concrete.

to build upwards and there are more skyscrapers in its small area than anywhere else in the world, giving the city an unmistakeable skyline.

To-day architects and engineers can design and erect buildings which do not rely on the outside walls for their strength. This is because all the weight is taken by the reinforced concrete girders. As a result the sides of some new buildings are completely glass; while others have coloured panels between the windows and the different floor levels. One of the newest and most imaginative buildings is the Pirelli Tower in Milan in Italy. Although it is very tall it is also very narrow and the side walls at each end nearly meet in a point like the bows of a ship.

In the last few years a number of countries, which used to be ruled by Great Britain or France, have become independent. Many new government buildings have had to be built for these countries, and the architects have designed them to suit the climate.

MODERN ARCHITECTS

The most important English architect before the Second World War was Sir Edwin Lutyens. He did not design buildings in the modern style, but was a *traditionalist*. A traditionalist is one who bases his designs on those of the past. Many of his buildings are particularly handsome and have an eighteenth-century aspect. His largest and finest work is at New Delhi where he designed the government buildings.

POST-WAR ARCHITECTURE

One of the first really modern buildings to be erected in London after the war was the Royal Festival Hall, a large concert hall. The style of to-day is called *contemporary* and most new churches are built in this style. The new Coventry Cathedral, built to replace the one bombed during the war, was designed by Sir Basil Spence. Several of Britain's leading artists have designed the fittings for the new cathedral.

Walter Gropius was an architect who did much to help found modern architecture. Before the war he worked in Germany, where he was born, but later he went to live in America. There he became professor of Architecture at Harvard and designed the Pan-American Building in New York, one of the biggest office blocks in the world.

Still in progress at the moment are two completely new capital cities. One is Brasilia, which is now the new capital of Brazil. The other is Chandigar in the East Punjab in India. Two architects are designing Brasilia. Lucio Costa, is responsible for the housing and shopping districts; Oscar Niemeyer has designed the government buildings and the cathedral. Brasilia is like a city out of the future. The Parliament Buildings are two very tall, thin blocks set close together. Nearby are two council chambers. One is like a dome without any windows, while the other is like a huge saucer standing on the ground.

In Chandigar the government buildings such as the Law Courts were designed by the architect Le Corbusier. Le Corbusier, born in Switzerland, was one of the most progressive of all modern architects. Most of his buildings are made of reinforced concrete, and they look massive and strong. Some seem rather strange because they stand on legs. A huge block of flats at Marseilles in France does not have a ground floor with walls. The whole building stands on thick columns, leaving an open space beneath. Other architects are now copying this idea. Among the other buildings Le

The Bauhaus, *or Trades and Guilds House, at Dessau was designed by Walter Gropius. On the right is a ground floor plan of the same building.*

Corbusier designed is a monastery in France, which is thought by some to be one of his best works.

Another architect whose work has caused a great deal of argument is the American, Frank Lloyd Wright. In New York he designed for works of modern art, a remarkable looking building called the Guggenheim Museum. Many of his houses, especially those built in the country, seem almost to be a part of the rocks and trees of the surrounding landscape.

Perhaps the most important construction work done in Britain since the war is the rebuilding of older towns and cities. Out-of-date houses are being pulled down and blocks of flats and housing estates being built in their place. In the old days, architects did not always take care to make their houses easy to run. For example, very often the architects used to put the kitchen in the basement, and the dining-room upstairs, which meant a great deal of running up and down. Now flats and houses are designed to be labour-saving, and warm in winter. To-day the appearance of a building is less important. What is important is that it is properly designed for the job it has to do. This is called *functional architecture.*

Conceived and built in 1937-39, the house "Falling Water" is a magnificent example of Frank Lloyd Wright's work.

Le Corbusier designed this villa near Paris. The house rests on pillars and the garden extends under the building.

VINCENT VAN GOGH

Vincent Van Gogh was born in the small Dutch village of Zundert, where his father was a clergyman. A devoted group, Vincent and his brothers and sisters were cut off socially from the peasant community because of their father's position. In later years, the family were not so close and Van Gogh corresponded only with his eldest brother and, to a lesser extent, with his eldest sister. The correspondence between Vincent and his brother, Théo, forms one of the most important collections of letters ever written.

On leaving school at the age of 16, Vincent was apprenticed to Goupil and Co., art dealers in Paris. He entered through family connections, his uncles being directors of the firm. Starting work in the Hague branch of this concern he remained there until he was 20, when he was transferred to London. In the same year Theo entered the firm's branch in Brussels. It was when he was in London that Vincent began to show the first signs of the inner conflicts that were to pursue him throughout his life. He became withdrawn and increasingly difficult in his relations with other people. At his parents' request he was transferred to Paris, but the disturbed mental condition persisted and he now devoted himself almost exclusively to studying the Bible. In the early part of 1875, when he was 22, the lack of interest Vincent showed in his work resulted in his dismissal from Goupils.

MISSIONARY WORK

Returning to England in April, 1876, Vincent accepted a post as a teacher in a school at Ramsgate, where he received only board and lodging. Next, he acquired a similar position, with a salary this time, in a school in Isleworth on the outskirts of London. He worked there until the autumn, when he returned to Holland and found employment in a bookshop in Dordrecht. After only a short time there, he decided to enter the Church and become a minister. He studied with exceptional devotion for over a year, but he became impatient before his first examination and decided to study at a missionary school in Brussels. At the end of the three month course, Vincent was to take up an appointment in the Borinage, a coal-min-

ing area in the south of Belgium. Failing to satisfy the authorities that he was a suitable person to work as an evangelist, he went there of his own accord and gave Bible lessons and visited the sick. This prompted the evangelical committee to give him a six months contract, which only substantiated their previous disapproval of his suitability. Overzealous to a degree, Vincent not only gave away his clothes, but worked night and day with such an intensity that the, authorities fearing for his sanity, did not renew his contract.

ARTISTIC TALENTS

Still persistent, Vincent stayed on in the Borinage for a further six months, living off the little money his parents or Theo could afford to send him. He now began to draw and in this activity he began to understand himself more. The subjects he drew were the everyday happenings around him, usually people at work. Encouraged and financed by Theo, he decided to become an artist. Returning to Brussels he worked hard at his new profession. During this phase of his career he made several friends and, for once, was happy. However, Vincent soon longed for the country, and in the summer of 1881 he went to stay with his parents. In January, 1882, after a series of family upsets, he left for the Hague.

This period marks the beginning of Van Gogh's artistic achievements. The works that he produced were mainly drawings of simple subjects, a man or a woman at work, or standing at a street corner. These drawings are essentially character studies of poor, working-class people, whose gaunt faces and gnarled hands testify to their hardships. The constant urge to help the more unfortunate around him, resulted in his taking into his house a woman off the streets. Expecting a child, and homeless, she could scarcely have been more fortunate, for her plight aroused the utmost compassion in Vincent who married her and looked after her with tender care and devotion. This was what he had always wanted, a family who depended on him. The fact that he was solely dependent on

Evening Walk *by Vincent Van Gogh is now in the art gallery at Sao Paolo, Brazil.*

At 16, Van Gogh worked in an art-dealer's gallery.

the small allowance that Theo could afford to send him, never crossed his mind. Once the child was born, the woman returned to her former ways and Vincent's illusions of having a family and home of his own were destroyed. In November, 1883, he left the Borinage to live in Drenthe. Physically weak through lack of food and a recent illness, he was unable to withstand the harsh winter, and after only a few weeks he was obliged to return to his parents.

His family now lived in the north Brabant region of Holland, in the village of Neunen. The surrounding countryside with its peasant population was ideal subject matter for Vincent. For two years he worked unceasingly, producing a large number of drawings and paintings of landscapes, figures in a landscape setting, portraits and still life. Painted in dark, sombre colours in the Dutch tradition these works were akin to Rembrandt, both in feeling and the quality of the paint. His final achievement at Nuenen was the large composition " The Potato Eaters ", his most important painting to date. With this painting Vincent felt that he had at last accomplished something, and feeling more confident he decided to study at the Academy in Antwerp. Temperamentally unsuited to the Academy, he left to study in the museums. Eventually, exhausted through overwork and malnutrition, he departed again for Paris in August, 1887.

On arrival in Paris, Vincent went to live with Theo, who had an apartment in Montmartre. The understanding and companionship of his brother helped to restore his health and in a comparatively short time he settled down and was working with all his usual vigour. In Paris, he was immediately influenced by Impressionist painting. He lightened his palette and, for a time, adopted the Impressionist technique of using small brush marks. The pictures he painted were mainly landscapes of the different aspects of Montmartre. He soon began to feel restricted with this method and he turned towards large areas of flat colour—a feature of Japanese paintings which he admired. He had always been interested in Japanese prints since the days when he worked for Goupils. In Paris, this interest was widened and developed into his painting. During this period his subjects were mainly still-life and portraits, the best-known pictures probably being " The Breakfast Table " and " Père Tanguy ".

In February, 1888, when he was 35, Vincent left Paris for Provence and settled in the small town of Arles. The vigour

with which he portrayed the spring landscape continued into the heat of the summer. The almost frenzied urgency with which he worked resulted in a series of landscapes of the utmost beauty, ranging from the paintings of orchards to the pictures of the wooden bridge over the river at Arles. He also painted many still-life and portrait studies, including the important series of " Sunflowers " and the portrait of the postman " Roulin ".

The effect of this vast output of work, combined with general physical neglect, led to Vincent's first serious mental breakdown. After a quarrel with his friend Paul Gauguin, he cut off part of his ear and had to be taken to the local hospital in Arles. On his release he immediately began work again, the most notable pictures being the self-portraits showing his ear swathed in bandages.

Previous to this episode, he had suffered from slight bouts of mental disorder. These disturbances now became more acute, and Vincent decided to have hospital treatment. In May, 1889, he was admitted to the asylum at Saint-Rémy, not far from Arles. In the hospital he somehow managed to continue painting. His creativeness continued to grow and the development of his paintings and drawings seems unimpaired by his illness. Characterised by the swirling, writhing quality of their conception, these works have a direction and force of expression only to be found in the greatest works of art.

In the spring of 1890, feeling better, but depressed by the asylum, Vincent went to stay with Théo in Paris. Through his brother he was introduced to Dr. Gachet, a man familiar with mental healing, who lived in the small town of Auvers-sur-Oise. Dr. Gachet, himself an amateur painter, knew most of the Impressionist painters and was an ardent collector of their works. Vincent was unable to paint in Paris and missed the country, so on Théo's suggestion he went to live in Auvers-sur-Oise under the care of the sympathetic Dr. Gachet. The paintings of still-life, landscapes and magnificent portraits, particularly the last self-portrait and the two portraits of Dr. Gachet, testify to his industry during this period.

However, the intolerable burden of his illness finally became too much, and on 27th July, 1890, Vincent attempted to end his life. Theo, summoned from Paris, was with him when he died two days later. Unable to recover from his grief, Théo became ill and six months later he was laid to rest with his brother in the cemetery of Auvers-sur-Oise.

Van Gogh's sitters were often poverty-stricken peasants.

ANTON CHEKHOV

Anton Chekhov, who was to become one of the greatest dramatists in the world, was born in 1860 in the small town of Taganrog on the Sea of Azov, on the southern borders of Russia. His grandfather had been a serf but by diligent saving he had managed to buy his freedom and that of his three sons. Pavel Chekhov, the author's father, was a shop-keeper and a talented amateur artist, both as a musician and painter. He seems, however, to have been rather a violent man and Chekhov later wrote, " I could never forgive my father for beating me as a child ". He also describes how his father used to drag his young family in all weathers and at all hours from church to church to sing as a little choir. Anton's two elder brothers later reacted to this mixture of harshness and religion by becoming alcoholics but the author himself was made of sterner stuff.

When he was sixteen, his father went bankrupt and to avoid his debtors set off for Moscow where the two elder sons were by now students. Anton, however, remained in Taganrog to finish his schooling, suffering a good deal of hardship and frequent illness, no doubt due to the beginnings of the tuberculosis from which he was to die at the age of 44. Three years after his father's departure Chekhov, who was by this time determined to become a doctor, joined his family in Moscow. He found the family in poor straits. The eldest son was living away from home. The second son was no more effective a head of the family than his father and Anton entered upon his medical studies with the added problem of providing for the household. His medical studies would scarcely allow a regular part-time occupation, so he began to write stories.

EARLY WORKS

His elder brother, a journalist, would presumably put Chekhov in touch with the publishers and editors who accepted the short stories Chekhov wrote at the rate of two or three a week. In 1884 he graduated as a doctor and practised medicine in Moscow. But his five-year-old habit of writing, originally a hard necessity to pay his way and support his family, had become an addiction. Even in his first busy year in practice he wrote 129 stories and sketches. The sketches were generally light in character, vaudeville sketches and short comic plays. The stories varied from pot-boiling anecdotes to works full of profound observation of character, some of which remain among his major literary achievements.

So considerable an output could not fail to make an impression on the literary world of Russia in those days, and on a visit to St. Petersburg (Leningrad), Chekhov was surprised to find himself being treated as a writer of merit and significance. His reception by the writers and critics of St. Petersburg in 1885 marked an important step in his writing career.

It is one thing to turn out hundreds of stories for money and another thing to find oneself regarded as a leading writer in one's own country. Chekhov was, by all accounts, a man of extremely balanced mind for, although he must have seen the possibility of attaining greater heights by abandoning everything for writing, he also appreciated that the wild south-Russian temperament (one has only to see their dances to grasp their nature), unless severely disciplined could run easily to excess. He had two examples in his own family. So, while he devoted more time to writing and attempted other literary forms, notably plays, he continued, until towards the end of his life when illness prevented him, to engage in the routine of medical practice. He was to write to his brother at a later period, " What one needs is constant work, day and night, incessant reading, study and exercise of the will. Every hour is precious."

Chekhov's first full-length play *Ivanov* was produced in

Anton Chekhov was born in Russia on 17th January, 1860, and died in Germany on the 2nd July, 1904.

In 1879, Chekhov went to the University of Moscow and graduated as a doctor of medicine in 1884.

Moscow in 1887, but was a success only on its second production, two years later, in St. Petersburg. The year 1889 also saw the production, in Moscow, of his second play *The Wood Demon*, but as was almost to become a custom with Chekhov's plays, its first production was not well received. The success of the second production of *Ivanov*, however, added to Chekhov's reputation and he was becoming famous. He must have been a reasonably wealthy bachelor at this period for he was evidently a lavish host, his house always being full of friends, many of whom he compelled to stay for days or weeks on end. The only cloud on his horizon at this time was his tuberculosis which was again giving him trouble. The following year he did an extraordinary thing.

JOURNEY ACROSS SIBERIA

Perhaps he felt that he was becoming too settled, too comfortable. Perhaps he had had an unfortunate love affair that he wished to forget. In spite of the fact that he was becoming established successfully in both his professions, and in spite of his illness, he set off in 1890 for the convict settlement on the island of Sakhalin to spend some months studying the conditions of the prisoners.

Now, Sakhalin is a large island lying north of Japan off the coast of eastern Siberia, north of Vladivostok. It is some three thousand miles from Moscow and in those days there was no trans-Siberian railway. The invalid doctor, armed with a sheepskin, a revolver and a penknife (" for cutting sausages and killing tigers "), made his weary way across the vast wild continent, spent three months in the settlement, interviewed ten thousand convicts and returned by way of Singapore and Ceylon.

Whatever Chekhov's reasons for this journey, and whatever its effects, it is to the remaining fourteen years of his life that we owe the great dramatic masterpieces which are his last four plays, *The Seagull*, *Uncle Vanya*, *Three Sisters* and *The Cherry Orchard*.

" THE SEAGULL "

The Seagull was first produced in St. Petersburg in 1896. It was coldly received. Both critics and audience expressed themselves confused and bored by it. The Russian theatre was not yet ready for Chekhov's new way of writing plays. Chekhov, from his experiences in south Russia as a doctor and from his journey to Sakhalin, knew more about life than most people, and he was not satisfied with the way characters in plays were made to behave on the stage. People could be angry without throwing themselves about on the hearthrug. People could be sad without screaming and tearing their hair, or happy without embracing everyone in sight. Chekhov wanted to put people on the stage as they really were.

CHEKHOV AND THE MOSCOW ART THEATRE

The year after the unfortunate performance of *The Seagull*, an important meeting took place, a meeting which was to influence the whole future of the European, and indeed American, theatre right up to the present day. The theatre director Constantine Stanislavsky met the writer Nemirovitch Dantchenko and after an all-night conversation they decided to found a theatre company to put on plays in a new way. Their ideas were very much the same as Chekhov's. This was the beginning of the famous Moscow Art Theatre.

The first half dozen productions of the new company were more or less failures; then Nemirovitch-Dantchenko persuaded Chekhov to allow them to revive *The Seagull*. It was a nervous first night for everybody. However author, actors and director seemed to have come together to form something like an ideal production of the play. It was a tremendous success. The atmosphere behind and in front of the curtain was electric, and at the end everybody was weeping or dancing with emotion. The Moscow Art Theatre still has the symbol of the seagull on its stage curtain in memory of that first night, 17th December, 1898.

Chekhov then completely re-wrote his early play *The Wood Demon* and retitled it *Uncle Vanya*. The Moscow Art Theatre presented it in 1899 and although at the beginning, it was not such a success as *The Seagull*, it became quite successful later and has remained no less admired than the other three later plays. By this time Chekhov, at the peak of his fame, was forced by his advancing illness to leave Moscow and live in the warmer and drier climate of the south near

Leo Tolstoy and Anton Chekhov met and became close friends. Nevertheless, between these two writers, there was not only a difference in age but also a conflict of ideas.

Chekhov had to leave the harsh winter climate of Moscow because of ill-health. He lived the greater part of the year abroad, first in Nice and finally in the Crimea.

Chekhov reading his first play to the cast.

Yalta, on the Black Sea. He remained in close touch with the Company, however, and in 1901 he married Olga Knipper, one of their leading ladies, who had played Arcadina in *The Seagull*.

FINAL YEARS

Stanislavsky and Nemirovitch-Dantchenko kept trying to persuade Chekhov to write more plays for them. In his early days in Yalta, when he was too ill to return to the theatre in Moscow, they brought the Company to him. There, in addition to making a highly successful tour of the Crimea, they enjoyed their author's celebrated hospitality. As a result of this visit Chekhov wrote *The Three Sisters*, a fine, wistful piece about three cultured ladies living in a small garrison town in the provinces and yearning for the bright lights of Moscow. Like *Uncle Vanya* it took some time to establish itself with the Moscow audience and Chekhov himself felt that it was too gloomy.

So he determined that his next play—it was to be his last—should be a comedy. The last three years of his life were largely devoted to planning and writing *The Cherry Orchard*. In rapidly deteriorating health, his wife much of the time working with the Company in Moscow, himself in Yalta, he struggled on with the play. " I write about four lines a day," he wrote to Nemirovitch-Dantchenko, " and even that costs me an intolerably painful effort," and yet he was adamant that it should be " a comedy, almost a farce."

Stanislavsky could never quite see *The Cherry Orchard* as a farce, and neither have most critics since Chekhov's time. There is an unavoidable sadness hanging over Madame Ranevsky's old country house. Partly by her own ineptitude and unwillingness to plan ahead, the house is doomed to be sold and the cherry trees cut down to make room for workers' houses. Chekhov did not judge his characters. And although his view of them was perhaps, as he maintained, essentially humorous, they come alive to such a degree on the stage that it is impossible not to sympathise with them.

Nowadays in Russia, the play is performed almost as an attack on Madame Ranevsky, the idle, rich ladies and gentlemen who surround her, and the ineffectual hangers-on who support her. Trofimov, the eternal student, is played as the hero of the piece because he looks forward to a great new Russia of the future. And yet Trofimov is always losing his galoshes and failing in his examinations. Chekhov had no heroes: he regarded people in their full, human variety, neither good nor bad, neither heroes nor villains.

The first night of *The Cherry Orchard* was planned for Chekhov's birthday, 17th January, 1904, when he would be 44 years old. The play was rapturously received and Chekhov appeared on the stage to long applause and bouquets of flowers. Unfortunately he had a spasm of coughing just as he stepped on to the stage, and, although the audience shouted to him to sit down, he remained standing while speeches and presentations were made.

Five months later his wife took him to the German spa of Badenweiler for a holiday. On 30th June he was in good form and made her roar with laughter as he sat up in bed in the evening. During the night, however, he sent for the doctor and told him he was dying. The doctor gave him a glass of champagne. Chekhov smiled at his wife and said, " It's a long time since I last drank champagne," finished the glass, lay back on the pillow, and died.

The plot of The Seagull *is based on two characters, Constantine and Nina. Both have dreams of fame, which never reach fruition. The symbol of their unrealised hopes is the white seagull, which falls to earth, dead, accidentally shot by Constantine.*

THE IMPRESSIONISTS

The small group of artists known as the Impressionists took their name from a criticism written about their first group exhibition, which was held in Paris in 1874. The word Impressionism implied ridicule, and was taken from the title of one of the pictures exhibited.

The artists concerned with this movement were all closely connected with Paris, the exceptions being Paul Cézanne and Camille Pissaro. Three members of the group, Edouard Manet, Edgar Degas and Alfred Sisley, were born and brought up in Paris. Pierre-Auguste Renoir and Berthe Morisot both came to Paris as children, and were essentially Parisians. Claude Monet, although born in Paris, spent his boyhood at Le Havre and, like Cézanne and Pissaro, came to Paris as a young man to study painting.

In painting, prior to Impressionism, artists relied on the drawing in the subject matter to tell the story, and imply the particular type of atmosphere. The most obvious examples are the Dutch marine artists, who painted ships, lashed by raging gales, at sea. The spectator is aware, through the exaggerations of the happenings in the picture, that a storm is taking place. Rope ladders and rigging are hanging loose, and masts are broken off, huge waves batter the ships, all helping to suggest stormy conditions. The whole scene is depicted in dark colours symbolic of these conditions, and the drama is further emphasised by contrasts of small areas of light colour usually representing a literal image, forked lightning, a fire on board ship or white edges to the waves.

TECHNIQUES OF THE IMPRESSIONISTS

Impressionism aimed at achieving a more natural or truthful sensation of atmosphere. By direct observation of nature, the Impressionist artists studied the effects of the play of light on the surface of objects. The technique for achieving these aims was in direct contrast to the traditional ideas of drawing and painting. The artists relied on small brush marks of bright, pure colours applied closely together to describe the sensations of light as they saw it. The outline of the objects became less defined, and the picture depended on the vibration of colour through the harmonies created for its effect. This style of painting also had the advantage of being quick. The very nature of Impressionism demanded rapid execution.

To catch the fleeting effects of nature meant working out of doors. The limited time at the artist's disposal, through the movement of the sun and the ever changing weather, necessitated a fast technique.

The scorn and derision with which the public greeted these paintings was levelled at two artists in particular, Edouard Manet and Claude Monet. Entirely different in conception and subject matter, the works of these two men formed the rock on which Impressionism was founded. Manet, unconcerned with moral or intellectual preoccupations, expressed himself with a freedom and frankness reminiscent of Velasquez and Hals. Essentially, he was a painter of portraits and figure compositions. Through the contrasts of light to dark and with as little half-tone as possible, he introduced a way of seeing that was at once spontaneous and reactionary. Never an Impressionist painter in relation to technique, his contribution to the movement was to remove the barriers of Classical and Romantic concepts. Monet was the artist who slowly developed and evolved the Impressionist technique of the small brushwork and the use of close tonal and colour relationships, which was to become the method adopted by the majority of the group. Appropriately, it was his painting "Impression-Sunrise" that gave rise to the title Impressionism.

EDOUARD MANET

Edouard Manet, born in 1833, began painting in the studio of Couture, an accomplished artist, who was unfortunately torn between Romanticism and Classicism. This back-

The Impressionists were a group of young painters who rebelled against the tyranny of conventional forms of painting.

A distinguished member of the Impressionist group, Camille Pissaro was a French artist of Spanish extraction.

ground only served to convince Manet that he must look elsewhere for the guidance he needed, so he began to study the works of Velasquez and Goya in the Louvre.

SALON DE REFUSÉS

In 1861, Manet exhibited his first paintings in the French Royal Academy, known more widely as the Salon. The following year his works were rejected. In 1863, although again rejected, he exhibited in the now famous exhibition, the " Salon de Refusés ". This exhibition resulted because of the many protests which had been made over the large numbers of works rejected by the jury of the Salon. Manet's main contribution, " The Picnic ", referred to as indecent by Napoleon III, aroused a public outcry. In 1865, the Salon jury accepted his painting " Olympia ", which again aroused public indignation because of its alleged indecent subject matter. For several years after this his paintings were either rejected, or if accepted, hung so high as to pass unnoticed.

From 1870 onwards, Manet adopted the Impressionist palette.

Retaining his original technique, he painted pictures which were more acceptable in subject matter. His painting of " The Bar at the Folies-Bergère " completed in 1882, a year before his death, illustrates a basic principle of Impressionism which is the searching pursuit of colour in the shadow and in the light.

CLAUDE MONET

Claude Monet, born in Paris in 1840, spent most of his boyhood at Le Havre where he saw the paintings of Boudin, Jongkind, and Corot. He returned to Paris as a young man and entered the studio of Gleyne, where he formed a close friendship with Renoir and Sisley. On leaving Gleyne's studio in 1862, these three companions painted together in the forest region of Fontainebleau—a spot made famous by Courbet and the Barbizon school. Although similar in manner to their predecessors of the Barbizon school, they showed a preoccupation for an entirely different aspect of nature. They were already concerned with presenting an atmospheric light effect particular to a certain time of day, as opposed to the more generalised concepts of the Barbizon school.

In comparison with his friends, Monet's paintings are much freer in their handling, and he shows a more natural affinity towards landscape. It is significant that at this point of his career, Monet turned towards the painting of Manet. Renoir, on the other hand, shows a marked influence of Courbet.

In 1865, Monet painted " The Picnic ", the first of two large figure compositions. " The Picnic " was obviously meant to rival Manet's picture of the same title. By painting this picture out of doors, Monet hoped to create a less theatrical version. He finally destroyed this picture, preserving only two fragments of the whole. The second picture " Women in the Garden " was refused by the Salon in 1867. The landscapes he painted during this time show the slow development towards the style of painting which was, in 1874, labelled " Impressionism ".

From this time onwards he devoted himself almost entirely to the painting of landscapes, in which the different aspects of light were always his principal concern. In order to pursue this even farther he began to paint several versions of the

The Impressionists had several patrons who tried to help them, including Vollard and Durant-Ruel.

Richard Wagner, who had previously refused to be painted, consented to sit for Renoir, a leading Impressionist.

The Press and public reaction to the works of the Impressionists was one of ridicule, horror and disgust.

same subject under different conditions of light. The better known of these series are the " Haystacks ", " The Poplars ", and " Rouen Cathedral ". The final achievements of his life are the very large paintings of " Water Lilies " on which he was still working at his death in 1926. These paintings, the climax of his research into the properties of light and colour, opened up a completely new field in the history of painting.

CAMILLE PISSARO

Camille Pissaro, the oldest member of this group, came to Paris from the West Indies in 1855. Of all the Impressionists he was the most consistent. Although he became interested in the theories of Seurat in 1884, and for a short time painted in a pointillist style, he soon returned to Impressionist principles and methods, which he continued to explore until his death in 1903. He differs from Monet in that he always shows more consideration for the literal descriptive values of painting. Always concerned with light, he never lets this dominate to the exclusion of the objects in his picture. He used the objects that form his subject matter purely for story-telling reasons; houses, trees and other particular

aspects of nature are experienced visually as opposed to emotionally. Also, he uses a traditional perspective to express depth as opposed to the optical colour perspective of Monet. Pissaro's space nearly always depends on the drawing in the design leading the eye along a diagonal towards a central focus in the picture.

In his early works, Pissaro's technique of working with a subdued palette, using fluid colours and semi-impasto, is reminiscent of Corot. From 1872 onwards, he uses a combination of his former methods and the Impressionist technique to express a joy of painting and a sympathy for nature, which characterises his work.

Throughout his life he devoted himself to the painting of landscapes. Between 1870 and 1876, he painted views of house- and tree-lined roads, but in 1877 he went on to more condensed landscapes, such as " Red Roofs " in the Louvre. After his minor diversion into pointillism between the years 1886 and 1888, he painted numerous studies of town and city life. These are entirely Impressionist in conception and treatment and guarantee this movement of a place in the history of painting.

At the age of 16, Edouard Manet served as a cabin-boy on the ship, Guadeloupe, *sailing to South America.*

ALFRED SISLEY

Alfred Sisley, born in 1840, was exclusively a landscape painter, his work having an affinity with Corot and the Barbizon school. Although never developing away from Impressionist ideas, he contributed to this movement a refined sensitivity and poetic restraint which was entirely personal. The paintings he produced are similar to Pissaro in their general design. Never imaginative in terms of subject matter and expression, he relied on an acute vision and subtle colour harmonies to describe the beauty contained in nature.

Although associated with the Impressionist movement, Renoir, Cézanne, Degas and Berthe Morisot were never Impressionist painters in the true sense. After passing through a short Impressionist phase in their early years, they soon abandoned this, finding the method and type of vision employed insufficient for their purpose.

BERTHE MORISOT

Berthe Morisot, born in 1841, nearly always painted subject matter that did not lend itself to Impressionist methods. Her real interest was in the painting of figure compositions, usually of a domestic nature, which show the influence of Manet, Degas and Renoir. In the best of her paintings, for example " The Cradle " in the Louvre, she imparts a touch of sentiment and charm that is always natural and never vulgar through over-emphasis.

RENOIR

Pierre Auguste Renoir, born in 1841, was apprenticed at the age of thirteen as a painter of porcelain in a china factory. It is probable that the scenes he copied on to porcelain were his first introduction to the painting of Watteau, Boucher and Fragonard. The admiration he felt for these artists is reflected in his work throughout his life. He painted many landscapes and still-life subjects, but first and foremost he was a painter of the nude figure. Always an ardent student of the museums, his early paintings, for example the " Diana " he painted in 1867, show the influence of Courbet's realism, allied to the classicism of Ingres. From 1868 onwards, his colour became lighter and higher in key as a result of painting out-of-doors and Monet's influence. For a time he adopted Impressionist methods developing his painting in terms of light and colour. The painting of a " Duckpond " in 1873 is identical to Monet's picture of the same subject.

Feeling that mere atmospheric effects limited his expression he renounced Impressionism and turned to figure compositions and portraits; and from 1876 until his death in 1919, he moved towards an art form reminiscent of Rubens.

PAUL CÉZANNE

Paul Cézanne, born in Aix-en-Provence in 1839, came to Paris in 1861, where he studied at the Académie Suisse. In his early days as a painter, until he was about 33 years of age, he was inspired by Delacroix and Manet to paint sombre, romantic pictures. In these, he used a thick impasto technique, sometimes laying on the pigments with a palette knife.

He exhibited at the first Impressionist Exhibition in 1874 and the erotic nature of his paintings, particularly his version of Manet's " Olympia ", antagonised the public. For the next seven years he was much influenced by Pissaro and he introduced an Impressionist palette and technique into his paintings. The nearest he came to painting a true Impressionist picture was at the age of 34, when he completed " The Hanged Man's House ".

Never content with only an impression, Cézanne's work is an analysis of tone and colour defining form and space. Like Degas and Renoir he was concerned with the solid object in relation to space.

EDGAR DEGAS

Edgar Degas, born in 1834, studied at the Ecole des Beaux-Arts where he came into contact with the Ingres tradition of painting. He differed from his contemporaries in that he composed his pictures in the traditional classical sense through the drawing and design. He was never solely dependent on direct observation of subject matter and colour.

A painter of people, his art is a commentary on human behaviour and situations. His best known works are the numerous studies he painted of racecourse scenes, ballet dancers and women dressing or washing, themes he continued to develop in various media until his death in 1917.

Included in the group known as the Impressionists was one woman, Berthe Morisot. She was a pupil of Manet and later she married his brother.

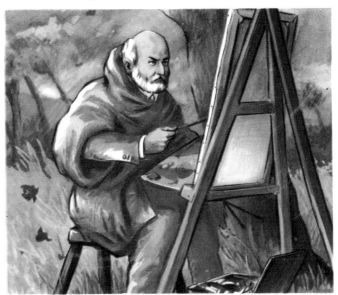

Dissatisfied with the limitations of the Impressionist techniques, Paul Cézanne became, with Van Gogh and Gauguin, one of the leaders of the Post-Impressionist movement.

JACK LONDON

Jack London, American author, was born John Chaney in San Francisco on 12th January, 1876, and died forty years later on 22nd November, 1916. His birth was tragic in the extreme. His mother was neurotic and unstable before he was born, and his father deserted her. Jack was illegitimate. This added a feeling of shame and confusion to the poverty and struggles of his childhood which was to affect him all his life. In his later years, in spite of fame and success, he was still bewildered about his birth and his father.

HIS PARENTS

His father was William H. Chaney, born in Maine and generally believed to be an Irishman which might have accounted for the Irishness of Jack's temperament. His mother, Flora Wellman, was born in Ohio, the emotional and spoiled daughter of good Anglo-Saxon stock. Eight months after being deserted by Chaney she married John London, a widower, of Pennsylvania, from whom Jack took his name—John Griffith London.

Chaney, his father, had lived principally on his claims to be able to tell people's fortunes by horoscopes and astrology. The new step-father was an ineffectual wage-earner in a variety of jobs, for whom nothing ever came off. In the grinding poverty which dogged them there was no real childhood for Jack London, only continual hunger.

HIS BOYHOOD

He was able to read at a very early age, and when he was ten he discovered that books could be borrowed from the Oakland Public Library. He began to read every adventure, travel and sea story he could find. He also had the good fortune to meet Miss Ina Coolbrith, the head librarian and poet laureate of California, who encouraged him to read Flaubert, Tolstoy and Dostoievski.

To help at home the eleven-year-old Jack did odd jobs such as swabbing the decks of boats in the harbour, deliver-ing newspapers and working in a bowling alley. In an old boat he indulged his first love of the sea, sailing far out into the bay, alone with his dreams and his hatred of drudgery. He laboured in a cannery and a jute mill, working 12 hours a day for 10 cents an hour.

JOHN BARLEYCORN

By scrimping and saving and borrowing some money he bought the sloop *Razzle Dazzle*, and with a tough, hard-drinking bunch of thugs he became a pirate, raiding by night the oyster beds on the shoals of the Lower Bay. He was his own man at 15, drinking, fighting, living recklessly on the wrong side of the law and piling up experiences for his books of adventure that were soon to thrill millions of readers in every country of the world. His addiction to alcohol, on which he came to depend so much, is described in his book *John Barleycorn*. His feelings of inferiority and shame, and his deep resentment at his lot, compelled him to challenge all comers in strenuous living, in proving his rugged manhood, in drinking.

FIRST SUCCESS

He signed on with an 80-ton schooner to slaughter seals in the hunting grounds off the Siberian and Korean coast, a grim and bloody experience. Returning to San Francisco he found the whole country suffering another economic depression, described later in *The Valley of the Moon*, and his socialistic and rebellious feelings strengthened. Then came the gleam of light. The San Francisco newspaper *Call* offered a 25-dollar prize for an article describing a personal experience. Jack sat up all night writing an account of a hurricane that took place on the Japanese coast. He was 17. He won the prize and the article was published.

But he had still a long way to go. He took to the road as a tramp and rode the freight-trains with " Kelly's Army ", a raggle-taggle mob bound for Washington to draw attention

At 15, Jack London bought the Razzle Dazzle *and became an oyster pirate, carrying out raids on the oyster nursery-ponds.*

At 17, London won first prize for a story about a typhoon.

to the plight of the underprivileged and give vent to their discontent—all to be set down eventually in his book *The Road*. He was arrested as a vagrant near Niagara Falls and sentenced to 30 days hard labour in the Erie County Jail. This was a turning point in his life. His observations at close quarters of how savagely society revenges itself on its delinquents and his reading of Karl Marx's *Das Kapital*, guided him towards socialism and his career as a writer.

BACK TO SCHOOL

He plunged into the works of Darwin, and Nietzsche, and at 19 he entered Oakland High school determined to have more education. With his life of adventure behind him, the conventional, well-scrubbed boys and girls in his classes must have seemed like children to him. But in himself, he was a muscular, attractive young man, with pale blue eyes in a sunburned face, lightish-brown curly hair, a soft voice, and a great deal of boyish charm, which stayed with him to the end of his life. But he drank with " bums ", and earned the title " The Boy Socialist " because of his nightly meetings at the City Hall Park. Soon the police pounced and charged him with being a public nuisance. However, he appeared in court before a liberal-minded judge who cautioned him and gave him a suspended sentence.

He studied for only a year at Oakland, left to cram for the University of California and passed the entrance examination with flying colours. He was 20 when the great Klondike gold rush hit the United States. All over the continent men abandoned everything—work, home, families—to rush to the cold waters of the forlorn Yukon to hunt for gold. It was a fever in the blood, a mass migration, the like of which had never been seen before and will never be seen again.

GOLD RUSH

It was one more adventure with life in the raw that Jack London could not miss. With his pack weighted down with the books of Kipling, Stevenson, and Spinoza, he was off over the Chilkoot Pass. It was his grimmest experience of all. He discovered no gold; there was only suffering and struggle and illness and near starvation but as he said afterwards, it was here that he discovered himself.

It was there that the material for many books, principally *The Call of the Wild*, was gathered and jotted down. He

intended it to be only a short story of a few thousand words but became so carried away by Buck, the great dog-wolf animal who is the hero of the story, that he made it a book— his most popular book, which sold over two million copies after its publication in 1903.

Before that, in 1900, he had published his first book, a collection of short stories, *The Son of the Wolf*. In the 16 years between then and his death he wrote a total of fifty books. An early one, *A Daughter of the Snows* (1902), brought out his belief in Anglo-Saxon superiority, a belief which was to be expressed often and emphatically in his work. He believed in Nietzschean theory of the Superman, the superior type of man who could conquer everything and rule supreme. If this appears to be a contradiction of his violently-expressed socialism, we must remember that he was a man continually in conflict with himself. Early influences left bitter wounds that went with him to the grave. But they did not destroy his instinctive generosity.

HIS EXTRAVAGANCE

As his success grew and publishers fought for his work, London was insatiable in his demand for money in advance. He was a prodigious spendthrift, again a compensation for early deprivations. He was always good for a " touch " and scores of old friends, relatives and associates lived handsomely on his hospitality. He made over a million dollars from his writings and spent it all.

He fell in love with a delicate and cultured girl, Mabel Applegarth, attending the University of California. Nothing came of it, but the character named Ruth Morse in his autobiographical novel, *Martin Eden*, is said to be this " pale, gold flower ". After writing *The Son of the Wolf*, he married Bessie Madern, a cousin of the actress Minnie Madern Fiske. Three years later he left her and their two daughters to marry Charmian Kittredge. He always saw himself as the great adventurer, the great romantic, the greatest at everything, continually trying—like Hemingway in a later generation—to prove his masculinity.

THE HEIGHT OF SUCCESS

London was a supreme egoist, always believing that he could do anything better than anyone else. Everything he wrote was himself. In the full flood of creation and success,

The main character of The Call of the Wild *is Buck, the dog.*

In 1906, Jack London and his second wife, Charmian, set sail in the Snark *for a cruise round the world, which he described in his novel,* The Cruise of the Snark.

the books poured out of him, and all that he had lived and loved and hated ran riot in their pages. His output was fantastic, his popularity was world-wide.

In 1904 he reported the Russo-Japanese war for the Hearst newspapers in America. A previous newspaper assignment in 1902 to cover the aftermath of the Boer war left him stranded in London for a while. As always, he put the time to good account and gathered material for his grimly realistic story *People of the Abyss*. He built a ketch, the *Snark*, and sailed it to Hawaii and the South Seas, but his past life was beginning to tell on him and he was frequently ill during the voyage.

One of his most remarkable books was *The Iron Heel* (1907) which had an introduction by Anatole France. It dealt with a revolution in the far-off-year-to-come, 1932, and anticipated in an extraordinary way the Fascism that actually came to blight the world through Hitler and Mussolini in the 1930s.

He lived like a lord, gave lavish hospitality at his large ranch in California, and then squandered vast sums of money in building a fantastic castle called The Wolf House which was destroyed by fire before it was completed. He had to write incessantly to meet the bills, although by 1913 he was the highest paid and most popular writer in the world.

His disenchantment with the world was bitterly set out in *The Valley of the Moon*, and more and more London retreated from it to try to find solace and peace of mind on his ranch. This was a vast property, swallowing up more than he earned by his writing. Yet he went on frantically adding to it, buying more land, desperately seeking to put the world and its ways farther away from him.

Overwork, financial difficulties, illness, heavy drinking, over-eating, and the eternal inner fires of self-destruction, caused his work to deteriorate. He was a very sick man on the night of 21st November, 1916, cruelly afflicted with rheumatism in his legs and a deadly kidney disease. During the night he committed suicide with an overdose of morphine tablets. He was only forty.

Of all London's semi-autobiographical novels, Martin Eden, *first published in 1909, is the most autobiographical. It is about a rough sailor who has ambitions to be a writer.*

In 1904, Jack London went to Japan to report on the Russo-Japanese war as American war-correspondent for the Hearst group of newspapers.

POISONS IN WILDLIFE

Poisons have been used for a very long time in wildlife control in this and other countries, and in Britain to-day it is still legal to use certain poisons to kill insects, invertebrates, rats, mice, and what the law calls "other small ground vermin." It is, however, illegal to use phosphorus or red squill for killing animals of any description, and strychnine may be used only to kill moles.

In fact, strychnine is still widely, and illegally, used for killing foxes, crows, jackdaws, ravens, buzzards, eagles and others. It is illegal to use any poison to kill any wild bird in any part of Britain, and illegal to kill buzzards or eagles in any way whatsoever, at any time, for any reason. If, however, one can show that a wild bird was poisoned inadvertently, by eating bait put down for a rat, that is a defence so long as the poison was not phosphorus, red squill or strychnine.

Although it is illegal to put down poison baits for foxes, or badgers, or other large mammals, it is legal to gas foxes and rabbits, and this method is often used. It is not legal to gas badgers, but badgers are often gassed. In the United States the deadly poison, familiarly known as 1080, has been used with devastating effect on wolves, and has been responsible for the near extermination of this predator in many parts.

Poisoning of large predators, bird or mammal, is usually done with bait. A fowl dressed with strychnine is a much used bait for foxes, and works with deadly effect. But, since strychnine can be legally bought only for moles, it has to be obtained illegally, or under false pretences, for foxes. This poison, used in dead rabbits or hares or in deer or sheep carcasses, will kill anything from mice and shrews to foxes

and eagles. Once it is put down it cannot be controlled. Anything that eats it dies.

In modern times man has achieved spectacular success with poisons and antibiotic repellents in his war against rats. Rats are usually extremely suspicious of poison but the new poisons, mixed with oatmeal, are readily taken over a period of time so that a temporary reduction or even elimination of rats can take place. Food or water contaminated with the new repellents is not touched by rats, however hungry or thirsty they may be.

But the poisoning of birds and mammals (apart from rats) does not take place on a great scale, and is certainly not to be compared with the great war, which is going on all the time on many fronts and on a vast scale, against insects and soil pests. Furthermore, in their effects, the old-type poisons used against birds, mammals and soil pests cannot be compared with the modern organo-chlorine group.

ORGANO-CHLORINES

The old poisons killed individuals or groups of a species, and there was seldom any threat to the species as a whole. Other species were often poisoned accidentally, but here again there was no real threat to the existence of these species. This cannot be said of the organo-chlorines, which have had an effect never foreseen on many species. The organo-chlorines group of poisons are threatening the very existence of species which were never intended to suffer.

The term *pesticide* has now acquired an importance far beyond its mere meaning, which is simply "killer of pests." The control of pests, plant or animal, is essential in the

In order to get maximum results for farm produce, the control of pests is necessary.

The significance of a food chain is apparent when you consider that the owl is a predator and the last link in an eating chain. The owl preys on rats, mice, voles, shrews and an occasional weasel. If an owl eats a weasel that has eaten a rat which has eaten grain containing pesticide . . .

interests of increased food production, and there is no doubt that the pesticides do this job. The trouble is that some of them do far more than that. The group known as organo-chlorines have side effects that are causing alarm from ground level to the highest levels of government.

We are now aware of the dangers, but it remains to be seen whether we can act quickly enough to avert disaster to many forms of wildlife. The problem is being kept under constant watch and review by the Government, The Nature Conservancy, The Royal Society for the Protection of Birds, The Council for Nature, Naturalists' Trusts, The National Farmers' Union, and other bodies, and much research is presently being done.

It was an American biologist, the late Rachel Carson, who flashed the warning light with her book *Silent Spring* (published in Britain in 1963). Its effect in both countries was explosive. It is a documented indictment of the wholesale and unregulated use of pesticides. The theme of the book might be summarised as follows:

1. The widespread use of toxic chemicals can cause long-term ecological and genetic upset;

2. That residues of these toxins are left in the soil, in water, and in food chains;

3. That resistant strains of pests are left to build up and make pesticides less effective in the future, thus leading to the need for still more potent varieties;

4. That the destruction of predators at the ends of food chains permits an increase in the very pests which the pesticides are designed to control.

The evidence of research in this country to date supports the arguments put forward in *Silent Spring*.

FIRST VICTIMS

In the first instance, the new toxic chemicals were used in Britain mainly as seed dressings, especially against the wheat bulb fly. In 1955 and 1956 birds began to die, the first

victims being mainly woodpigeons. This was sufficient cause for alarm, but it was not until a variety of small birds, as well as pheasants and partridges, began to suffer that the truth began to be seen.

Most of this mortality was reported from southern and eastern England, and the Midlands. In 1961 a voluntary ban was placed upon the use of persistent seed dressing—except in autumn when a serious threat from wheat bulb fly was more likely. It has to be said that the ban was honoured, and is being honoured, and the results have been encouraging. There is now very little direct poisoning. But wildlife faces more subtle dangers from the organo-chlorines, which are still widely used in other ways.

The difference between the new organo-chlorines (for example aldrin, dieldrin and heptachlor) and the older poisons is that the organo-chlorines are persistent. That is to say they build up in the body until a lethal dose is reached. They are not metabolised in the ordinary way. The evidence shows that sub-lethal doses of organo-chlorines can cause reproduction upset, infertility of eggs, behaviour upset and failure to breed.

FOOD CHAINS

The organo-chlorines are widely used in sprays, and some are used in sheep-dips, although the sale of dieldrin was banned from the end of 1965. As a result of this widespread use many species of birds now carry sub-lethal doses, and the eggs of many species are contaminated. The most notable sufferers at present are the predators at the end of food chains.

To understand the full significance of this it is necessary to understand what is meant by a food chain. A food chain can be described as the links in the order of eating. An owl eats a weasel that has eaten a mouse that has eaten dressed grain. Weasel and mouse may contain sub-lethal doses of the toxin, but the owl is left with both sub-doses after it has

. . . then the owl will be the last in the food chain. Both weasel and rat will contain sub-lethal doses of poison. The rat has eaten grain which has been sprayed, and the weasel has eaten the rat and perhaps other prey containing sub-lethal doses. The owl, therefore, will receive both sub-doses of toxin and if it continues to eat poisoned prey, will eventually die.

Other species affected by toxic substances in pesticides are the falcon, osprey and sparrowhawk.

eaten the weasel. If it keeps on eating contaminated prey the dose builds up and up until a lethal dose is reached. The bird then dies.

Otters that eat fish that eat small aquatic animals are at the end of another food chain. Hawks that eat birds that have eaten caterpillars that have eaten sprayed vegetation are at the end of another. Whatever organo-chlorines have been eaten by the prey species end up in total in the body of the predator. And, being persistent, they remain there.

So far, current research shows that predators are worse affected than other species. This is to be expected, since predators are at the end of food chains and, therefore, consuming toxins which are the sum of the toxins in their prey. Thus eagles, falcons, hawks, owls, herons and grebes are seriously affected. The rare osprey in Scotland is affected. The rare kite in Wales is affected.

The sparrowhawk, once the *bete noire* of gamekeepers, is now a rare bird in most parts of Britain.

THE RARE PEREGRINE FALCON

The peregrine falcon, once the pride of kings, still a favourite with falconers and until recently represented in fair strength in suitable parts of Britain, is now in an alarming state of decline. This species has received much attention in the past few years, especially from researchers like Derek Ratcliffe.

Before the war, the population of British breeding peregrines was estimated to be a steady 650 pairs. The species lost ground during the war, when it was often killed on sight because of its predations on carrier pigeons. After 1945 it was left to breed and it soon regained its former status.

The decline set in around 1955. In 1961 only 82 pairs of peregrines reared young, and something like two fifths of the pre-war birds had vanished. In 1962 only 68 pairs reared young, and birds were found on only half the original territories. There has been no improvement since, and the peregrine falcon can now be considered a rare bird.

Four different chlorinated hydrocarbons were found in the egg of a Perthshire peregrine in 1963. These toxins have since been identified in eggs from other Scottish birds and from falcons in the Lake District. All the evidence points to

contamination of the falcon through eating affected prey. This led to the breaking of eggs by the parent birds, infertility of eggs, and breeding failure.

Much the same thing is happening to the golden eagle, and in 1964 a high proportion of Scottish golden eagles failed to breed. Others broke their own eggs. In 1963, the eggs of eight golden eagles were tested, and in them were found four toxins of the organo-chlorine group. These eggs were taken under special licence for testing, in 1963 and 1964, by J. D. Lockie, formerly of The Nature Conservancy, now of Edinburgh University.

How does the eagle, inhabiting wild hill country where there is no spraying or seed dressing, become contaminated? Contrary to the popular notion that eagles prey on lambs, many of these birds, especially in winter, live largely on mutton and deer carrion. Modern sheep-dips contain dieldrin, one of the organo-chlorines, and the eagles ingest the poison with the mutton. Dieldrin was not available after 1965, but there was no law to prevent anyone from building up a stock for use in future years, so this kind of contamination could go on.

CONTAMINATION OF FISH

Pesticide residues are being increasingly identified in fish, so we can look for upsets among fish-eating birds. But it has also been pointed out by the Scottish Department of Agriculture and Fisheries that salmon now run an increasing risk of death from chemicals used on land adjacent to the rivers up which they run.

In some parts of the country there is already a notable reduction in the number of barn owls and kestrels, and the circumstantial evidence points to their contamination from pesticides.

Given that the evidence means what we think it means, what is the position of human beings in all this? Man is at the end of a great variety of food chains. He eats fish, he eats game, he eats mutton, he eats venison, and many kinds of agricultural food from all over the world, where crops are sprayed with these chemicals. Is it conceivable that man will escape serious contamination when so many other predators are affected?

178

MAN IN INDUSTRY : II

Great changes have transformed the industrial picture in Britain since the end of the Second World War, and these changes have led to a profound alteration in the position of labour within industry. The living, working, and whole social conditions of the vast mass of industry's workers have taken on a completely new look since 1945.

A glance at pre-war industry will show vividly how different the situation has become to-day. Before war broke out in 1939, Britain was one of a small group of countries in the world that had become predominantly industrial. Many workers were involved in some way in manufacturing industry, whether they worked in a factory, a workshop, or an office. But industry was not prosperous. The nineteen-twenties and thirties had seen widespread depression among many of Britain's leading industries, for the manufacturing firms were unable to sell their products. Thus, with lack of adequate markets, production was reduced. And because production was lowered, industry needed fewer workers.

And so unemployment became a general feature of Britain's industry between the two world wars, 1919-39. It was a terrible time for the working man. Usually, about one in ten of the entire labour force was without work. When times were very bad, as in the "Great Depression" of the early nineteen-thirties, as many as one worker in every four or five was without a job.

Unemployment was never spread evenly throughout the country. It affected certain industries and regions more than others. In particular, depression was severe in those industries providing the backbone of the British economy—those trades that had grown rapidly during the nineteenth century, and set the pace for the rest of industry to follow. Industries like cotton and woollen textiles, coal-mining, iron and steel production, and shipbuilding were all important in the economy, for large numbers of men depended on them for a livelihood. These industries all suffered a depression, which put tens of thousands of workers out of a job.

These depressed industries influenced the whole economy, because they were so large. And unless these basic industries were prosperous, the economy as a whole suffered. The inter-war years was consequently a difficult period throughout British industry.

Unfortunately the industries that suffered most were concentrated in a few areas, for as they had developed, so whole towns had grown up around them. Thus the prosperity of a region was often dependent upon the prosperity of just one branch of industry. When coal-mines were shut down in the mining villages of South Wales for example, nearly the entire town would be without work for there were no other industries to turn to.

Depressed industries led to depressed areas, and before 1939 the main pockets of unemployment in the country were in South Wales, South Lancashire, Cumberland, Lanarkshire, North Eastern England, and Northern Ireland. All these regions suffered greatly, especially in the nineteen-thirties. At worst, more than three out of every four workers would be unemployed. This happened in towns such as Jarrow and Merthyr Tydfil.

And because labour was plentiful—for jobs were few—the workers found it difficult to combine in order to improve their conditions. The inter-war years were disastrous for the trade unions, and their bargaining power was weak. A strike for higher wages or shorter hours could have little effect when there were always out-of-work men willing to undertake a job on almost any conditions.

Unemployment, dole queues, hunger marches, weak unions: these were among the major features of social and economic conditions in industry during the twenties and thirties. Yet all was not so discouraging. New industries did grow, many of them rapidly. Electrical engineering, synthetic fibres, chemicals, building and construction all expanded. Radios, gramophones, and electric heating and lighting all became common. And as these industries and trades grew, so Britain came to be less dependent on the old depressed "staple" industries. Moreover the new industries looked more to the home market, whereas the staples had been geared largely to sales abroad. And the expanding industries therefore tended to develop around the main centres of population, such as London and the Midlands.

Manufacturing industry—those occupations in which something is actually made—continued to expand in some areas. But there was also expansion in those jobs which are not directly productive. These industries were mainly those providing a service, and are called tertiary industry (just as agriculture and mining are known as primary, and manufacturing, secondary industry).

MASS-PRODUCTION

Within industry, great technological advances took place, above all in the manufacture of motor vehicles. And the important breakthrough came with the adoption of mass-

During the "Great Depression" years, unemployment was rife and, in Britain, one person in four was out of work.

production, based on the assembly-line. This new system, as momentous as that brought about by the steam engine, profoundly altered the working lives of industrial men, as we shall see later.

The post-1945 changes in working and living conditions must be seen in relation to the dire experiences of the inter-war years. And a comparison shows aspects both of continuity and contrast. Many of the changes taking place in the first period have continued in the second. Among these have been the further decline in the once important basic industries, and the rise of automobiles, aircraft production, electrical engineering, and many others. Industry has become more diversified as dependence on a few major branches of production has diminished. The growth of industry has also been accompanied by an expansion in those "white-collar" jobs away from the factory bench, while the proportion of total workers engaged in tertiary industry has also risen continuously. Above all, methods of mass-production have spread so that the assembly-line system has become more general throughout industry. And with the growth in mass-production has come an increased scale and size of operations in business and firms, so that larger numbers of workers than ever before were employed under the same roof.

A comparison of the situation existing in pre- and post-war industry thus reveals similarities and differences. The Second World War in many cases quickened the pace of changes that were already taking place before. But even more striking in such a comparison are the contrasts between modern industry and that of the inter-war years, for there have been great changes throughout industry both in living and working conditions.

Most important, the period since 1945 has not witnessed anything like the vast unemployment of the thirties. Wages have risen rapidly, and living standards have improved. Places of work are becoming more attractive with airy, clean workshops and factories. The working week has become shorter, so that greater leisure is enjoyed by industrial workers. Trade Unions have flourished and their membership has grown, so that they have been able to play an important part in improving living standards for their members.

Life in industry has changed considerably since 1945, and a new development may well bring about an even more dramatic transformation. This new feature is the growth of automation, and it will have a profound effect upon industrial labour. For now it seems that we are on the threshold of an age when even the most complex processes and decisions will be undertaken, not by men, but by machines.

FULL EMPLOYMENT

The end of mass unemployment since 1945 has been a great step forward. For now almost anyone who seeks work can find it. And equally important has been the development of new techniques of preventing unemployment, so that the conditions of the nineteen-thirties will not reappear. For after the terrible unemployment between the wars much study and research went into the problem of how to prevent such great industrial slumps. The remedy suggested, which has been adopted since 1945, was for the government to take on responsibility for maintaining full employment. When industry becomes depressed and unable to provide sufficient jobs, the government steps in and spends money on various public works like road construction. By these means work is found for the unemployed.

Of course, there has been unemployment since 1945 and

there always will be. Firms still sometimes go out of business, and it takes time to absorb their workers into other jobs. Sometimes, also, workers leave one industry to look for another job elsewhere, hence they are for a time voluntarily unemployed. Slumps in industry still occur and in declining sectors such as cotton-textiles, shipbuilding, and coal mining, men become redundant. But compared to the days when over 20 per cent. of workers were without employment, the situation since 1945 has improved beyond all measure. The following table will show how low the level of unemployment has been in the ten years since 1958:

TABLE I
Percentage of unemployed workers in the U.K. yearly averages, 1958-68.

1958	1959	1960	1961	1962	1963	1964	1965	1966	1967	1968
2·1	2·2	1·6	1·5	2·0	2·5	1·8	1·5	1·7	2·6	2·5

Source: Ministry of Labour statistics.

Full employment has also been accompanied by better working conditions. The government, employers, and unions have all taken steps to ensure that work-places are as pleasant and safe as possible. Many firms provide sickness insurance benefits, recreation facilities, subsidised canteens, pension schemes, and many other amenities. At the same time holidays with pay are now granted throughout industry. Conditions have also been improved by shorter working hours. Many industrial employees work a forty hour week or less, instead of over fifty hours as before the war. Similarly many workers have a five day week instead of the previous six. The downward trend in the normal working week in British industry is shown in Table II.

TABLE II
Normal weekly hours of work per worker in industries in the United Kingdom, 1951 and 1968.

1951	1968
44·6 hours per week	40 hours per week

Source: Ministry of Labour Statistics.

Great improvements in standards of living have taken place in post-war Britain; and workers in industry have

Britain's archaic road system cannot cope with present-day traffic and the building of more major motorways is essential to the solution of the serious traffic problem.

shared fully in the general progress throughout the country. Better conditions of employment and more leisure time have raised living standards, and so has the introduction of the Welfare State. The development of social services such as health, pensions and education have given people greater security, and means that the state now provides many services which previously had to be shouldered by the individual.

Above all, however, better living standards have come with increasing wages and salaries. Higher incomes have led to greater comfort and families are now able to afford goods previously considered luxuries. The improvements can be seen in better housing conditions, and more and higher quality food being bought. Increased earning power has led to a big growth in the number of car owners, while washing-machines, refrigerators, vacuum-cleaners and other time-saving household devices are finding their way into homes all over the country. Television sets became as common in the 1950s as radios were in the 1930s, and these too are a sign of increasing wealth in Britain. More families have holidays abroad. There are countless examples of the higher living standards which the post-war affluence has brought to Britain, as people now have more to spend than ever before. The rise in earnings since the war has been partly offset by rising prices, but wages and salaries have gone up faster than prices. The following table illustrates the growth in average weekly earnings by men in manufacturing industry from 1956 to 1968:

TABLE III
Average weekly earnings by men in manufacturing industry.

1956		1968	
£	s	£	s
12	3	23	12

Source: Ministry of Labour Gazette.

GROWTH OF UNIONS

Full employment and the growth of industry have given great opportunities to industrial workers. They have frequently been able to obtain better conditions by collective bargaining with employers. Sometimes peaceful negotiations have resulted in satisfactory arrangements, but often workers have resorted to strike action, or threat of such strikes, to force employers to meet their demands. The years since 1945, and especially since 1950, have seen great increases in the number of industrial strikes. The strikes have often been called by the unions in support of their claims, but there have also been a growing number of "unofficial" strikes as action has frequently been taken by groups of workers independently of the trade unions.

The importance of unions is reflected in the continuous growth of their membership during and since the war. Whereas in 1940 there were some six million trades unionists in Britain, the figure had grown to eight million by 1945. In 1952 membership was more than nine million, while a continued growth brought the number to over ten million by 1968.

Recent years have seen continued changes throughout British industry. In overall employment, the numbers engaged in agricultural occupations have been declining, while those in manufacturing industry have been growing slowly. By far the largest increase however has come in tertiary employment. With the growing prosperity all over the country, society has come to demand and depend far more upon services. Thus there has been an increase in the pro-

portion of the labour force employed in transport and communications, in the Civil Service and Local Government, and in professions such as the law, teaching, medicine, accountancy, and estate management. There has similarly been a sharp rise in the numbers engaged in advertising and in retail trading. In fact, of the total working-force in Britain in 1963, 48 per cent. were providing services of some description; 38 per cent. were working in manufacturing industry; while the remaining 14 per cent. were distributed in agriculture, construction, and public utilities such as gas, water, and electricity.

Within secondary industry, more are now finding work in the engineering, electronics, automobile, and chemical industries, while there is declining employment in agriculture, mining and quarrying, shipbuilding, and textiles.

Employment within individual firms has also undergone striking changes. Among these has been the ever-increasing proportion of white-collar workers. As firms have grown in size, so they have tended to create more desk jobs. The increasingly complex problems on sales and marketing employment policy, output schedules, adoption of new technology, advertising, and other matters are all generally worked out in firms' offices. For manufacturing to-day, with the vast outlays necessary for large-scale production, involves more risks and requires more planning and long-range forecasting. And it therefore needs a greater number of skilled executive and administrative staff to keep the business efficient and competitive. The proportion of these white-collar to total workers in manufacturing industry has increased to such an extent in recent years that in 1968 they actually formed one quarter of all employees.

TECHNOLOGY

Among the many reasons making for greater industrial prosperity since the war, one of the most important has undoubtedly been the rapid progress of technology and scientific management. One aspect of this has been the great developments in the production of new and improved machines. And there has also been a widespread adoption of the techniques of mass-production.

Mass-production, though significant before the war, has spread throughout industry since. And the methods used in

Technological advances have made life easier for the housewife who now has many domestic appliances at her command.

181

mass-production have made a big impact on the life of the industrial worker. "Continuous flow" of production is the principle underlying these methods. Instead of manufacturing an article in a number of independent and separate stages, each process is linked through an assembly line. The first important application of this system came in the American motor-car industry about the time of the First World War. Henry Ford, a manufacturer of cars, found that great increases in productivity could be obtained if workers, standing at a moving conveyor belt, each performed a simple task over and over again in exactly the same manner to each part of the car.

Gradually this technique has spread. Simple processes performed at a conveyor-belt, have resulted in astonishing increases in production in many different industries. And this has presented an important problem for industrial workers. For although increases in output have led to prosperity, good working conditions, high wages and living standards, yet the work itself tends to become elementary and dull. Doing the same minute task day after day, year after year, has raised the question of the status of human labour in the manufacturing industry. There is a danger of men becoming automatons, like machines. Traditional craftsmanship and pride in work have been ousted by the new techniques of standardisation based on a "continuous flow" of production, with the complex operations of manufacture being broken down into a very large number of simple components.

But the problem is not only one of the dignity of labour. For the simplicity of each individual operation at an assembly line with the labour force performing merely mechanical tasks, has inevitably led to the substitution of machines themselves in place of men. Machines are often cheaper, more reliable, and capable of longer and more intensive work than men. So various operations in industry increasingly are undertaken by automatic machines.

The position of man in industry has thus been challenged by the organisation of production on the "continuous flow" system. From threatening to make him merely a cog in the wheel of manufacturing, the growth of new machinery since 1945 now threatens to displace him altogether.

The growing use of computers in British industry is an important step on the way to factory automation.

To some extent the spread of mass-production accounts for the increase in numbers of white-collar as opposed to manual workers in industry. The very techniques of production require an enormous output, with great problems of management, control and decision-making. Constantly the firm's managers and directors are having to decide what should be produced and in what quantities, and they try to foresee and forestall likely bottle-necks in production. The problems of big industry producing on a mass scale has thus led to the expansion of these executive and research groups.

But a momentous development since the war has raised the issue of employing even decision makers and operation controllers within industry. And this new factor is automation. The spread of automation may in the years to come alter the whole position of industrial workers, for it means that the whole productive process can be carried on without human agency. Instead of men reading and digesting information and making decisions on the basis of such data, it can now be fed into machines.

Automation involves the use of electronic computers which are able to use data fed to them to make decisions with far greater speed and accuracy than men. The computers can thus control production, and they can even allow for errors in the information they are given. Thus, not only can the actual productive processes be carried on by automatic machines at the assembly line, but their operation can be controlled and guided automatically. Automation can lead to spectacular improvements in production, for it gives greater output in a shorter time. Work which took a skilled iron forger eight hours in 1908 can be done to-day with automation in a mere twenty seconds.

The use of electronic computers has developed quickest in the United States of America. From only a few dozen such computers in 1955, there were over eleven thousand in operation in 1960. Computers are found not only in manufacturing industry, but in clerical work, the Post Office, and even in laundries. Their use is spreading rapidly in Britain.

Automation holds out enormous possibilities to civilisation, for the day when manufacturing is done almost entirely by automatic machines at the push of a button may not be far away. When this happens, what will happen to the industrial worker? He will cease to exist as he is known to-day, for there will be no work for him to do. But if automation ends employment in some jobs, it will create many new, exciting, and highly skilled ones. Machines will have to be designed, maintained, and improved, and the data to feed into the computer will have to be selected and checked. And automation will lead to greater output, and may lead to undreamed-of improvements in living standards. Then new industries will emerge, geared to the increased leisure, spending-power, and growing demands of society. Certainly machines will come more and more to perform the simple, standardised tasks necessary for mass-production, and the worker will therefore be released from the drudgery brought by the assembly-line.

All this is to come. The day of the steam-engine is not far behind us. That of the assembly-line is with us, while the age of automation is only dawning. The solid achievements of industrial labour since the Second World War have been spectacular enough with rising incomes, better living and working conditions, shorter hours, and longer holidays. And with the coming of automation we may be living through yet another "Industrial revolution."

WILDLIFE AND MAN

Every form of human activity connected with land-use affects wildlife in some degree—its numbers, its stability, its breeding success, its future and, perhaps, its very existence. Since man is forever changing the face of the countryside his influence is being increasingly felt. In his struggle to get the most out of life he has destroyed many forms of wildlife, directly by killing them off, and indirectly by destruction of their habitats, which has meant leaving them without a suitable place to live.

DESTRUCTION OF HABITATS

Obvious examples of this come readily to mind. If a great area is flooded for purposes of water catchment to produce hydro-electricity, every form of wildlife that can't live in water disappears, and if fish are then put in the artificial lake you have trout where you once had, perhaps, grouse, curlews, plovers, hares, roe deer, larks and lizards. Since such a change of land-use is likely to be permanent, all these species are permanently excluded from the flooded ground.

The change of land-use also works in reverse. If an area of marshland is reclaimed for agriculture you have corn and grass with the wildlife suited to such a habitat (larks, plovers, partridges, hares and so on) and the disappearance of gulls, ducks and waders, water voles and otters, and perhaps even frogs and newts if every pond is dried up.

In the same way, the ground taken over for new towns, aerodromes, roads, industrial estates, and such like, are lost to many forms of wildlife, although some may adapt and remain. Changes from pastoral husbandry to forestry, from forestry to pastoralism, from one form of agriculture to another, the influence of game preservation, sport, and tourism, can all make themselves felt, often with far-reaching results.

Large-scale tree-felling forces forest animals to change their habitat and sometimes leads to their extinction.

If we look at ground which has been switched from sheep rearing to forestry we can almost predict the wildlife changes that will follow, sooner or later. First of all the planted ground is enclosed to keep out rabbits and deer and, of course, sheep. When the trees are young and small there is a great growth of ground cover which suits field voles, and they begin to multiply, reaching plague numbers in some years. As the voles build up their numbers, weasels, stoats, foxes, kestrels and short-eared owls move in to prey on them, and for all of these at some time, and some of them at all times, the vole becomes the principal prey.

But voles fluctuate in numbers, with ups and downs in a four-year cycle, and we find that the species that prey on them fluctuate too. In years of vole abundance, short-eared owls may build up to great numbers on the ground, and rear big families; when the voles are low the owl numbers drop dramatically, and only two or three pairs may remain where forty pairs bred the year before. Weasels and stoats move out as the vole numbers fall, but are replaced by others when the vole numbers come up again. A sort of balance, or equilibrium, therefore develops in the new habitat.

This, however, changes as the trees grow. Once the trees have joined heads, as it were, forming what is known as closed canopy, the ground vegetation is smothered and the voles drop in numbers. Then the trees, grown taller, are thinned, and some ground cover appears again. This suits small mammals. When the trees begin to produce cones they provide food for red squirrels, which begin to move in. The mature forest can then support, and cover, deer, pine marten, wildcat, capercaillie, black grouse, and others. All this is a long way from the former sheep runs.

We know what happens in the reverse case—when forests are cut down and the ground turned over to pastoralism—because we have the historical record. Scotland provides a first-class example, and one that has received much attention from ecologists from all over the world.

FELLING OF FORESTS

Much of Scotland was formerly covered by the great Forest of Caledon. Bears existed there until the ninth or tenth centuries, at which time serious destruction of the forests had hardly begun. The reindeer disappeared some time in the twelfth century. Later still the wild boar and the wolf were killed off. But the really dramatic changes, as distinct from the extermination of a few native species, began much later when the great forest was almost cleared.

With great tracts of hill laid bare, the wildcat and the pine marten retreated to the most remote fastnesses, the latter to cling precariously to existence. The capercaillie, the giant forest grouse, became extinct. The red squirrel disappeared. The squirrel was reintroduced from England, and the capercaillie from Sweden. Both became re-established because new forests were growing up to give them a suitable habitat. The pine marten, which held on through grim days, was saved in the twentieth century by the big plantations in the north-west, and its spread is being helped by the activities of the Forestry Commission.

The felling of the great forest had other effects. The cleared ground produced fresh, clean grass, and these endless areas of green attracted the southern flockmasters who began to bring in their sheep. The coming of the sheep meant the going of the people, and thus began the notorious Highland Clearances: the driving out of a people to make way for a type of livestock that needed little labour. With the sheep in and the people out the long story of West Highland deterioration began, bringing with it war on foxes, eagles, wildcats, buzzards and pine martens, or anything that could be considered dangerous to the new livestock.

DELIBERATE DESTRUCTION OF SPECIES

The white-tailed eagle disappeared, the golden eagle became rare, the wildcat and marten held on precariously. The fox kept his numbers up and war is still waged on him to-day. But the greatest disaster, apart from the depopulation, was the impoverishment of the hill grazings. Bracken spread, ground became eroded, and rabbits became a plague. Burning became the order of the day to keep grass and heather right for sheep. There was no regeneration of trees. In the end sheep farming became uneconomic in many places, and is still a precarious occupation.

Deer stalking became a fashionable sport in the nineteenth century and sheep areas were often cleared to make room for deer. Sport became the main activity of many parts of the country, and this led to further destruction of wildlife, especially predators. In Glen Garry, between the years 1837 and 1840, the following were destroyed as a routine in the interests of game: 11 foxes, 198 wildcats, 78 house cats, 106 polecats, 301 stoats and weasels, 67 badgers, 48 otters, 15 golden eagles, 27 white-tailed eagles, 18 ospreys, 63 goshawks, 275 kites, 107 peregrine falcons, 11 hobbies, 6 jerfalcons, 78 merlins, 462 kestrels, 285 common buzzards, 371 rough-legged buzzards, 3 honey buzzards, 475 ravens, 1,431 hooded crows, 63 hen harriers, and 109 owls of three kinds.

This was direct, deliberate destruction, and a look at the list shows species that no longer exist in Scotland, and others that are rare or staging a difficult come-back, like the osprey.

To encourage grass to send out new shoots, old grass and heather are burnt under carefully controlled conditions.

Deer-stalking and grouse-shooting became fashionable sports in the nineteenth century. One of the side effects was the senseless persecution of other forms of wildlife.

Imagine a time when 275 kites and 63 goshawks could be killed in three years on one estate!

Of course, England had her great upheavals too, if none so spectacularly for ill, or so all-embracing as the devastation of the Highlands. The drainage of the fenlands created a new granary for England, and made possible the raising of cattle, sheep, poultry, pheasants and partridges where once had been marsh and salt water: but it also helped to drive out such species as the spoonbill, avocet and marsh harrier by destroying their special habitats.

Game preservation in England reached the highest level in Europe, with vast areas of Yorkshire devoted to grouse, and others such as East Anglia, to partridges, pheasants and hares. There, too, predatory birds and mammals were killed as routine. We used the term "vermin" for them, but it is now discredited outside the circle of the most backward game-preservers and keepers.

To-day more and more people—from country landowners to townsmen—are becoming conservation-minded. But conservation of what is left of our wildlife becomes more and more difficult at the same time as the new outlook is growing, because an expanding human population requires greater and greater living space, which means that less and less is available for wildlife. We can no longer afford to be prodigal or careless if we are to save what we have left.

Even tourism, which is now such a source of foreign currency, and considered so important, brings its own problems. Too many feet trampling an area of botanical interest can destroy the very sights people come to see, just as too many visitors can disturb a rare species of bird or mammal. This danger can be met, with foresight and planning, as the Royal Society for the Protection of Birds has proved in the case of the ospreys nesting on Speyside. These birds bred while receiving 20,000 visitors! The threat to them now comes not from people, but from poisons used on the land.

No doubt other problems of a similar nature will be solved; but they have to be solved in good time, before the damage begins. Two sites in need of this kind of forward thinking are Speyside and the Western Isles in Scotland. The first is now seeing a boom in tourism, with ski-ing attracting more and more people on to ground that is one of Britain's great Nature Reserves. The second holds the breeding ground of the grey lag goose. Unrestricted movement of tourists could destroy much of the attraction of these places.

Despite the dangers, however, we are far better equipped than ever before to spot dangers in time, and do something about them before it is too late. There is, first of all, the growing conservation-mindedness at all levels, including that of government: the growing conviction that wildlife has a place, a right, and even a function, and should not therefore lightly be destroyed because of some short-term interest. Then there are a number of bodies acting as researchers and watchdogs.

The Nature Conservancy is the Government body concerned with basic research, including research into wildlife management and control. It advises the Government on lines of policy. It will advise and help anybody seeking its advice or help, and work with all kinds of organisations, or individuals. Then there are all the private organisations concerned with protection, legislation, safeguarding of threatened sites or species, and research. These bodies include the Mammal Society of the British Isles, The British Deer Society, The Council for Nature, the Country Naturalists' Trusts in England, the Wildlife Trust in Scotland, The Fauna Preservation Society, The Universities' Federation for Animal Welfare, and the long established Royal Society for the Protection of Birds.

In England, all deer now have legal status and a Close Season (except for roebucks). In Scotland only the red deer has a legal Close Season. In both countries the Forestry Commission operates its own Close Season for roe deer of both sexes, which is an advance on government action, and one for which the Forestry Commission deserves full credit. In Scotland, where colonising red deer can be a problem, there is now the Red Deer Commission, concerned with control and management in the field. We may soon see other mammals given this kind of attention.

Besides deer, much research has recently been devoted to the grey seal, a rare animal on a world scale. The world population is estimated at 46,000; the number in British waters is 35,000. A cull of these seals is now taking place in the Farne and Orkney Islands, as part of a short-term attempt at control in the interests of salmon fisheries. The grey seal is a special problem, because it is by no means a common species, and must therefore be watched carefully. There has been much disquiet about the cull, which may yet prove to be unnecessary. But the present authorised cull (restricted to two breeding stations) is a great advance on a former method when the answer to a problem animal was unrestricted and absolute war.

Other countries have made the same mistakes; some are still making the old mistakes; and most are at varying stages of conservation-mindedness. To-day the World Wildlife Fund, financed by public subscription and donations, exists to help in the preservation of threatened species in any part of the world. Already it has done much good work. At considerable cost it helped to save the famous Coto Donana in southern Spain as a perpetual Nature Reserve. Among many other rare and interesting species, the Coto holds the Spanish Imperial eagle and the Spanish lynx.

The Arabian oryx, one of the rarest mammals on earth is near extinction in its native land, largely because of unrestricted hunting in motor cars. When it became obvious that this species was liable to disappear altogether, The Fauna Preservation Society made the first move towards saving a remnant. The Sultan of Muscat was in favour of protecting the species, but could do nothing to cover the vast area of desert used by the animals. So it was decided to fly out a breeding herd. Three were caught up and flown to Phoenix, Arizona, where the climate suited them. Later four others were lent by private owners to help in the building of a herd. Now the herd is producing calves and apparently doing so well that their future is certain.

Operation Oryx, as it has been called, was helped by the R.A.F., a private airline, a London newspaper, private individuals, the World Wildlife Fund, a ruler in the oryx's home area, an American hunting association, an oil comp-

In an effort to preserve this species from extinction, the Arabian oryx was air-lifted to the Arizona desert.

any, three zoos, and others. It was a wonderful example of modern will in action, and is notable for the fact that the major effort, almost the whole effort, came from outside the country concerned, many of whose so-called sportsmen were actively engaged in killing the last animals as quickly as they could.

When a species disappears from the earth it disappears for all time, and not all threatened ones have been saved at the last hour like the oryx. The American bison (called buffalo) was saved almost by accident until its future was made the responsibility of government. The great auk disappeared; so did the American passenger pigeon, whose millions used to darken the sky, and which hunters imagined would last for ever. It can now be seen only in museums, stuffed: a salutary reminder of what can happen. Zoos are now performing a most important function in rescuing other threatened species, but time is running out for some of them, and every rescue is an eleventh hour one. The orang-utan is seriously threatened: mothers are killed so that their young can be caught for zoos. This traffic is now being stopped. Because of the modern fashion for spotted furs, the leopard is now threatened.

The threat to wild life in Africa, which is still the world's greatest reservoir of big game, is becoming increasingly recognised by the governments of the emergent African nations. After the famous Arusha Conference of September, 1961, President Nyerere of Tanganyika (now of Tanzania) made a declaration of intent concerning the future of wild life in that country and its conservation. Other African States recognise the needs and the problems, and in some instances wise conservation of certain species will provide a food resource for the nation as, for example, the lechwe which until recently was being over-hunted.

MAN'S INTERFERENCE

In the past, man has created serious problems for himself, often with the best of intentions. He has done so by interfering with wild populations before he knew how to manage them, and by introducing species from other countries. There are plenty of examples of these because the mistakes were so often made.

A classic example of the results of interference is that of the deer of the Kaibab Plateau in Arizona, reported by Aldo Leopold, one of the great American Conservationists.

At the beginning of this century there were 4,000 deer on the plateau which extends to 127,000 acres. Pumas, wolves and coyotes lived there, and preyed upon the deer. A war began on the predators, with the intention of protecting and conserving the deer. The results were staggering, and the reverse of what was expected.

The pumas were practically killed out, the kills being 600 between 1907 and 1917, 74 up to 1923, and 124 between 1924 and 1939. By 1926 the wolves had been exterminated, and over 7,000 coyotes had been killed between 1907 and 1939. This was killing on a vast scale, and the results soon became evident. In 1905 there had been 4,000 deer. By 1920 the number had increased to 60,000. In 1924 it was 100,000, a twenty-five fold increase. With all these mouths to be fed the range soon suffered deterioration, and food resources declined. The deer felt the pinch, and 60,000 perished between 1924 and 1925, leaving 40,000 head. This number fell to 30,000 in 1929 and had fallen to 10,000 by 1939.

Man has learned a great deal about the effects of predation in the past two decades, and this has been responsible for the new ideas we have concerning predators. It has now been shown, for example, that eagles and falcons make little difference to the number of grouse on a moor, and that stoats and weasels, even when preying entirely on voles, cannot prevent a vole plague.

ESTABLISHMENT OF ALIEN ANIMALS

It is an obvious fact of history that the biggest problems posed by wild animals have been of man's own creating. When the Normans brought the rabbit to England, it was never foreseen that this beast would one day become the major pest of agriculture and forestry. Imported as a food species, it was at first confined in warrens. Then it became feral, and was deliberately transported to other parts of the

*In Borneo and Sumatra, the orang-utan (*man of the woods*), is seriously threatened with extinction because many adult animals are killed so that their young may be more easily captured for zoos.*

The South American coypu was introduced into Britain for fur-farming purposes. Many escaped and breeding colonies are now well established in parts of south-east England.

country. Later it became a sporting animal as well as a food species. Later still it became an important crop on marginal lands. Then, during the Second World War, real war on it began. But none of the traditional methods of killing made any great inroad on its numbers, and it took the disease known as myxomatosis to cut it down to the status of an uncommon animal. Now the stocks are slowly building up again, presumably because some rabbits are immune to the disease, or are able to recover from it. An exotic species once out of control is difficult to bring under control again.

Irresponsible but well-meaning people took the rabbit to Australia where it became the greatest single pest in the country, and vast sums of money have been spent on attempted control.

The grey squirrel, which is now such a pest of forests, orchards and gardens, was deliberately turned loose in England, mainly by people who liked the look of it. One American turned 100 of them loose! The grey, an American, has since spread over most of England and into many parts of Scotland. For a time the Forestry Commission paid a bounty for the destruction of grey squirrels, but this has been stopped because the problem was not being solved. Apart from its depredations on trees and fruits, the grey squirrel has been partly responsible, in some mysterious way, for driving out the native red squirrel.

Another introduced species is now emerging as a problem, although until now it was considered no problem at all. This is the fat dormouse, often familiarly known by its Latin name of *Glis glis*. Found over most of Europe where it lives mainly in deciduous woodland, it is a big dormouse, with a squirrel-like tail. In England it often invades houses, hibernating and sometimes breeding in lofts and attics. It is strongly attracted by stored apples. But it was not considered a problem, and people who killed *Glis glis* in their houses did so mainly because of the noise it made in the roof.

Now word comes from the Forestry Commission that *Glis glis* is attacking Norway spruce by barking the tree high up, and thus causing considerable damage. If the bark of a tree is ringed, the tree dies. Apart from the damage, *Glis glis* is now showing a change of habit to fit in with it. Instead of living in holes in trees, or in the ground, it is now building a drey like a squirrel's high up in the spruce canopy, where it cannot be readily seen. This makes control difficult, and the present technique of listening at the bottom of trees for sounds of activity and shooting at the sound, is hardly satisfactory.

Another species, this time a South American one, has now become established in England under its own power. This is the coypu, a species of water rat formerly farmed for its fur, which is *nutria*. Many coypus escaped, and colonies have become established in some parts of South East England. So far no great damage has been done, and none may be done, but the history of exotic species leaves little room for optimism.

The case of the reindeer, which has been reintroduced into Scotland in the Cairngorm area, is different. This animal was once a native, and the present herd is an experimental one. Although living free on the hill, it is under full control and its numbers are building up slowly. It is thought that the reindeer may one day become a source of venison, and it is hoped that it will graze mostly on the highest ground never used by sheep and rarely by the red deer. But this remains to be seen.

Another alien introduced by man and now established, if somewhat precariously, is the mink. Escapees from fur farms in certain parts of Britain have been reported to be breeding wild, and there seems to be no reason why the mink should not settle down in this country. So far, most mink are reported after they have killed poultry, but this is the easy road for an escaped mink to take, and there must be others which have settled into a niche where they can live on wild prey.

It is clear then that the management and conservation of wildlife is a complex business, not a matter of killing what you don't like and encouraging what you like, or killing pest species all the time which may not be pest species most of their time. Nothing in nature is as simple as that, and this is one field where zoologists are learning that nothing is as simple as it looks.

187

INDEX